face2face

Starter Teacher's Book

Chris Redston

CAMBRIDGE UNIVERSITY PRESS
Cambridge, New York, Melbourne, Madrid, Cape Town,
Singapore, São Paulo, Delhi, Tokyo, Mexico City

Cambridge University Press
The Edinburgh Building, Cambridge CB2 8RU, UK

www.cambridge.org
Information on this title: www.cambridge.org/9780521712750

First published 2009
Reprinted 2011

Printed in the United Kingdom by Latimer Trend

A catalogue record for this publication is available from the British Library

ISBN 978-0-521-71275-0 Teacher's Book
ISBN 978-0-521-71273-6 Student's Book with CD-ROM/Audio CD
ISBN 978-0-521-71274-3 Workbook with Key
ISBN 978-0-521-71277-4 Class Audio CDs

Contents

Welcome to face2face!

face2face

face2face is a general English course for adults and young adults who want to learn to communicate quickly and effectively in today's world.

face2face is based on the communicative approach and combines the best in current methodology with special new features designed to make learning and teaching easier.

The **face2face** syllabus integrates the learning of new language with skills development and places equal emphasis on vocabulary and grammar.

face2face uses a guided discovery approach to learning, first allowing students to check what they know, then helping them to work out the rules for themselves through carefully structured examples and concept questions.

All new language is included in the interactive *Language Summaries* in the back of the **face2face** Student's Books and is regularly recycled and reviewed.

There is a strong focus on listening and speaking throughout **face2face**.

Innovative *Help with Listening* sections help students to understand natural spoken English in context and there are numerous opportunities for communicative, personalised speaking practice in **face2face**. The *Real World* lessons in each unit focus on the functional and situational language students need for day-to-day life.

The **face2face** Starter Student's Book provides approximately 60 hours of core teaching material, which can be extended to 90 hours with the photocopiable resources and extra ideas in this Teacher's Book. Each self-contained double-page lesson is easily teachable off the page with minimal preparation.

The vocabulary selection in **face2face** has been informed by the *Cambridge International Corpus* and the *Cambridge Learner Corpus*.

face2face is fully compatible with the *Common European Framework of Reference for Languages* (CEF) and gives students regular opportunities to evaluate their progress. **face2face** Starter covers level A1 (see p13).

face2face Starter Components

Student's Book with free CD-ROM/Audio CD

The Student's Book provides 40 double-page lessons in 10 thematically linked units, each with 4 lessons of 2 pages. Each lesson takes approximately 90 minutes.

The free CD-ROM/Audio CD is an invaluable resource for students, with over 200 exercises in all language areas, plus video, recording and playback capability, a fully searchable *Grammar Reference* section and *Word List*, all the sounds in English, customisable *My Activities* and *My Test* sections, and *Progress* sections where students evaluate their own progress. The free Starter CD-ROM/Audio CD also contains all the new language drills from the Student's Book, so students can practise their pronunciation at home. Help students to get the most out of the CD-ROM/Audio CD by giving them the photocopiable instructions on p10–p12.

Class Audio CDs

The three Class Audio CDs contain all the listening material for the Student's Book, including conversations, drills and the listening sections of the *Progress Tests* for units 5 and 10.

Workbook

The Workbook provides further practice of all language presented in the Student's Book. It also includes a 20-page *Reading and Writing Portfolio* based on the *Common European Framework of Reference for Languages*, which can be used either for extra work in class or for homework.

Teacher's Book

This Teacher's Book includes *Teaching Tips*, *Teaching Notes* and photocopiable materials: 29 *Class Activities* (p100–p146), 10 *Vocabulary Plus* worksheets (p147–p160) and 10 *Progress Tests* (p161–p175).

Website

Visit the **face2face** website www.cambridge.org/elt/face2face for downloadable word lists, placement tests, sample materials and full details of how **face2face** covers the language areas specified by the CEF.

The face2face Approach

Listening

A typical listening practice activity checks students' understanding of gist and then asks questions about specific details. The innovative *Help with Listening* sections in **face2face** Starter take students a step further by focusing on the underlying reasons why listening to English can be so problematic. Activities in these sections:

- introduce the concept of stress on words and phrases
- focus on sentence stress and its relationship to the important information in a text
- explain why words are often linked together in natural spoken English
- help students to identify and understand contractions
- introduce some common weak forms
- show students how these features of connected speech combine to give spoken English its natural rhythm.

For *Teaching Tips* on Listening, see p18.

Speaking

All the lessons in **face2face** Starter and the *Class Activities* photocopiables provide students with numerous speaking opportunities. Many of these activities focus on accuracy, while fluency activities help students to gain confidence, take risks and try out what they have learned. For fluency activities to be truly 'fluent', however, students often need time to formulate their ideas before they speak. This preparation stage is incorporated into the *Get ready ... Get it right!* activities at the end of each A and B lesson.

For *Teaching Tips* on Speaking, see p19.

Reading and Writing

In the **face2face** Starter Student's Book, reading texts from a variety of genres are used both to present new language and to provide reading practice. There are also a number of writing activities which consolidate the language input of the lesson.

For classes that require more practice of reading and writing skills, there is the 20-page *Reading and Writing Portfolio* in the **face2face** Starter Workbook. This section contains 10 double-page stand-alone lessons, one for each unit of the Student's Book, which are designed for students to do in class or at home. The topics and content of these lessons are based closely on the CEF reading and writing competences for level A1. At the end of this section there is a list of 'can do' statements that allows students to track their progress.

Vocabulary

face2face Starter recognises the importance of vocabulary in successful communication. There is lexical input in every lesson, which is consolidated for student reference in the *Language Summaries* in the back of the Student's Book. The areas of vocabulary include:

- lexical fields (*a teacher, a doctor, an actor, a manager,* etc.)
- collocations (*go on holiday, go to the beach, take photos,* etc.)
- sentence stems (*Would you like ... ?, Can I have ... ?,* etc.)
- fixed and semi-fixed phrases (*See you soon., Not for me, thanks.,* etc.)

In addition, each unit in **face2face** Starter includes at least one *Help with Vocabulary* section. These sections are designed to guide students towards a better understanding of the lexical systems of English.

For longer courses and/or more able students, this Teacher's Book also contains one *Vocabulary Plus* worksheet for each unit. These stand-alone worksheets introduce and practise new vocabulary that is **not** included in the Student's Book.

For *Teaching Tips* on Vocabulary, see p19.

Grammar

Grammar is a central strand in the **face2face** Starter syllabus and new grammar structures are always introduced in context in a listening or a reading text.

We believe students are more likely to understand and remember new language if they have actively tried to work out the rules for themselves. Therefore in the *Help with Grammar* sections students are often asked to focus on the meaning and form of the structure for themselves before checking with the teacher or in the appropriate *Language Summary*. All new grammar forms are practised in regular recorded pronunciation drills and communicative speaking activities, and then consolidated through written practice.

For *Teaching Tips* on Grammar, see p19.

Functional and Situational Language

face2face Starter places great emphasis on the functional and situational language students need to communicate effectively in an English-speaking environment. Each unit has a double-page *Real World* lesson that introduces and practises this language. Typical functions and situations include:

- functions: greetings, saying goodbye, making suggestions
- situations: in a café, in a shop, in a restaurant, at a station.

Pronunciation

Pronunciation is integrated throughout **face2face** Starter. Drills for all new vocabulary, grammar structures and *Real World* language are included on the Class Audio CDs and indicated in the Student's Book and Teacher's Book by the icon ⓟ. These drills are also included on the CD-ROM/Audio CD, allowing students to practise their pronunciation at home.

In **face2face** Starter there is also a *Help with Sounds* section at the end of each unit. These sections present and practise sounds that are often problematic for students. These drills are also included on the CD-ROM/Audio CD.

For *Teaching Tips* on Pronunciation, see p20.

Reviewing and Recycling

We believe that regular reviewing and recycling of language are essential and previously taught language is recycled in every lesson. Opportunities for review are also provided in the *Quick Review* sections at the beginning of every lesson, the *Review* sections at the end of each unit, and the 10 photocopiable *Progress Tests* in this Teacher's Book.

For *Teaching Tips* on Reviewing and Recycling, see p20.

The Student's Book

Lessons A and B in each unit introduce and practise new vocabulary and grammar in realistic contexts.

Menu boxes list the language taught and reviewed in each lesson.

Help with Grammar sections ask students to focus on the rules of form and use for themselves before checking with the teacher or in the *Language Summary*.

6 Towns and cities

6A My home town

QUICK REVIEW ●●●
Write sentences about things that you: always, usually, sometimes, never do on Saturday. Work in pairs. Tell your partner your sentences:
A *I always get up late on Saturday.* B *Me too. / Oh, I usually get up early.*

Vocabulary places in a town or city (1)
Grammar *a, some, a lot of; there is / there are*: positive
Review frequency adverbs; Present Simple; adjectives (1)

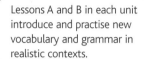

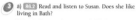

3 a) [R6.2] Read and listen to Susan. Does she like living in Bath?

b) Read about Bath again. Tick (✓) the true sentences. Correct the false sentences.

1 Bath is in the USA. *England*
2 It's a very beautiful city. ✓
3 Susan goes to the Thermae Bath Spa every Friday.
4 The Jane Austen Centre is a theatre.
5 There are trains to London every 30 minutes.
6 Bath doesn't have an airport.

I live in Bath, a city in England. It's a very beautiful place. There are a lot of old buildings in the centre and there are some very nice parks. Bath is famous for its hot springs, and you can swim in the hot water at the Thermae Bath Spa. I go there every Sunday, it's great! In the centre of Bath there are five theatres and some very good museums, including the Roman Baths and the Jane Austen Centre, about the famous English writer. There are also a lot of good restaurants and hotels, and there's a big new shopping centre called SouthGate. There are trains to London every half an hour, and there's an airport in Bristol, only 15 miles away. I think Bath is a great place to live.

Susan

Places in a town or city (1)

1 a) Match these words to pictures 1–9.

a building 4   a museum   a theatre   a shopping centre
a park   a river   a station   a bus station   an airport

b) [R6.1] [P] Listen and practise.

My city

2 a) Check these words with your teacher.

famous   great   hot springs   swim   a train   a mile

b) Look at the photos of Bath, a famous city in England. Which things from 1a) can you see in the photos?

Help with Grammar *a, some, a lot of; there is / there are*: positive

4 a) Match sentences 1–3 to pictures A–C.

1 There's **a person** in the park.
2 There are **some people** in the park.
3 There are **a lot of people** in the park.

A   B   C

b) Fill in the gaps with 's (= is) or *are*.

SINGULAR
There _____'s_ **a** big new shopping centre.
There _____ **an** airport in Bristol.

PLURAL
There _____ **five** theatres.
There _____ **some** very nice parks.
There _____ **a lot of** old buildings.

[G6.1] p111

5 a) Look at these sentences about Bath. Fill in the gaps with 's or *are*.

1 There _'s_ a beautiful river.
2 There _____ two cinemas.
3 There _____ a bus station.
4 There _____ some hot springs.
5 There _____ a nice cafe near the station.
6 There _____ two five-star hotels.
7 There _____ a famous restaurant called Sally Lunn's.
8 There _____ a lot of trains to London every day.

b) [R6.3] Listen and check. Notice how we say *there's* and *there are*.

There's /ðəz/ a beautiful river.
There are /ðeərə/ two cinemas.

c) [P] Listen again and practise.

6 a) Choose the correct words.

1 There's *a* / *some* station.
2 There are *a* / *three* parks.
3 There are *a* / *some* good museums.
4 There's *a* / *some* bus station.
5 There are *some* / *a* beautiful buildings.
6 There's *a* / *an* old theatre.
7 There are *an* / *a lot of* very good restaurants.
8 There are *some* / *a* nice hotels.

b) Work in pairs. Compare answers. Which sentences are true for the town or city you are in now?

Get ready … Get it right!

7 Write sentences about a town or city you know (**not** the town or city you're in now). Use *there is, there are* and words from 1a).

In … there are some beautiful parks.
There are a lot of nice restaurants.
There's a big shopping centre.

8 a) Work in pairs. Tell your partner about your town or city in 7.

b) Tell the class two things about your partner's town or city.

The [P] icon indicates a drill or a practice activity designed to improve students' pronunciation. The integrated pronunciation syllabus includes drills for all new vocabulary and grammar.

New grammar structures are always presented in context in a listening or a reading text.

Controlled practice exercises check students have understood the meaning and form of new language.

Reduced sample pages from **face2face** Starter Student's Book

Quick Reviews at the beginning of each lesson recycle previously learned language and get the class off to a lively, student-centred start.

New vocabulary is usually presented visually. Students are often asked to match words to pictures before checking with their teacher or in the Language Summary.

 6B Are there any shops?

QUICK REVIEW ● ● ●
Work in pairs. Say sentences about the town or city you are in now. Use there is and there are: A There are some good restaurants in the centre. B Yes, and there's a nice park.

Vocabulary places in a town or city (2)
Grammar there is / there are: negative, yes / no questions and short answers; any
Help with Listening linking (1)
Review a, some, a lot of; there is / there are: positive

Places in a town or city (2)

1 a) Match these words to pictures 1–9.

a road 3   a post office
a chemist's   a bank
a market   a supermarket
a bus stop   a square
a cashpoint   an ATM

b) **R6.4** **P** Listen and practise.

c) Work in pairs. Test your partner.

> What's picture 3?

> It's a road.

Welcome to my home

2 a) **R6.5** Look at the photo of Susan and her friend, Isabel. Listen to their conversation. Put these things in the order they talk about them.

Susan's flat   1
restaurants
shops
trains and buses
banks

b) Listen again. Choose the correct words.

1 Susan (likes) / doesn't like living in her flat.
2 There are some / a lot of shops in Susan's road.
3 There's a cashpoint at the supermarket / post office.
4 It's a mile / two miles to the centre of Bath.
5 There are buses to the centre of Bath every ten / twenty minutes.
6 There are some nice restaurants near Susan's house / in the centre.

c) Work in pairs. Compare answers.

Isabel

Susan

3 a) Fill in the gaps with aren't or isn't.

NEGATIVE (–)

1 There _____ a station near here.
2 There _____ any good restaurants near here.

b) Fill in the gaps with is, are, isn't or aren't.

YES / NO QUESTIONS (?)	SHORT ANSWERS
Is there a bank?	Yes, there _____ . No, there _____ .
_____ there any shops?	Yes, there are. No, there _____ .

c) Look again at the sentences in 3a) and 3b). Then choose the correct word in this rule.

● We use some / any in negatives and questions with there are.

C6.2 p111

Help with Listening Linking (1)

4 **R6.6** Listen to these sentences. Notice the linking between the consonant sounds and the vowel sounds.

1 There's an expensive market.
2 There are some old buildings.
3 There isn't an airport.
4 There aren't any museums.
5 Is there a post office?
6 Are there any nice old cafés?

5 **R6.7** **P** Listen and practise the sentences in 4 and the short answers.

There's an expensive market.

6 a) Write sentences about places near Susan's flat.

1 (✓) a supermarket
   There's a supermarket.
2 (✗) a shopping centre
   There isn't a shopping centre.
3 (✓) a market
4 (✗) any museums
5 (✓) a park
6 (✗) a square
7 (✗) any nice cafés
8 (✓) a lot of old houses

b) Work in pairs. Compare answers.

7 Work in the same pairs. Student A → p86. Student B → p92.

Get ready ... Get it right!

8 Look at the picture and the places (a cinema, hotels, etc.) Write eight questions to ask another student about places near his / her home. Use Is there a ... ? and Are there any ... ?.

Is there a cinema near your home?
Are there any hotels?

a cinema   hotels
shops   a park   a post office
a supermarket   a shopping centre
good restaurants   a station
nice cafés   a market   a bus stop
old buildings

9 a) Work in pairs. Ask your questions from 8. Make notes on your partner's answers. Give more information about places near your home if possible.

> Is there a cinema near your home?

> Yes, there is. It's five minutes away.

b) Work in new pairs. Talk about places near your first partner's home.

> There's a cinema near Gabi's home, but there aren't any hotels.

Help with Listening sections focus on the areas that make spoken English so difficult to understand and help students to listen more effectively.

Get ready ... Get it right! sections are structured communicative speaking tasks that focus on both accuracy and fluency. The Get ready ... stage provides the opportunity for students to plan the language and content of what they are going to say so that they can Get it right! when they do the communicative stage of the activity.

Reduced sample pages from **face2face** Starter Student's Book

Lesson C *Real World* lessons focus on the functional and situational language students need to communicate effectively in an English-speaking environment.

Real World sections focus on the language that students need in a particular situation or context, often using easy-to-follow flow charts.

The integrated pronunciation syllabus includes drills for all new *Real World* language.

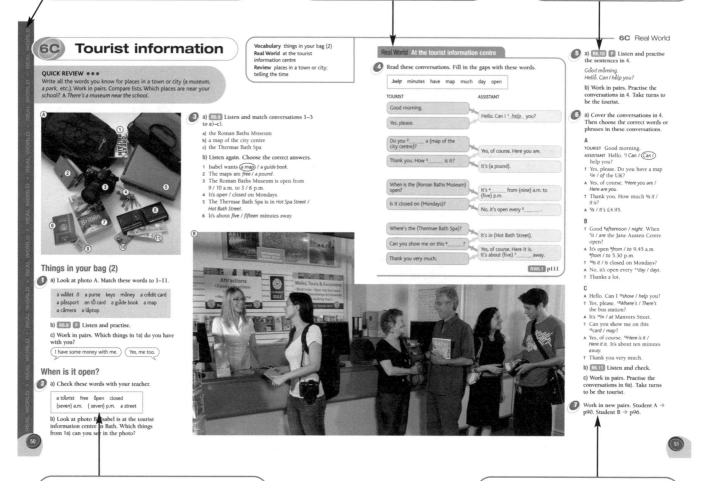

6C Real World

6C Tourist information

QUICK REVIEW ● ● ●
Write all the words you know for places in a town or city (*a museum, a park*, etc.). Work in pairs. Compare lists. Which places are near your school? A *There's a museum near the school.*

Things in your bag (2)

1 a) Look at photo A. Match these words to 1–11.

a wallet   a purse   keys   money   a credit card
a passport   an ID card   a guide book   a map
a camera   a laptop

b) [R6.8] [P] Listen and practise.

c) Work in pairs. Which things in 1a) do you have with you?

I have some money with me.   Yes, me too.

When is it open?

2 a) Check these words with your teacher.

a tourist   free   open   closed
(seven) a.m.   (seven) p.m.   a street

b) Look at photo B. Isabel is at the tourist information centre in Bath. Which things from 1a) can you see in the photo?

3 a) [R6.9] Listen and match conversations 1–3 to a)–c).
a) the Roman Baths Museum
b) a map of the city centre
c) the Thermae Bath Spa

b) Listen again. Choose the correct answers.
1 Isabel wants *a map* / *a guide book.*
2 The maps are *free* / *a pound.*
3 The Roman Baths Museum is open from 9 / 10 a.m. to 5 / 6 p.m.
4 It's *open* / *closed* on Mondays.
5 The Thermae Bath Spa is in *Hot Spa Street* / *Hot Bath Street.*
6 It's about *five* / *fifteen* minutes away.

Vocabulary things in your bag (2)
Real World at the tourist information centre
Review places in a town or city; telling the time

Real World At the tourist information centre

4 Read these conversations. Fill in the gaps with these words.

help   minutes   have   map   much   day   open

TOURIST	ASSISTANT
Good morning.	Hello. Can I ¹ *help* you?
Yes, please.	
Do you ² ____ a (map of the city centre)?	Yes, of course. Here you are.
Thank you. How ³ ____ is it?	It's (a pound).
When is the (Roman Baths Museum) open?	It's ⁴ ____ from (nine) a.m. to (five) p.m.
Is it closed on (Mondays)?	No, it's open every ⁵ ____ .
Where's the (Thermae Bath Spa)?	It's in (Hot Bath Street).
Can you show me on this ⁶ ____ ?	Yes, of course. Here it is. It's about (five) ⁷ ____ away.
Thank you very much.	

[RW6.1] p111

5 a) [R6.10] [P] Listen and practise the sentences in 4.
Good morning.
Hello. Can I help you?

b) Work in pairs. Practise the conversations in 4. Take turns to be the tourist.

6 a) Cover the conversations in 4. Then choose the correct words or phrases in these conversations.

A
T Good morning.
ASSISTANT Hello. ¹*I Can* / *Can I* help you?
T Yes, please. Do you have a map ²*in* / *of* the UK?
A Yes, of course. ³*Here you are* / *Here are you.*
T Thank you. How much ⁴*is it* / *it is*?
A ⁵*Is* / *It's* £4.95.

B
T Good ⁶*afternoon* / *night*. When ⁷*is* / *are* the Jane Austen Centre open?
A It's open ⁸*from* / *to* 9.45 a.m. ⁹*from* / *to* 5.30 p.m.
T ¹⁰*Is it* / *Is* closed on Mondays?
A No, it's open every ¹¹*day* / *days.*
T Thanks a lot.

C
A Hello. Can I ¹²*show* / *help* you?
T Yes, please. ¹³*Where's* / *There's* the bus station?
A It's ¹⁴*in* / *at* Manvers Street.
T Can you show me on this ¹⁵*card* / *map*?
A Yes, of course. ¹⁶*Here is it* / *Here it is.* It's about ten minutes away.
T Thank you very much.

b) [R6.11] Listen and check.

c) Work in pairs. Practise the conversations in 6a). Take turns to be the tourist.

7 Work in new pairs. Student A → p90. Student B → p96.

50   51

New vocabulary that students need for a listening or reading text is always pre-taught, enabling the students to complete the comprehension tasks successfully.

The *Pair and Group Work* section in the back of the Student's Book provides a wide variety of communicative speaking practice activities.

Reduced sample pages from **face2face** Starter Student's Book

Lesson D *Vocabulary in Context* lessons present and practise new vocabulary through visual contexts and reading texts.

Help with Sounds sections present and practise sounds that are often problematic for learners of English.

The *Review* sections provide revision of key language from the unit. These activities can be done in class or for homework and will help students prepare for the *Progress Test* for the unit (see p161–p175 of this book).

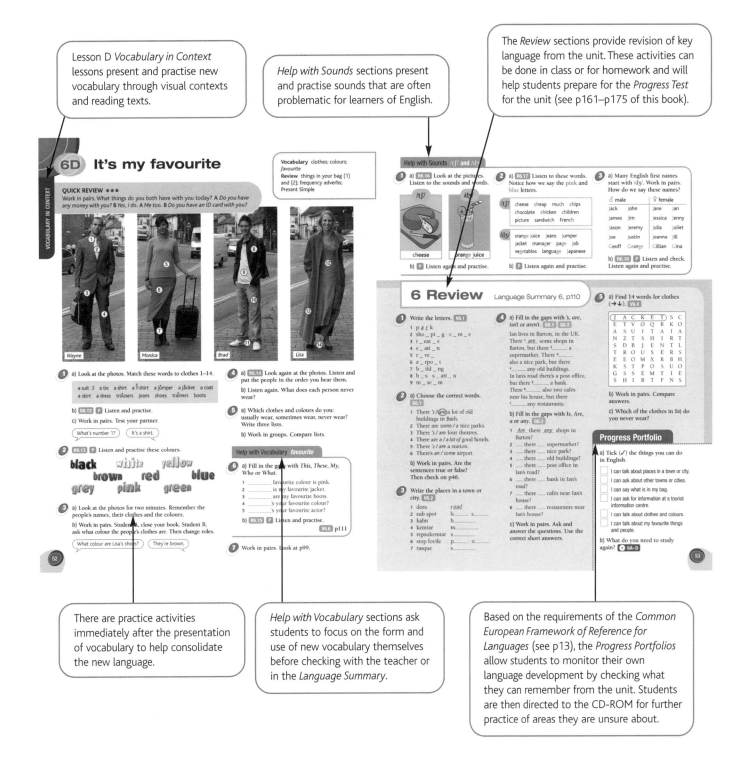

There are practice activities immediately after the presentation of vocabulary to help consolidate the new language.

Help with Vocabulary sections ask students to focus on the form and use of new vocabulary themselves before checking with the teacher or in the *Language Summary*.

Based on the requirements of the *Common European Framework of Reference for Languages* (see p13), the *Progress Portfolios* allow students to monitor their own language development by checking what they can remember from the unit. Students are then directed to the CD-ROM for further practice of areas they are unsure about.

Reduced sample pages from **face2face** Starter Student's Book

The CD-ROM/Audio CD: Instructions

- Use the CD-ROM/Audio CD in your computer to practise all the new language from the Student's Book.

- Use the CD-ROM/Audio CD in CD players at home or in your car. You can practise the language from the *Real World* lessons (lesson C in each unit).

Look at the *Language Summary* reference for the *Grammar* and *Real World* language you have learned in the lessons. You can also add your own notes.

Read, listen and record yourself saying any word or phrase from the Student's Book.

Learn the phonemic symbols and practise saying the sounds.

Check your progress.

Make your own *Tests* from over 500 questions.

Practise the language from the Student's Book in over 200 different activities.

Listen and record yourself saying example sentences and words from the Student's Book.

Read and listen again to the main recordings from the Student's Book.

Watch video clips which recycle language learned in the *Real World* lessons in the context of a story. You can also record yourself speaking the conversations.

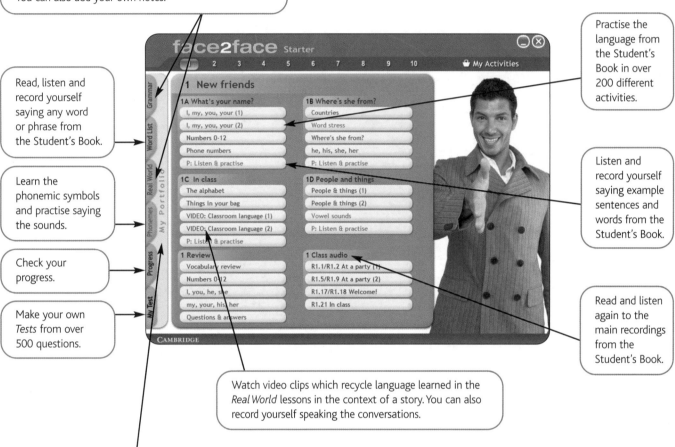

How to use *My Portfolio*

Grammar

Click on the *Grammar* tab to open the *Grammar* screen. It gives all the information from the *Language Summaries* in the Student's Book.

Click on the name of a grammar area to find the information you need.

You can write your own grammar notes.

When you are working on an activity, you can click on *Grammar* to get help.

Two screenshots from **face2face** Starter CD-ROM/Audio CD

face2face Starter Photocopiable

Phonemes

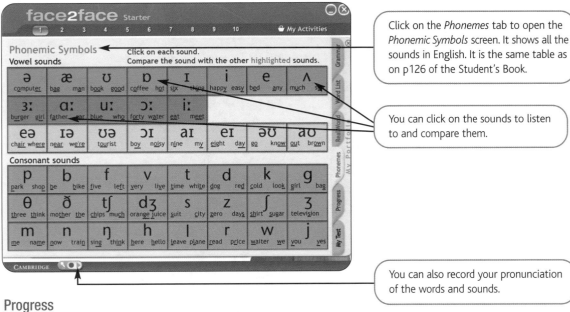

Click on the *Phonemes* tab to open the *Phonemic Symbols* screen. It shows all the sounds in English. It is the same table as on p126 of the Student's Book.

You can click on the sounds to listen to and compare them.

You can also record your pronunciation of the words and sounds.

Progress

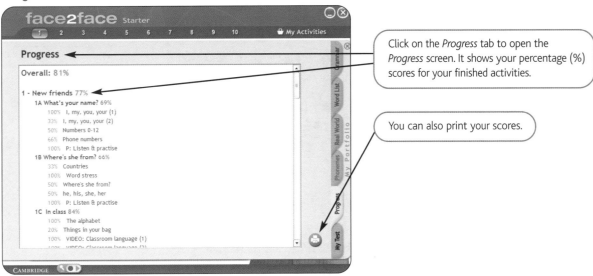

Click on the *Progress* tab to open the *Progress* screen. It shows your percentage (%) scores for your finished activities.

You can also print your scores.

My Test

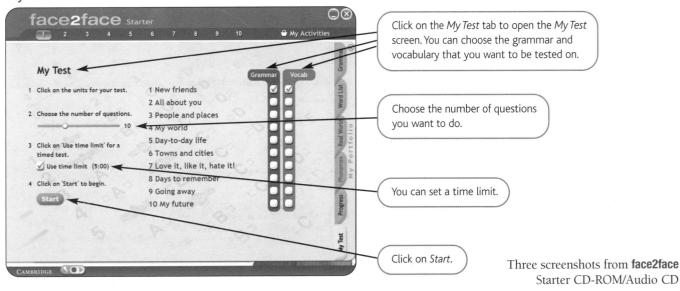

Click on the *My Test* tab to open the *My Test* screen. You can choose the grammar and vocabulary that you want to be tested on.

Choose the number of questions you want to do.

You can set a time limit.

Click on *Start*.

Three screenshots from **face2face** Starter CD-ROM/Audio CD

The CD-ROM/Audio CD

How to practise new language

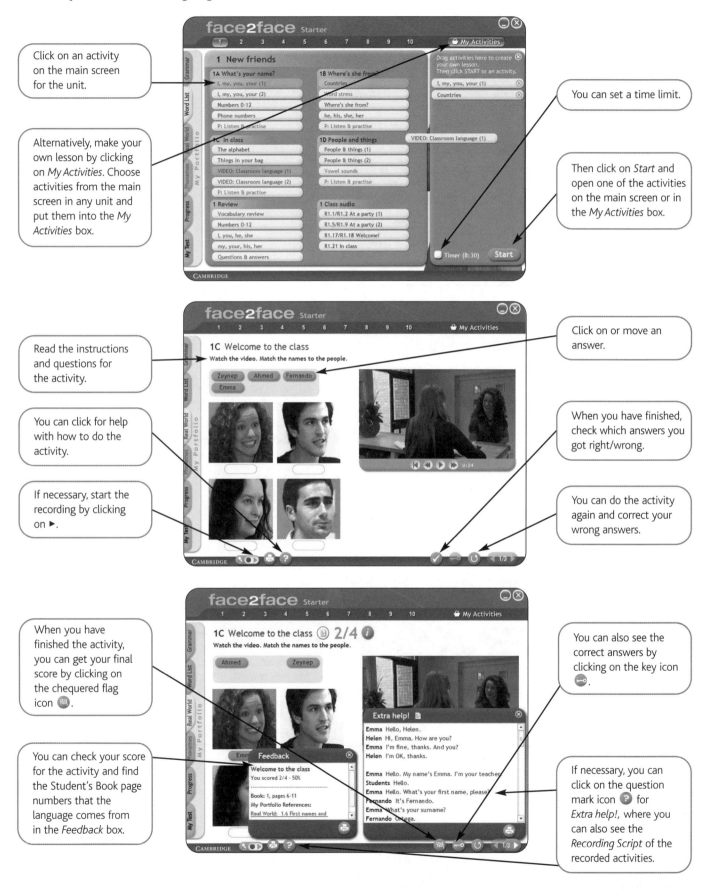

Click on an activity on the main screen for the unit.

Alternatively, make your own lesson by clicking on *My Activities*. Choose activities from the main screen in any unit and put them into the *My Activities* box.

You can set a time limit.

Then click on *Start* and open one of the activities on the main screen or in the *My Activities* box.

Read the instructions and questions for the activity.

You can click for help with how to do the activity.

If necessary, start the recording by clicking on ►.

Click on or move an answer.

When you have finished, check which answers you got right/wrong.

You can do the activity again and correct your wrong answers.

When you have finished the activity, you can get your final score by clicking on the chequered flag icon.

You can check your score for the activity and find the Student's Book page numbers that the language comes from in the *Feedback* box.

You can also see the correct answers by clicking on the key icon.

If necessary, you can click on the question mark icon for *Extra help!*, where you can also see the *Recording Script* of the recorded activities.

Three screenshots from **face2face** Starter CD-ROM/Audio CD

face2face Starter Photocopiable

The Common European Framework (CEF)

What is the Common European Framework (CEF)?

Since the early 1970s, a series of Council of Europe initiatives has developed a description of the language knowledge and skills that people need to live, work and survive in any country or environment where the main language of communication is different form their own language. *Waystage 1990*[1], *Threshold 1990*[2] and *Vantage*[3] detail the knowledge and skills required at different levels of ability.

The contents of these language specific documents served as the basis for the more general *Common European Framework of Reference for Languages: Learning, teaching, assessment* (CEF)[4] which was officially launched by the Council of Europe in 2001 and includes sets of 'can do' statements or 'competences'. A related document, *The European Language Portfolio*, encourages learners to assess their progress by matching their competences against the 'can do' statements.

The **face2face** series has been developed to include comprehensive coverage of the requirements of the CEF. The table above right shows how **face2face** relates to the CEF and the examinations which can be taken at each level through University of Cambridge ESOL Examinations (Cambridge ESOL), which is a member of ALTE (The Association of Language Testers in Europe).

face2face Student's Book	CEF level	Related examinations	Council of Europe document
Starter	A1		*Breakthrough*
Elementary	A2	KET Key English Test	*Waystage*
Pre-intermediate	B1	PET Preliminary English Test	*Threshold*
Intermediate			
Upper Intermediate	B2	FCE First Certificate in English	*Vantage*
Advanced	C1	CAE Cambridge Advanced Certificate	

In the spirit of *The European Language Portfolio* developed from the CEF, **face2face** provides a *Progress Portfolio* at the end of every Student's Book unit. Students are encouraged to assess their ability to use the language they have learned so far and to review any aspects by using the CD-ROM/Audio CD. In the Workbook there is a 20-page *Reading and Writing Portfolio* section linked to the CEF and a comprehensive list of 'can do' statements in the *Reading and Writing Progress Portfolio*, which allows students to track their own progress.

face2face Starter and CEF level A1

The table on the right describes the general degree of skill required at A1 of the CEF. Details of the language knowledge required for A1 are listed in *Breakthrough*. The 'can do' statements for A1 are listed in the *Common European Framework of Reference for Languages: Learning, teaching, assessment*.

face2face Starter covers level A1. The Listening, Reading, Speaking and Writing tables on p14–p17 show where the required competences for level A1 are covered in **face2face** Starter.

More information about how **face2face** Starter covers the grammatical, lexical and other areas specified for A1 by *Breakthrough* can be found on our website: www.cambridge.org/elt/face2face

U N D E R S T A N D I N G	Listening	I can recognise familiar words and very basic phrases concerning myself, my family and immediate concrete surroundings when people speak slowly and clearly.
	Reading	I can understand familiar names, words and very simple sentences, for example on notices and posters or in catalogues.
S P E A K I N G	Spoken Interaction	I can interact in a simple way provided the other person is prepared to repeat or rephrase things at a slower rate of speech and help me formulate what I'm trying to say. I can ask and answer simple questions in areas of immediate need or on very familiar topics.
	Spoken Production	I can use simple phrases and sentences to describe where I live and people I know.
W R I T I N G	Writing	I can write a short, simple postcard, for example sending holiday greetings. I can fill in forms with personal details, for example entering my name, nationality and address on a hotel registration form.

[1] *Waystage 1990* J A van Ek and J L M Trim, Council of Europe, Cambridge University Press ISBN 978-0-521-56707-7

[2] *Threshold 1990* J A van Ek and J L M Trim, Council of Europe, Cambridge University Press ISBN 978-0-521-56706-0

[3] *Vantage* J A van Ek and J L M Trim, Council of Europe, Cambridge University Press ISBN 987-0-521-56705-3

[4] *Common European Framework of Reference for Languages: Learning, teaching, assessment* (2001) Council of Europe Modern Languages Division, Strasbourg, Cambridge University Press ISBN 978-0-521-80313-7 © Council of Europe

Listening

A language user at level A1 can:	1	2	3
understand basic greetings and phrases (*Hello*, *Excuse me*, etc.)	1A 1C	2A 2C 2D	3C
understand simple questions about themselves	1A 1B 1C	2B 2C 2D	3B
understand very short dialogues	1A 1B 1C	2B 2C 2D	3B 3C 3D
understand numbers, prices and times	1A	2D	3C
understand short simple directions			

Reading

A language user at level A1 can:	1	2	3
understand very short, simple texts, a single phrase at a time	WBP1		3A
pick out familiar names, words and phrases in very short, simple texts			3A
pick out information from catalogues, posters and calendars of public events about the time and place of films, concerts, etc.			
get an idea of the content of simpler informational material and short, simple descriptions (especially if there is visual support)			
understand information about people in newspapers, etc. (age, place of residence, etc.)			
understand simple forms well enough to give basic personal details		2C WBP2	
understand common commands	This competence is practised throughout the course in the rubrics.		
follow instructions that have clear pictures and few words	This competence is practised throughout the course in the rubrics.		
follow short, simple written directions			
understand short, simple messages on postcards			WBP3
understand simple messages written by friends or colleagues about everyday situations (text messages, invitations, etc.)			

1A = **face2face** Starter Student's Book unit 1 lesson A   WBP1 = **face2face** Starter Workbook Reading and Writing Portfolio 1

4	5	6	7	8	9	10
4B 4C	5C	6C	7B 7C 7D			10B 10C
4B	5A	6D	7A 7B	8B 8C	9B 9D	10B 10C
4B 4C 4D	5B 5C	6B 6C	7B 7C 7D	8B 8C	9C	10B
4C 4D	5A 5C	6C		8C 8D	9C	
			7C			

4	5	6	7	8	9	10
4A 4B WBP4	5A 5D WBP5	6A	7A WBP7	8A	9A 9B 9D	10A
4A 4B WBP4	5D WBP5		7A WBP7	8A	9A 9B 9D	10A
4D		6C		WBP8		
WBP4		6A WBP6		8A 8D	9A 9B WBP9	10A
4B	5D WBP5				9A	
			7C			
						WBP10

Speaking

A language user at level A1 can:	1	2	3
introduce someone and use basic greeting and leave-taking expressions	1A	2C	
ask and answer simple questions and initiate and respond to simple statements in areas of immediate need or on very familiar topics	1A 1B 1C 1D	2A 2B 2C 2D	3A 3B 3C
ask and answer questions about themselves and other people, where they live, things they have, people they know	1B	2B 2C 2D	3B 3D
give personal information (address, telephone number, etc.)	1A 1B 1C	2A 2B 2C 2D	3B
describe where he/she lives			
handle numbers, quantities, costs and times	1A	2C 2D	3C
make simple purchases			3C
ask people for things and give people things			3C
indicate time by such phrases as *next week, in November, on Monday,* etc.			
say when he/she doesn't understand	1C		
ask someone to repeat what they say	1C		

Writing

A language user at level A1 can:	1	2	3
copy familiar words and short phrases	This competence is practised throughout the Student's Book and Workbook.		
spell his/her address, nationality and other personal details	1B 1C WBP1	2A 2C WBP2	
write sentences and simple phrases about themselves and others (where they live and what they do, etc.)	WBP1		3D
fill in a questionnaire or form with personal details		2C WBP2	
write a greetings card			
write a simple postcard			WBP3
link words or groups of words with very basic linear connectors (*and, but, so, because,* etc.)			WBP3

1A = **face2face** Starter Student's Book unit 1 lesson A

WBP1 = **face2face** Starter Workbook Reading and Writing Portfolio 1

4	5	6	7	8	9	10
						10C
4A 4B 4D	5A	6A 6B	7A 7C	8A 8B	9A 9B 9C 9D	10A 10B 10C
4B	5A 5B	6B 6D	7A 7B 7D	8B 8C	9B 9C 9D	10B 10C
4A	5A 5D			8A 8C	9A	10A
4B		6A 6B				
4C 4D	5C	6A 6B		8C 8D	9C 9D	
4C		6C			9C	
4C	5C	6C			9C	
	5A 5B 5D	6C		8A 8B 8C	9A 9B	10A 10B 10C

4	5	6	7	8	9	10
4A 4B WBP4	5A 5B 5D WBP5	6A 6D WBP6	7A 7B WBP7	8A WBP8	9A 9B 9C WBP9	10A 10B
						WBP10
	WBP5		WBP7		WBP9	

Teaching Tips

Teaching Starter Classes

Teaching Starter classes can often be challenging as well as rewarding. Starter students can lack confidence and might not have studied a language formally before. Here are some tips to help you teach Starter classes.

- Each lesson in the Student's Book is carefully staged and takes students step-by-step from presentation to practice. Go slowly and methodically through the material exercise by exercise, making sure that students understand each point before moving on.

- Keep your instructions in class short, clear and to the point. Students can often get lost if the teacher talks too much in English. It is perfectly acceptable to use imperatives to give instructions (*Look at exercise 3. Work in pairs.*, etc.). Teach the words and phrases in Classroom Instructions, SB p127 early in the course.

- Most exercises in the Student's Book have an example already filled in. Use these examples to check that the class knows what to do before asking students to work on their own or in pairs.

- Take time to demonstrate communicative activities with the class. At Starter level, demonstration is often a more effective way to give instructions than describing what to do. You can demonstrate activities yourself or by using a confident student as your partner.

- Do a lot of drilling. This helps to build students' confidence and allows them time to practise new language in a controlled way. All new vocabulary, grammar and *Real World* language is included on the Class Audio CDs to provide clear models of new language. See the tips on drilling on p20.

- Using the board is particularly important with Starter students. In the Teaching Notes (p21–p99) this icon 🖉 indicates a point in the lesson where it may be useful for you to use the board.

- When using the board, try to involve students in what you are writing by asking questions (*What's the next word?*, *Where's the stress?*, etc.). Give students time to copy what you have written and leave useful language on the board so that students can refer to it during the lesson.

- Show students the *Language Summaries* on SB p100–p119 early on in the course and encourage them to refer to these in class and when doing homework.

- Starter students need a lot of revision and recycling throughout the course. See the tips on reviewing and recycling on p20.

- It is, of course, very useful to know the students' first language. If you have a monolingual class, you may want to use the students' language to give or check instructions for speaking activities, or to deal with students' queries. However, try to speak to the class in English as much as possible, as this will help establish the classroom as an English-speaking environment.

- Remember that at Starter level, encouragement and praise are very important, particularly for weaker students.

Teaching Mixed Levels

In Starter classes teachers are often faced with a mixture of real beginners and 'false' beginners. Here are some tips to help you deal with teaching low-level mixed-ability classes.

- Work at the pace of the average student. Try not to let the fastest or slowest students dictate the pace.

- To prevent stronger students from dominating, nominate the quieter ones to answer easier questions.

- Ask stronger and more confident students to demonstrate activities for the whole class.

- Allow time for students to check answers in pairs or groups before checking with the whole class.

- Encourage stronger students to help weaker ones; for example, if a student has finished an activity, ask him/her to work with a slower student.

- Give students time to think by asking them to write down answers rather than calling them out. This helps prevent the more able students from dominating the class.

- When monitoring during pair and group work, go to the weaker students first to check that they have understood the instructions and are doing the activity correctly.

- Plan which students are going to work together in pair and group work. Vary the interaction so that stronger students sometimes work with weaker students, and at other times (for example, during freer speaking activities) students work with other students of the same level.

- Don't feel that you have to wait for everyone in the class to finish an exercise. It is usually best to stop an activity when most of the class has finished.

- Vary the amount and type of correction you give according to the level of the student, in order to push stronger students and to avoid overwhelming those who are less confident. Remember to praise successful communication as well as correct language.

- Give weaker students extra homework from the Workbook or the CD-ROM/Audio CD to help them catch up with areas of language the rest of the class is confident with.

Listening

- For most Starter students, listening to spoken English is usually very challenging. Be sensitive to the difficulties that students might be having and play a recording several times if necessary.

- At this level, activities where students listen and read at the same time are very useful, as they allow students to 'tune in' to spoken English and make the connection between what they hear and the written word. Make full use of the 'listen and read' activities in the Student's Book in your classes. For other listening activities, you can ask students to read the Recording Scripts (SB p120–p125) when they listen and check their answers.

- Before asking students to listen to a recording, establish the context, the characters and what information you want them to listen for.

- Give students time to read the comprehension questions in the Student's Book and deal with any problems in these questions before playing a recording.
- Make full use of the *Help with Listening* sections in the Student's Book, which help students to understand natural spoken English.
- Encourage students to listen again to the classroom recordings on their CD-ROM/Audio CD at home. These can be found in the Class Audio section for each unit. Note that students can only listen to these classroom recordings on a computer, not on a CD player.

Speaking

Pair and Group Work

- Make full use of all the communicative speaking activities in the Student's Book, particularly the *Get ready ... Get it right!* sections. These allow students to work out what language to use before they do the communicative stage of the activity, which will help them to retain the accuracy that has been built up during the lesson.
- Help students with the language they need to do speaking tasks by drawing their attention to the 'transactional language' in the speech bubbles.
- Try to ensure that students work with a number of different partners during a class. If your students can't swap places, ask them to work with students behind or in front of them as well as on either side of them.
- It is often useful to provide a model of the tasks you expect students to do. For example, before asking students to talk about their family in pairs, you can talk about your family with the whole class to give students a model of what they are expected to do.
- Go around the class and monitor students while they are speaking in their pairs or groups. At this stage you can provide extra language or ideas and correct any language or pronunciation which is impeding communication.
- When giving feedback on speaking, remember to praise good communication as well as good English, and focus on the result of the task as well as the language used.
- Use the *Class Activities* (p100–p146) to provide extra communicative speaking practice in class.

Correction

- When you hear a mistake, it is often useful to correct it immediately and ask the student to say the word or phrase again in the correct form, particularly if the mistake relates to the language you have been working on in the lesson.
- Alternatively, when you point out a mistake to a student you can encourage him/her to correct it himself/herself before giving him/her the correct version.
- Another approach to correction during a freer speaking activity is to note down any mistakes you hear, but not correct them immediately. At the end of the activity write the mistakes on the board. Students can then work in pairs and correct the mistakes. Alternatively, you can discuss the mistakes with the whole class.

Vocabulary

- Most of the new vocabulary in **face2face** Starter is presented pictorially and students are usually asked to match words to pictures themselves. If all your class are real beginners, consider introducing new vocabulary yourself first by bringing in pictures, flashcards, objects, etc. and teaching the words one by one. You can then use the first exercise in the Student's Book as practice.
- Point out the stress marks (*) on all new words and phrases in the vocabulary boxes in the lessons and the *Language Summaries*. Note that these show only the **main** stress on words and phrases.
- Make full use of the *Help with Vocabulary* sections in the Student's Book. These focus on lexical grammar and help students to understand the underlying patterns of how vocabulary is used in sentences. You can either go through each point with the whole class or ask students to do the exercises themselves before you check answers with the class, as shown in the *Teaching Notes* for each lesson.
- Make students aware of collocations in English (e.g. *start work, have dinner, go to the beach,* etc.) by pointing them out when they occur and encouraging students to record them as one phrase in their notebooks.
- Review and recycle vocabulary at every opportunity in class, using the *Reviews*, the *Language Summaries* and the *Class Activities*.
- Use the photocopiable *Vocabulary Plus* worksheets (p147–p160). These worksheets introduce and practise extra vocabulary which is **not** included in the Student's Book. They can be used for self-study in class or as homework, or as the basis of a classroom lesson. There is one *Vocabulary Plus* worksheet for each unit in the Student's Book.

Grammar

- Make full use of the *Help with Grammar* sections in the Student's Book. These highlight the rules for form and use of each grammar point. You can either go through each point with the whole class, or ask students to do the exercises themselves before you check answers with the class, as shown in the *Teaching Notes* for each lesson.
- Sentences in the grammar tables in the Student's Book are often colour-coded. When using these tables, use the pink and blue words to highlight the underlying grammatical patterns of the new language.
- Teach your students useful grammatical terms (e.g. noun, verb, Present Simple, etc.) when the opportunity arises. This helps students become more independent and allows them to use grammar reference books more effectively. However, try not to overload students with terminology at this level.
- If you know the students' first language, highlight grammatical differences between their language and English. This raises their awareness of potential problems if they try to translate. It is also useful to highlight grammatical similarities when a structure in English is the same as in the students' own language.

Pronunciation

Drilling

- Make full use of the pronunciation drills on the Class Audio CDs. These drills are marked with the icon **P** in the Student's Book and give standard British native-speaker models of the language taught.

- Note that there are already sufficient pauses built into these recorded drills for students to repeat chorally without you having to pause the recording. If students are finding a particular word or sentence difficult to pronounce, you can pause the recording and ask each student to repeat individually before continuing.

- Point out that all the recorded drills are also on the **face2face** CD-ROM/Audio CD. Encourage students to use these for pronunciation practice on their computer at home.

- For variety, you can model and drill the sentences yourself instead of using the recordings. When you model a phrase or sentence, make sure that you speak at normal speed with natural stress and contractions. Repeat the target language two or three times before asking the whole class to repeat after you in a 'choral drill'.

- After choral drilling it is usually helpful to do some individual drilling. Start with the strongest students and drill around the class in random order.

- As the aim of drilling is accuracy, you should correct students when they make a mistake. However, avoid making the students feel uncomfortable and don't spend too long with one student.

- After drilling new language, you can ask two students to practise alternate lines of a conversation from where they are sitting, with the rest of the class listening. This 'open pairs' technique is very useful to check students' pronunciation before they go on to practise in 'closed pairs'. It can also be used after students have worked in closed pairs to check their performance of the task.

- Praise students for good/comprehensible pronunciation and acknowledge weak students' improvement, even if their pronunciation is not perfect.

- Students can also listen to the audio component of the CD-ROM/Audio CD on their CD players. This contains *Real World* drills from each lesson C in the Student's Book.

Helping students with stress and intonation

- Point out the stress marks on all new vocabulary in the vocabulary boxes and the *Language Summaries*. Note that only the **main** stress in each new word or phrase is shown. For example, in the phrase *finish work*, the main stress on *work* is shown, but the secondary stress on *finish* is not. We feel this simplified system is the most effective way to help students stress words and phrases correctly.

- When drilling new vocabulary, pay particular attention to words that sound different from how they are spelt. Words that students often find difficult to pronounce are highlighted in the *Teaching Notes* for each lesson.

- When you write words or sentences on the board, mark the stress in the correct place or ask the students to tell you which syllables or words are stressed.

- When you model sentences yourself, it may be helpful to over-emphasise the stress pattern to help students hear the stress. You can also 'beat' the stress with your hand or fist.

- Emphasise that intonation is an important part of meaning in English and often shows how we feel. For example, a falling intonation on the word *please* can sound very impolite to a native English speaker.

- Encourage students to copy the intonation pattern of model sentences on the recorded drills, particularly in the *Real World* sections in lesson C of each unit.

Helping students with sounds

- Make full use of the *Help with Sounds* sections at the end of each unit in the Student's Book. These focus on sounds in English that most learners find difficult to pronounce.

- If students are having problems making a particular sound, you can demonstrate the shape of the mouth and the position of the tongue in front of the class (or draw this on the board). Often students can't say these sounds simply because they don't know the mouth position required. The mouth positions for all sounds in the *Help with Sounds* sections can be found in the *Teaching Notes* for each unit.

- Draw students' attention to the English sounds which are the same in their own language(s) as well as highlighting the ones that are different.

- Encourage students to use the pronunciation activities in each unit of the CD-ROM/Audio CD at home. Students can also use the phonemes section of the CD-ROM/Audio CD to practise individual sounds.

Reviewing and Recycling

- Use the *Quick Reviews* at the beginning of each lesson. They are easy to set up and should take no more than five to ten minutes. They are a good way of getting the class to speak immediately as well as reviewing what students have learned in previous lessons.

- Exploit the *Review* sections at the end of each unit. They can be done in class when students have finished the unit, or set for homework. Note that the *Review* exercises are organised in lesson order, so that individual exercises can be used as fillers at the beginning or end of a lesson.

- After a mid-lesson break, ask students to write down in one minute all the words they can remember from the first part of the lesson. These quick 'What have we just learned?' activities are very important for helping students transfer information from their short-term memory to their long-term memory.

- Encourage students to use the **face2face** CD-ROM/Audio CD to review each lesson at home. Also encourage students to review new language by reading the *Language Summary* for the lesson.

- Set homework after every class. The **face2face** Starter Workbook has a section for each lesson in the Student's Book, which reviews all the key language taught in that particular lesson.

- Give students a *Progress Test* (p161–p175) after completing each unit of the Student's Book. These can be done in class or given for homework.

1 New friends

Student's Book p6–p13

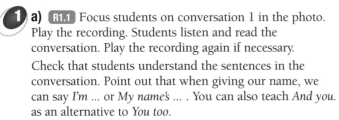

1A What's your name?

Hello!

1 a) **R1.1** Focus students on conversation 1 in the photo. Play the recording. Students listen and read the conversation. Play the recording again if necessary.

Check that students understand the sentences in the conversation. Point out that when giving our name, we can say *I'm …* or *My name's …* . You can also teach *And you.* as an alternative to *You too*.

P (= pronunciation activity) Play the recording again, pausing after each sentence for students to repeat. Alternatively, model each sentence yourself and ask students to repeat chorally and individually. For tips on drilling, see p20.

b) Demonstrate the activity yourself by role-playing the conversation with a confident student. Then ask students to practise the conversation with four other students, either by moving around the room or by talking to students sitting near them. Students should use their own first names.

— EXTRA IDEA —

- Before asking students to practise the conversation in pairs, choose two confident students and ask them to practise the conversation for the class. Students don't have to leave their seats. Correct students' pronunciation as necessary, then ask them to practise the conversation again. Repeat this 'open pairs' procedure with other students. If this technique works well with your class, use it when appropriate in future lessons.

c) Focus students on the speech bubbles. Students take turns to introduce themselves to the class.

— EXTRA IDEA —

- ✎ Draw a plan of the class seating arrangements on the board and write in the students' names as they introduce themselves to the class. Leave the plan on the board for students to refer to during the lesson.

2 a) **R1.2** Focus students on conversation 2 in the photo. Play the recording. Students listen and read.

Check students understand all the sentences in the conversation. Point out that *Hi = Hello* and *I'm fine = I'm OK*. You can also point out that *Hi* is more informal than *Hello*.

P Play the recording again, pausing after each sentence for students to repeat. Alternatively, model each sentence yourself and ask students to repeat chorally and individually.

Vocabulary numbers 0–12
Grammar *I, my, you, your*
Real World saying hello; introducing people; phone numbers; saying goodbye

b) Demonstrate the activity yourself by role-playing the conversation with a confident student. Then ask students to practise the conversation with four other students, either by moving around the room or by talking to students sitting near them. Students should use their own first names.

Help with Grammar *I, my, you, your*

- Help with Grammar boxes help students to examine examples of new language and discover the rules of meaning, form and use for themselves. Students should usually do the exercises on their own or in pairs before you check the answers with the class. For tips on how to teach grammar, see p19.

3 a)–b) Students do the exercises on their own or in pairs. Check answers with the class.

- **a)** 2 I 3 My
- **b)** 2 you 3 your
- Highlight the difference between *I/my* and *you/your*.
- Point out that we use *I/you* + verb (*I read*, **you** *listen*, etc.) and *my/your* + noun (**my** *name*, **your** *book*, etc.).
- Also point out that we always use a capital *I* when we refer to ourselves.
- You can also tell students that there is no polite form of *you* in English.
- Students may ask you about the meaning of *'m*, *are* and *'s* in the example sentences. Tell the class they are part of the verb *be*, but treat the new language as fixed phrases at this stage of the course. Note that the verb *be* is taught systematically in units 2 and 3.

— EXTRA IDEA —

- Highlight the Language Summary reference **G1.1** in the Help with Grammar box and then ask students to turn to Language Summary 1, SB p100–p101. Ask students to find **G1.1** and give them time to read the information. Point out that all the new language in each unit is included in the Language Summaries.

R1.3 Focus students on the sentences in **3**. Play the recording. Students listen and practise. Note that in most recorded drills there are already sufficient pauses for students to repeat chorally without you pausing the recording yourself.

5 **a)** Students do the exercise on their own, then compare answers in pairs.

b) **R1.4** Play the recording. Students listen and check their answers. Check answers with the class.

> **A**
> SUE   Hello, **my** name's Sue. What's **your** name?
> MARIO   Hello, **I'm** Mario.
> SUE   Nice to meet **you**.
> MARIO   **You** too.
> **B**
> ADAM   Hi, Meg.
> MEG   Hi, Adam. How are **you**?
> ADAM   I'm fine, thanks. And **you**?
> MEG   I'm OK, thanks.

c) Students practise the conversations in pairs. Ask a few pairs to role-play the conversations for the class.

Introducing people

6 **a)** **R1.5** Focus students on conversation 3 in the photo. Play the recording. Students listen and read the conversation.

Check students understand that we use *this is ...* to introduce people.

P Play the recording again, pausing after each sentence for students to repeat. Alternatively, model each sentence yourself and ask students to repeat chorally and individually.

b) Put students into groups of three. Students practise conversation 3 in their groups.

Ask a few groups to role-play their conversations for the class. Alternatively, ask students to move around the room and introduce people to each other.

Numbers 0–12

7 **a)** **R1.6** **P** Teach the word *number*. Play the recording. Students listen and repeat the numbers. Alternatively, model the words yourself and ask students to repeat chorally and individually.

Highlight the pronunciation of *zero* /ˈzɪərəʊ/ and *eight* /eɪt/. Repeat the drill if necessary.

b) Demonstrate the activity by saying four numbers and asking students to write them down. Check they have the correct answers. Students then do the exercise in pairs.

> ── EXTRA IDEA ──
> • Students work in pairs and count alternately from 0 to 12. They can then count backwards alternately from 12 to 0.

Phone numbers

8 **a)** **R1.7** Pre-teach *phone number*. Play the recording. Students listen and read the questions and answers.

Check students understand *mobile number* and *home number* by referring to the photos.

Point out the **TIP!** on how to say 0 and double digits (44, etc.) in phone numbers. Note that we can also use *zero* in phone numbers.

P Play the recording again, pausing after each sentence for students to repeat individually.

b) Students do the exercise in pairs.

9 **a)** **R1.8** Play the recording (SB p120). Students listen and write the numbers. Play the recording again if necessary.

b) Students compare answers in pairs. ✍ Check answers with the class by eliciting the phone numbers and writing them on the board.

You can also use the recording to teach the phrases *Yes, that's right. Thanks.* and *Thank you.*

> **A** 020 7599 6320
> **B** 07655 421769
> **C** 00 34 91 532 67 53

> ### Get ready ... Get it right!
>
> • There is a Get ready ... Get it right! activity at the end of every A and B lesson. The Get ready ... stage helps students to collect their ideas and prepare the language they need to complete the task. The Get it right! stage gives students the opportunity to use the language they have learned in the lesson in a communicative (and often personalised) context. These two-stage activities help students to become more fluent without losing the accuracy they have built up during the controlled practice stages of the lesson. For tips on how to teach speaking, see p19.

10 Put students into pairs, student A and student B. Student As turn to SB p86 and student Bs turn to SB p92. Check they are all looking at the correct exercise.

a) Focus students on the *you* column in the table. Students practise saying the numbers on their own.

b) Students do the exercise with their partner. They are not allowed to look at each other's books.

c) Students compare tables and check their partner has written the phone numbers correctly.

> ── EXTRA IDEA ──
> • Students move around the room and ask other students for their mobile numbers and home numbers. If you think that your students might be unwilling to tell each other their real phone numbers, prepare cards with fictitious phone numbers and give one to each student.

Goodbye!

 11 a) `R1.9` Focus students on conversation 4 in the photo. Play the recording. Students listen and read the conversation.

Check students understand the words and sentences in the conversation. Point out that *Bye = Goodbye*.

You can teach *See you tomorrow.* and *See you next class.* as alternatives to *See you soon.*

P Play the recording again, pausing after each sentence for students to repeat. Alternatively, model and drill the sentences yourself.

b) Students move around the room and say goodbye to other students, or say goodbye to students sitting near them.

EXTRA IDEA

- Ask students to do some of the practice activities from lesson 1A on the CD-ROM/Audio CD for homework. For photocopiable instructions on how to use the CD-ROM/Audio CD, see p10–p12.

EXTRA PRACTICE AND HOMEWORK

1 Review Exercises 1 and 2 SB p13

CD-ROM Lesson 1A

Workbook Lesson 1A p3

 # 1B Where's she from?

QUICK REVIEW ●●●

- Quick Reviews begin each lesson in a fun, student-centred way. They are short activities which review previously taught language and are designed to last about five or ten minutes. For tips on reviewing and recycling, see p20.

This activity reviews phone numbers. Students work on their own and write two phone numbers. These can be real or invented numbers. Students do the activity in pairs. Students then check that their partner's numbers are correct.

Vocabulary countries
Grammar *he, his, she, her*
Real World *Where are you from?*
Help with Listening word stress
Review phone numbers; *I, my, you, your*

Countries

 1 Check students remember numbers 1–12. Focus students on the map of the world. Pre-teach *country* and *map*.

Students do the exercise on their own or in pairs. Check answers with the class.

Point out that we use capital letters for countries (**I**taly, **B**razil, etc.). Also point out *the* in **the** USA and **the** UK.

Note that *the USA* is also called *the US, the States, the United States* or *America*. Also note that *the UK* refers to England, Scotland, Wales and Northern Ireland, and that we can say *the UK* or *Britain* /ˈbrɪtən/. The term *Great Britain* refers to the island that contains England, Scotland and Wales, not the country.

> 1 the USA 2 Mexico 3 Brazil 4 the UK 5 Germany
> 6 Spain 7 Italy 8 Turkey 9 Egypt 10 Russia 11 China
> 12 Australia

EXTRA IDEA

- When students have finished the matching activity in **1**, they can check their answers in Language Summary 1 `V1.2` SB p100.

Help with Listening Word stress

- Help with Listening boxes are designed to help students understand natural spoken English. They often focus on phonological aspects of spoken English which make listening problematic for students. For tips on how to teach listening, see p18.
- This Help with Listening section introduces students to the concept of word stress.

 2 `R1.10` Focus students on the word box in **1** and point out how stress is marked in the Student's Book (ˈ). Play the recording. Students listen and notice the word stress.

Use the countries to teach *syllable* and point out the number of syllables in each country (*Italy* = three syllables, *Brazil* = two syllables, etc.).

Also highlight that *Spain* doesn't have a stress mark because it is a one-syllable word.

 3 `R1.10` **P** Play the recording again. Students listen and practise. Check students copy the word stress correctly.

Highlight the pronunciation of *Egypt* /ˈiːdʒɪpt/, *Australia* /ɒsˈtreɪliə/ and *Turkey* /ˈtɜːki/. Repeat the drill if necessary.

 4 Students do the activity in pairs. While they are working, move around the room and correct any pronunciation mistakes that you hear.

Where are you from?

 5 **a)** **R1.11** Focus students on the photo of Stefan and Emel. Play the recording. Students listen to the conversation and fill in the gaps. Check answers with the class.

EMEL	Where are you from, Stefan?
STEFAN	I'm from **Russia**. And you?
EMEL	I'm from **Turkey**.

b) **R1.12** **P** Play the recording (SB p120). Students listen and practise. Repeat the drill if necessary.

c) Focus students on the speech bubbles. Check students know the countries *Japan, France* and *Colombia*, and which country *Moscow* is in (Russia). Pre-teach *city*.

Also highlight that we say *I'm from* + city: *I'm from Moscow.*, etc.

Drill *Japan, Colombia* and *Moscow*, highlighting the stress with the class.

Students take turns to tell the class which country they are from.

— EXTRA IDEAS —

- If you have a multilingual class, write all the students' countries on the board. Mark the stress on each country. Model and drill any new countries with the class.

- If your students are all from the same country or city, ask them to say which city, town or district they are from instead.

d) Students practise the conversation in groups. Alternatively, students move around the room and practise the conversation with six other students.

What's his name?

6 **a)** Students do the exercise on their own. Check answers with the class.

2a) 3d) 4c)

b) **R1.13** **P** Play the recording. Students listen and practise. Check that students pronounce the contractions (*What's, He's*, etc.) correctly. Repeat the drill if necessary.

7 **a)–b)** Students do the exercises on their own or in pairs. Check answers with the class.

- **a)** 2 His 3 he 4 He
- **b)** 2 Her 3 she 4 She
- Highlight the difference between *he/his* and *she/her*.
- Point out that we use *he/she* + verb (**he's**, etc.) and *his/her* + noun (**his** *name*, etc.).
- Also highlight the difference in pronunciation between *he's* /hiːz/ and *his* /hɪz/.

- Students may ask you about the meaning of *'s* in the example sentences. Tell that class that *'s* = *is* and is part of the verb *be*, but encourage students to treat the new language as fixed phrases at this stage of the course. Note that the verb *be* is taught systematically in units 2 and 3.

8 **a)** Focus students on photos 1–6 of famous people. Use the photos to teach *famous, actor* and *actress*. Don't ask students about the names or countries of the famous people at this stage. Students do the activity in pairs.

b) **R1.14** Play the recording (SB p120). Students listen and check their answers.

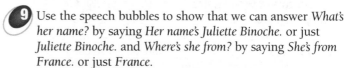 Check answers with the class by eliciting the sentences and writing them on the board.

2 His name's Daniel Craig. He's from the UK.
3 Her name's Nicole Kidman. She's from Australia.
4 His name's Will Smith. He's from the USA.
5 Her name's Penélope Cruz. She's from Spain.
6 His name's Jackie Chan. He's from China.

9 Use the speech bubbles to show that we can answer *What's her name?* by saying *Her name's Juliette Binoche.* or just *Juliette Binoche.* and *Where's she from?* by saying *She's from France.* or just *France.*

Students do the exercise in new pairs.

10 Put students into pairs, student A and student B. Student As turn to SB p87 and student Bs turn to SB p93. Check they are all looking at the correct exercise.

a) Focus students on the photo. Give students a few moments to read the names and countries of the people.

Students work with their partner. Student A in each pair asks about people 1, 3 and 5, as shown in the speech bubbles, and writes the answers in the correct places in his/her book. While students are working, move around the room and check their questions for accuracy.

Note that the names have been chosen as they are easy for most nationalities to spell. However, if the English script is new to your students, you may choose to do this Get ready … Get it right! activity after you have done lesson 1C, where the alphabet and the question *How do you spell that?* are taught and practised.

b) Student B in each pair asks about people 2, 4 and 6, as shown in the speech bubbles, and writes the answers in the correct places in his/her book. When they have finished, students can compare books with their partners and check their answers.

c) Give students one minute to memorise the people's names and countries.

d) Ask students to close their books. Students take turns to ask where the people are from, as shown in the speech bubbles.

Finally, ask students to tell the class where each person is from.

— EXTRA IDEA —

• Use the photocopiable **Class Activity 1B Where's he from?** p112 (Instructions p100).

┌─ EXTRA PRACTICE AND HOMEWORK ─
│ **Class Activity** 1B Where's he from? p112
│ (Instructions p100)
│ **1 Review** Exercises 3 and 4 SB p13
│ **CD-ROM** Lesson 1B
│ **Workbook** Lesson 1B p4
└─

1C In class

Vocabulary the alphabet; things in your bag (1); *a* and *an*
Real World first names and surnames; classroom language
Review *What's his/her name?*

QUICK REVIEW ●●●

This activity reviews *What's his/her name?* and the names of the students in the class. If you have a multilingual class, ask students to practise the question *Where's he/she from?* as well.

Pre-teach *I don't know*. Put students into pairs. Students take turns to ask the names of other students in the class, as shown in the examples.

— EXTRA IDEAS —

• If you have a monolingual class, highlight any differences between the English alphabet and the students' alphabet (extra letters, missing letters, the lack of accents, how particular letters are pronounced, etc.).

• Students work in pairs and take turns to say the letters of the alphabet in order.

The alphabet

1 R1.15 P Focus students on the letters Aa–Zz. Teach *the alphabet* /'ælfəbet/. Play the recording. Students listen and say the alphabet. Alternatively, model and drill the letters yourself.

Point out that the letters in pink are called *vowels* /vauəlz/ and the letters in blue are called *consonants* /'kɒnsənənts/.

If the English script is new for your students, point out that each letter has a capital form (A, B, C, etc.) and a lower-case form (a, b, c, etc.). For more guidance on when we use capital letters in English, see Reading and Writing Portfolios 1 and 2 on p52–p55 of the Workbook.

— EXTRA IDEA —

• If you have a class of false beginners, ask them to close their books and write down the English alphabet from memory. Check the answers by eliciting the alphabet from the class and writing it on the board. Then play R1.15 and ask students to practise saying the letters.

2 R1.16 Play the recording (SB p120). Students listen and write the letters in their lower-case form. There are two letters for each number. Play the recording again if necessary. Note that these letters have been chosen as they are often confused by learners of English.

Students check answers in pairs. Check answers with the class.

1 u v 2 y i 3 g j 4 b v 5 a r 6 e i 7 b p 8 t d 9 u q 10 v w

What's your first name?

3 a) Focus students on photo A. Ask who is the teacher (Kate) and who is the student (Pedro). Tell the class that Pedro is a new student in the class.

Students do the exercise on their own, then compare answers in pairs.

b) R1.17 Play the recording (SB p120). Students listen and check their answers. Check answers with the class.

Highlight the difference between *first name* and *surname*, and check students understand the verb *spell*. Note that this language is drilled in **5a)**.

Use the recording to teach *Thank you* and *Welcome (to the class)*.

4 a) R1.18 Play the recording (SB p120). Students listen and write the names of two more students in Kate's class. Play the recording again if necessary.

b) Students compare answers in pairs. Ask students to spell the names and write them on the board.

1 Magda Janowska 2 Hasan Yousef

— EXTRA IDEA —

• Ask students to look at R1.18, SB p120. Play the recording again. Students listen, read and check their answers.

5 **a)** [R1.19] [P] Focus students on the example drill. Play the recording (SB p120). Students listen and practise.

Highlight the pronunciation of *first name* /'fɜːs neɪm/ and *surname* /'sɜːneɪm/. Note that we don't usually pronounce the *t* in *first name*. Repeat the drill if necessary.

b) Students move around the room and ask three people the questions in **3a)**. Students should write the names in their notebooks and check that they have spelt them correctly before moving on to talk to a different student. If students can't move around the room, they should talk to three people sitting near them.

Ask a few students to tell the class the first names of other people in the class.

— EXTRA IDEA —
- If your students know each other well, give them role cards with new names on before they do **5b)**.

Things in your bag (1)

6 **a)** Focus students on photo B. Students do the exercise on their own or in pairs. Check answers with the class.

Point out that we can say *a mobile* or *a mobile phone*, although *a mobile* is more common in spoken English. Also teach students that we say *a cell* or *a cell phone* in American English.

Highlight that we can say *an iPod* or *an MP3 player*. Note that *iPod* is a brand name for personal stereos made by Apple® and *an MP3 player* is used for personal stereos in general. In practice, however, native speakers often use the words interchangeably.

2 an apple 3 a dictionary 4 a book 5 a notebook
6 a mobile 7 an iPod 8 an umbrella 9 a pencil
10 a pen

— EXTRA IDEA —
- If your students are all complete beginners, consider teaching this vocabulary yourself by bringing photos of the things in photo B or the items themselves to the class. Teach the words one by one, drilling each word in turn. You can then use **6a)** for practice.

b) [R1.20] [P] Play the recording. Students listen and practise. Highlight the pronunciation of *dictionary* /'dɪkʃənri/, *pencil* /'pensəl/ and *iPod* /'aɪpɒd/. Also check that students say the multi-syllable words with the correct stress. Highlight that *dictionary* is three syllables, not four. Repeat the drill if necessary.

7 Students do the exercise in pairs.

— EXTRA IDEA —
- Ask students which things in photo B they have with them. If you have a strong class, teach other words for things that your students have with them, for example, *glasses*, *make-up*, *a bottle of water*, etc.

- Help with Vocabulary boxes help students to explore and understand how vocabulary works, often by focusing on aspects of lexical grammar. Students should usually do the exercises on their own or in pairs before you check the answers with the class. For tips on how to teach vocabulary, see p19.

8 Focus students on the words in **6a)**. Tell the class that these words are called *nouns*. Point out the pink and blue letters at the beginning of each word.

Students do the exercise on their own. Check the answers with the class.

- We use ***a*** with nouns that begin with a **consonant** sound.
- We use ***an*** with nouns that begin with a **vowel** sound.
- You can highlight that we use *an* with *MP3 player* as this word starts with a vowel sound /e/.

9 Students do the exercise on their own, then compare answers in pairs. Check answers with the class.

Point out that we also use *an* with 'adjective + noun' (e.g. *an English dictionary*) if the adjective begins with a vowel sound.

2 a 3 an 4 a 5 an 6 a

Excuse me!

10 Focus students on photo C. Point out the teacher (Kate), Pedro (from photo A), Magda and Hasan (from the recording in **4a)**).

[R1.21] Play the recording (SB p120). Students listen and do the exercise. Check answers with the class.

1b) 2c) 3a)

- Real World boxes are designed to help students with functional and situational language that they can use in real-life social situations, often by teaching common fixed and semi-fixed phrases. Students should usually do the exercises on their own or in pairs before you check the answers with the class. For tips on how to teach speaking, see p19.

11 [R1.21] Play the recording again. Students listen and tick the sentences when they hear them.

Check students understand the meaning of the sentences and that they can change the words in brackets.

We suggest that you teach this language as fixed phrases, rather than focus on the grammar of these sentences at this stage of the course.

Point out that we can say *Can you repeat that, please?* or *Can you say that again, please?*.

EXTRA IDEA
- Write these sentences on cards and put them up around the classroom. Use these prompts in future lessons to remind students of this language when they are unsure what to say to you in class.

12 R1.22 P Focus students on the sentences in **11**. Play the recording. Students listen and practise. Play the recording again, pausing after each sentence for students to repeat individually.

13 a) Students do the exercise on their own, then compare answers in pairs. Check answers with the class.

2 mean 3 understand 4 repeat 5 sorry
6 know 7 What's 8 spell

b) Students practise the conversations in pairs, taking turns to be the teacher (Kate). Finally, ask a few pairs to role-play the conversations for the class.

EXTRA IDEA
- Ask students to turn to **Classroom Instructions**, SB p127. Use the pictures to teach the classroom instructions. Alternatively, ask students to study this page for homework.

EXTRA PRACTICE AND HOMEWORK
Ph **Class Activity** 1C Real names p113 (Instructions p100)
1 Review Exercise 5 SB p13
CD-ROM Lesson 1C
Workbook Lesson 1C p6

1D People and things

QUICK REVIEW ●●●
This activity reviews the alphabet. Students work on their own and write four English words they know. Students then complete the activity in pairs.

1 a) Focus students on the picture. Students do the exercise on their own or in pairs. Check answers with the class.

b) a man c) a woman d) a boy e) a girl

b) R1.23 P Play the recording. Students listen and practise. Highlight the pronunciation of *woman* /ˈwʊmən/. Alternatively, model the words yourself and ask students to repeat chorally and individually.

2 a) Focus students on the photo of Kate (the teacher from lesson 1C). Students do the exercise on their own or in pairs. Check answers with the class. Alternatively, ask students to check their answers in V1.7 SB p100.
If your students speak a language that doesn't have articles, highlight the use of *a* with the singular nouns in **1a)** and **2a)**.

1 a chair 2 a watch 3 a computer 4 a diary
5 a sandwich 6 a table 7 a camera

b) R1.24 P Play the recording. Students listen and practise. Highlight the pronunciation of *diary* /ˈdaɪəri/, *chair* /tʃeə/ and *sandwich* /ˈsænwɪdʒ/.

c) Students do the activity in pairs. Check answers with the class.

a bag, a pen, a book/books, an apple, a pencil,
a mobile (phone), a dictionary, an iPod

Vocabulary people; things; plurals
Review the alphabet

3 a) Give students one minute to memorise all the things in the photo.
Ask students to close their books. Students work on their own and write all the things in the picture they can remember.

b) Students compare their answers in pairs and check their partner's spelling.
Students can then open their books and check if they have remembered all the things in the picture. Find out which student in the class remembered the most words.

Help with Vocabulary Plurals

4 Focus students on the pictures and the table. Use the pictures to teach *singular* and *plural*. Students do the exercise on their own by referring to the other words in the table. 🖊 While they are working, draw the table on the board. Check answers with the class.

- **Answers** *things, boys, sandwiches, babies.*
  🖊 Elicit the answers from students and write them in the table on the board. Use the table to highlight the following rules.
- We usually make nouns plural by adding -s: *chairs, tables, things, boys*, etc.
- If a noun ends in -ch, we add -es: *watches, sandwiches*, etc.
- If a noun ends in consonant + y, we change -y to -ies: *diaries, babies*, etc. Point out that if a noun ends in vowel + y, we simply add -s (*boy* → *boys*, etc.).
- A few common nouns have irregular plurals: *men, women, people*, etc.

- Note that we also add -es to words ending in -s, -ss, -sh and -x: *bus* → *buses*, *class* → *classes*, *brush* → *brushes*, *box* → *boxes*, etc. Point out these plurals when students meet words with these endings later in the course.
- Also highlight that we don't use *a* or *an* with plural nouns.

5 R1.25 P Play the recording. Students listen and practise. Check that students say the -es /ɪz/ endings in *watches* and *sandwiches* correctly. Also highlight the pronunciation of *women* /ˈwɪmɪn/ and *people* /ˈpiːpəl/. Repeat the drill if necessary.

6 Students do the exercise on their own, then compare answers in pairs. Check answers with the class.

> 2 cameras 3 countries 4 watches 5 men 6 computers
> 7 women 8 apples 9 dictionaries 10 people

7 Put students into pairs. Ask all students to turn to SB p98. Check they are all looking at the correct exercise.

a) Focus students on the picture. Point out that some of the things in the picture are hidden. Students do the exercise in their pairs. You can set a time limit of five minutes.

b) Put two pairs together in groups of four. If this is not possible, ask students to work in new pairs. Students compare their answers and see who has found more things and people.

c) Ask students to turn to SB p126. Students check their answers. Point out that each group of things or people is in a different colour in the picture. Check answers with the class.

> 3 tables 5 men 2 women 10 books 3 pens
> 8 pencils 7 apples 4 bags 6 mobiles

--- EXTRA IDEA ---

- Use the photocopiable worksheet **Vocabulary Plus 1 Things in a room** p151 (Instructions p147) in class or give it to your students for homework.

--- EXTRA PRACTICE AND HOMEWORK ---

Ph **Class Activity** 1D Pictures and words p114 (Instructions p101)

Ph **Vocabulary Plus** 1 Things in a room p151 (Instructions p147)

1 Review Exercise 6 SB p13

CD-ROM Lesson 1D

Workbook Lesson 1D p7

Workbook Reading and Writing Portfolio 1 p52

Progress Test 1 p164

Help with Sounds /æ/ and /ə/

- Help with Sounds boxes are designed to help students hear and pronounce individual sounds that are often problematic for learners of English. For tips on how to help students with sounds, see p20.

1 **a)** R1.26 Focus students on the phonemes /æ/ and /ə/, the pictures and the words. Play the recording. Students listen to the sounds and the words.

Point out that *a* in *bag* is pronounced with an /æ/ sound, and *o* and *er* in *computer* are pronounced with an /ə/ sound. Point out that *r* at the end of a word is not usually pronounced in British English (*teacher, doctor*, etc.).

Note that the /ə/ sound is called 'the schwa' and is the most common sound in English.

Check students understand that /æ/ and /ə/ represent individual sounds and are not letters of the alphabet. Point out that phonemic script is always written between two parallel lines (/ /) and should not be confused with standard written English.

b) P Play the recording again. Students listen and practise. If students are having problems producing the sounds, help them with the mouth position for each sound.

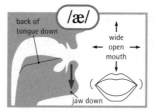

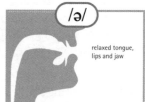

Point out that when we make the /æ/ sound, the mouth is wide open and the jaw down. When we make the /ə/ sound, the mouth is slightly open and the lips, tongue and jaw are relaxed.

2 **a)** Focus students on the boxes. Point out that all the pink letters are pronounced /æ/ and all the blue letters are pronounced /ə/.

R1.27 Play the recording. Students listen and notice how we say the pink and blue letters.

b) P Play the recording again. Students listen and practise.

3 **a)** R1.28 Play the recording. Students listen and read the sentences.

P Play the recording again. Students listen and practise. Check they say the pink letters with an /æ/ sound and the blue letters with an /ə/ sound.

b) Students practise the sentences in pairs.

Finally, ask students to say the sentences for the class.

--- EXTRA IDEA ---

- Tell your class that there is a chart of the phonemic symbols on SB p126. Also point out that students can practise the Help with Sounds drills at home on the CD-ROM/Audio CD.

Reading and Writing Portfolio

- There is a 20-page Reading and Writing Portfolio in the Starter Workbook. This section contains 10 double-page stand-alone lessons, one for each unit of the Student's Book, which are designed for students to do in class or at home. The topics and content of these lessons are based closely on the CEF reading and writing competences for level A1. At the end of this section there is a list of 'can do' statements that allows students to track their progress.
- **Reading and Writing Portfolio 1** (Workbook p52) can be used after you have completed unit 1 of the Student's Book.

Tips for using the Reading and Writing Portfolio in class

- Use the photos and illustrations to establish characters and context in each lesson.
- Go through the examples in each exercise with the class to check that students understand what to do.
- Ask students to compare answers in pairs or groups before checking answers with the class. The answers are in the Answer Key in the middle of the Workbook (pi–pviii).
- Go through the Help with Writing sections with the class and use the examples to highlight the relevant points. Note that all the examples in the Help with Writing sections come from the presentation texts.

- If you have a monolingual class, consider comparing the rules for writing in English with those of the students' language.
- The final activity of each lesson asks the students to do some personalised writing, using what they have learned from the lesson. These activities are preceded by a preparation stage, in which students are asked to decide what they are going to write by filling in a table, making notes, etc.
- Ask students to do the final writing activity on separate pieces of paper and collect them in at the end of the class. If you set the final writing activity for homework, collect the students' work at the beginning of the next class.
- When marking students' work, make sure you comment on examples of correct English, as well as highlighting errors. Remember to praise successful communication and interesting ideas as well as correct language.
- Consider asking students to write a second draft of their work, incorporating your corrections and suggestions. These can be put up around the classroom for other students to read.
- Remember that writing in a new language is a difficult skill to acquire, particularly if the students' first language is very different from English. At Starter level, it is important to encourage and praise students so that they view writing as a valuable and interesting part of the learning process.
- At the end of each lesson, ask students to tick the things they can do in the **Reading and Writing Progress Portfolio** (Workbook p72).

1 Review

- The Review section reviews the key language taught in the unit. It includes communicative and personalised speaking stages as well as controlled grammar, vocabulary and writing practice.
- This section is designed to be used in class after students have finished lesson D. Individual exercises can also be used as 'fillers' if you have a few minutes left at the end of a lesson. The **EXTRA PRACTICE AND HOMEWORK** boxes list which exercises are relevant to each lesson.
- The icons refer to the relevant sections in the Language Summary for each unit. Students can refer to these if they need help when doing the exercises.
- For tips on reviewing and recycling, see p20.

1a) 2 your 3 my 4 you 5 You 6 you 7 I 8 you 9 I

2 5 five 4 four 6 six 2 two 1 one 7 seven 12 twelve 9 nine 3 three 8 eight 11 eleven

3 2 Russia 3 Mexico 4 Germany 5 China 6 Brazil 7 Turkey 8 Spain

4a) 2 His 3 he 4 He 6 Her 7 she 8 She

5 2 an apple 3 a dictionary 4 an umbrella 5 a mobile 6 a notebook 7 a pencil 8 an iPod 9 a pen 10 a book

6a) → man, sandwich, girl, computer, table, woman
↓ diary, baby, chair, camera

Progress Portfolio

- Progress Portfolio boxes encourage students to reflect on what they have learned and help them decide which areas they need to study again.
- Note that the *I can ...* statements reflect communicative competences as set out in the *Common European Framework of Reference for Languages* (CEF) for level A1. For more information on the CEF, see p13–p17.

a) Students work through the list of *I can ...* statements on their own and tick the things they feel they can do. They can refer to Language Summary 1 SB p100–p101 if they wish.

Students can also work in pairs or groups and compare which statements they have ticked.

b) Students work on their own or in pairs/groups and decide which areas they need to study again. Encourage students to use the CD-ROM/Audio CD lessons 1A–D to help them improve in these areas. For photocopiable instructions for the CD-ROM/Audio CD, see p10–p12.

There is also further practice on all key language taught in the Student's Book in the **face2face** Starter Workbook.

2 All about you

Student's Book p14–p21

 2A # She's British

Vocabulary nationalities
Grammar *be* (singular): positive and negative
Review plurals; countries; *my, your, his, her*

QUICK REVIEW ●●●

This activity reviews plurals. Students work on their own and write five singular words. Put students into pairs. Students complete the activity with their partner.

Nationalities

1 a) Ask students which letters in the alphabet are vowels (*a, e, i, o, u*).

Students do the exercise on their own, then compare answers in pairs. Check answers with the class.

> 2 Brazil 3 Russia 4 the USA 5 Germany
> 6 Egypt 7 Australia 8 Mexico 9 Turkey
> 10 the UK 11 Spain 12 China

b) Pre-teach *nationality* and elicit the plural form (*nationalities*). Students do the activity on their own or in pairs.

Check answers with the class by writing the countries and nationalities on the board.

Highlight that nationalities often end in *-n, -an, -ian, -ish* and *-ese*.

You can also point out that we usually describe people from Brazil, Colombia, etc. as *South American*, not *American* (which we only use to refer to people from the USA).

> b)8 c)1 d)3 e)4 f)11 g)6 h)2 i)10 j)9 k)12 l)7

2 a) **R2.1** **P** Play the recording. Students listen and practise the countries and nationalities. Note that students should say both words together (*Italy, Italian*, etc.). Repeat the drill if necessary.

Point out that the same syllable is stressed in most nationalities (*Brazil, Brazilian*, etc.).

Highlight the different stress patterns in *Italy → Italian, Egypt → Egyptian* and *China → Chinese*.

b) Students do the exercise in pairs, as shown in the speech bubbles.

c) Write *I'm from* + country and *I'm* + nationality on the board. Elicit examples for each structure (*I'm from Italy. I'm Italian*, etc.).

Focus students on the speech bubbles and teach the nationalities *Japanese, French* and *Colombian*. Model and drill these words with the class, highlighting the different stress pattern in *Japan → Japanese*.

Ask students to tell the class their nationalities.

If you have students who have different nationalities from those already taught in the lesson, write them on the board and drill the words with the class.

— **EXTRA IDEAS** —

- If you have a monolingual class, teach the English words for the countries that border the students' own country, and any other countries that are of particular importance to them. Also teach students the corresponding nationalities.
- Use **Vocabulary Plus 2 Countries and nationalities** p152 (Instructions p147) in class or give it to your students for homework.

Around the world

3 a) Pre-teach *a car*. Focus students on photos A–D. Students do the exercise in pairs.

b) **R2.2** Play the recording. Students listen and check their answers. Check answers with the class.

> A British B Chinese C Brazilian D American

Help with Grammar *be* (singular): positive

4 Pre-teach *positive*. Tell the class that all positive verb forms in the Student's Book are marked with a (+) sign.

Students do the exercise on their own, then compare answers in pairs. Check answers with the class.

Note that the verb *be* is particularly problematic for students whose languages don't have an equivalent verb. If possible, check if your students' language(s) have the verb *be*, as this will help you understand why students might be making mistakes.

- **Answers** 1 'm 3 's 4 's 5 's
- Check students understand the subject pronouns *I, you, he, she* and *it*. Point out that we use *it* for things.
- Point out that *'m, 're* and *'s* are parts of the verb *be*. Check students understand which part of *be* goes with each subject pronoun.
- Highlight that *'m, 're* and *'s* are the contracted forms of *am, are* and *is*. Point out that contractions are very common in spoken and written English. Tell students to use contracted forms when speaking and writing, particularly after *I, you, he, she* and *it*.

5 [R2.3] [P] Focus students on the example. Play the recording (SB p120). Students listen and practise the sentences in **4**. Check that students pronounce the contractions correctly. Repeat the drill if necessary.

6 a) Students do the exercise on their own.

b) Students do the exercise in pairs. Check answers with the class. Ask students to give reasons for their answers.

1 's, photo C   2 'm, 'm, photo A   3 's, photo D
4 's, photo A   5 's, photo B   6 'm, photo D

Help with Grammar   *be* (singular): negative

7 Pre-teach *negative*. Tell the class that all negative verb forms in the Student's Book are marked with a (–) sign.

Students do the exercise on their own, then compare answers in pairs. Check answers with the class.

- **Answers** 1 'm not 3 isn't 4 isn't 5 isn't
- Point out that we use *not* to make a verb form negative.
- Also highlight that *aren't* is the contracted form of *are not* and *isn't* is the contracted form of *is not*. Remind students to use contracted forms when speaking and writing.
- Tell students that we can also say *you're not*, *he's not*, *she's not* and *it's not*, and write these forms on the board for students to copy.
- Point out that we can't say *I amn't*.

— EXTRA IDEA —
- Ask students to turn to Language Summary 2, SB p102–p103. Point out the vocabulary section [V2.1] and the grammar sections [G2.1] and [G2.2] from lesson 2A. Give students a few moments to read the sections. Remind students that all the new language from each lesson is included in the Language Summaries.

8 [R2.4] [P] Focus students on the example drill. Play the recording (SB p120). Students listen and practise the sentences in **7**. Check that students pronounce the contractions correctly. Repeat the drill if necessary.

True or false?

9 a) Pre-teach the vocabulary in the box, using examples that students are likely to know. Point out that we usually say *the capital*, not *the capital city* (*London is the capital of the UK.*, etc.).

Note that the aim of these boxes is to highlight which words you need to pre-teach to help students understand the exercise or text that follows. The vocabulary in these boxes is not included in the Language Summaries in the Student's Book.

b) Focus students on photos 1 and 2, and the corresponding examples. Use these to teach students *true*, *false* and *tick*. Drill these words with the class. Also point out that we use the pronoun *He* in the correct sentence in question 2, rather than repeating *Tiger Woods*.

Students do the exercise in pairs.

c) Students check their answers in the Answer Key on SB p126. Check answers by asking students to answer one question each around the class. Ask if any students got all the answers correct.

3 Cameron Diaz isn't Spanish. She's American.
4 ✓
5 ✓
6 Big Ben isn't in New York. It's in London.
7 Kylie Minogue isn't American. She's Australian.
8 Robbie Williams isn't an Australian singer. He's a British singer.
9 ✓
10 Hollywood isn't in San Francisco. It's in Los Angeles.

Get ready … Get it right!

10 Focus students on the examples. Ask students if they think the sentences are true or false. The first sentence is true (JK Rowling is British). The second sentence is false (Lacoste is a French company).

Put students into new pairs. Students work with their partner and write three true sentences and three false sentences. If necessary, direct students to **9b)** for examples of the types of sentence they can write. While they are working, monitor and check their sentences for accuracy.

11 a) Use the speech bubbles to teach *I think that's …* as a way to give your opinion, and the answers *Yes, you're right.* and *No, you're wrong.* Drill these sentences with the class.

Put two pairs together so that they are working in groups of four. Students take turns to read their sentences to the other pair, who must guess if the sentences are true or false. Tell students to keep a record of how many sentences they guess correctly. While they are working, monitor and correct any grammar or pronunciation mistakes you hear.

b) Finally, ask each pair to tell the class two of their true sentences.

— EXTRA PRACTICE AND HOMEWORK —
[Ph] **Vocabulary Plus** 2 Countries and nationalities p152 (Instructions p147)
2 Review Exercises 1 and 2 SB p21
CD-ROM Lesson 2A
Workbook Lesson 2A p8

2B What's your job?

Vocabulary jobs
Grammar *be* (singular): questions and short answers
Review countries and nationalities; *be* (singular): positive and negative

---

EXTRA IDEAS

- If your students are all complete beginners, you may choose to present the vocabulary yourself first. Prepare flashcards for the jobs and hold them up in front of the class as you teach the words. **1a)** can then be used as controlled practice.

- ✏️ If you have a strong class, teach the English words for students' jobs and write them on the board. You can also teach *I'm a housewife/househusband, I'm unemployed* and *I'm retired* /rɪ'taɪəd/. Check students remember *What's your job?*. Students then move around the room and ask each other what their jobs are.

Jobs

 a) Pre-teach *a job*. Focus students on pictures a)–i). Students do the exercise on their own or in pairs. Early finishers can check their answers in **V2.2** SB p102. Check answers with the class.

Point out that we say *an actor/a waiter* for men and *an actress/a waitress* for women (although nowadays *an actor* is often used for both men and women). All the other words can be used for both men and women. You can also teach students *a policeman* and *a policewoman*.

Also highlight that we always use *a* or *an* with jobs: *He's a doctor.* not *He's doctor*. This is particularly important if your students don't have articles in their language(s).

Draw students' attention to the **TIP!** in **1a)** and point out that only the **main** stress is shown in the vocabulary boxes and Language Summaries. We feel this is the simplest and most effective way to make sure students put the main stress in the correct place. For example, the main stress in *taxi driver* is on the first syllable of *taxi*, not on the first syllable of *driver* (which is also stressed).

> a) a shop assistant b) an actor/an actress c) a teacher
> d) a taxi driver e) a doctor f) a musician
> g) a police officer h) a manager i) a waiter/a waitress

b) **R2.5** **P** Play the recording. Students listen and practise. Alternatively, model each sentence yourself and ask students to repeat chorally and individually. Highlight the pronunciation of *manager* /'mænɪdʒə/ and *musician* /mjuː'zɪʃən/. Also highlight the /ə/ sound at the end of most of the jobs, for example, *doctor* /'dɒktə/, *actor* /'æktə/, *shop assistant* /'ʃɒp ə,sɪstənt/, etc.

c) Use the speech bubbles to teach *What's his job?* and *What's her job?*. Drill the questions and answers with the class. Teach and drill the question *What's your job?*.

Note that *What do you do?* is also a common question when asking about jobs. However, we feel at this stage of the course it is important to keep language as simple as possible. We suggest that you wait until students learn the Present Simple (in unit 4 of the Student's Book) before teaching this question.

Put students into pairs. Students take turns to point to pictures a)–i) and ask questions about the people. Remind students of the phrase *I don't know.* before they begin.

Photos of friends

 a) Pre-teach the vocabulary in the box. Drill the words with the class. Point out that *married, single* and *beautiful* are all adjectives and are used with the verb *be* (*I'm married. He's single. It's beautiful.*, etc.).

b) **R2.6** Focus students on the photo of Amy and Ben on SB p17 and point out photos 1–4 of Amy's friends on the computer screen. Play the recording (SB p120). Students listen and match the names in the box to photos 1–4. Check answers with the class.

> 1 Karl 2 Steve 3 Claire 4 Daniela

c) Play the recording again. Students listen and complete the table. Check answers with the class.

	Karl	Steve	Claire	Daniela
country	Germany	the USA	France	Italy
job	a doctor	a musician	a teacher	an actress

EXTRA IDEA

- Ask students to look at R2.6, SB p120. Play the recording again. Students listen, read and check their answers.

Help with Grammar *be* (singular): *Wh-* questions

 Pre-teach *a question*. Point out that all question forms in the Student's Book are marked with a question mark (?).

Students do the exercise on their own, then compare answers in pairs. Check answers with the class.

- **Answers** 2 are 3 's 4 's 5 's 6 's 7 's
- Highlight the word order in questions with *be*: question word + *am/are/'s* + person or thing + ...
- Remind students that we use *Where* to ask about a place and *What* to ask about a thing.
- Point out that *Where's* = *Where is* and *What's* = *What is*. Encourage students to use contracted forms when speaking and writing.
- Point out that we don't contract *am* or *are* in questions: *Where am I?* not ~~Where'm I?~~, *Where are you from?* not ~~Where're you from?~~, etc.
- Establish that we can also make questions with *How*: *How are you?*, etc.

4 **a)** [R2.7] [P] Play the recording. Students listen and practise the questions in **3**.

Check students pronounce the contractions *Where's* and *What's* correctly. Point out that *are* is usually pronounced /ə/ in questions, for example, *Where are* /ə/ *you from?*. Repeat the drill if necessary, pausing the recording after each question for students to repeat individually.

b) Ask students to cover the table in **2c)**. Focus students on the speech bubbles and drill the questions with the class. Students do the exercise in pairs.

Is he a musician?

5 **a)** Students do the exercise on their own.

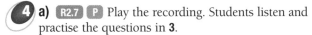

2a) 3b) 4a) 5 Students' answers 6 Students' answers

b) Students compare answers in pairs. Check answers with the class.

Help with Grammar *be* (singular): *yes/no* questions and short answers

6 Students do the exercise on their own, then compare answers in pairs. Check answers with the class.

- **Answers** See [G2.4] SB p103.
- Highlight the inverted word order in *yes/no* questions with *be*: *Am I ... ?*, *Are you ... ?*, *Is he ... ?*, etc.
- Point out that we don't usually answer these questions with just *Yes.* or *No.*, as this can sound impolite.
- Note that we don't use contractions in positive short answers: *Yes, you are.* not ~~Yes, you're.~~, *Yes, I am.* not ~~Yes, I'm~~, *Yes, he is.* not ~~Yes, he's.~~, etc.
- Point out that we can also say *No, you're not.*, *No, he's not.*, *No, she's not.* and *No, it's not.*. Also highlight that we don't usually use the uncontracted form in negative short answers: *No, you aren't.* not ~~No, you are not.~~, etc.

7 [R2.8] [P] Play the recording. Students listen and practise. Check that students pronounce the contractions correctly. Play the recording again if necessary, pausing after each question or short answer for students to repeat individually.

8 **a)** Students do the exercise on their own. Check answers with the class.

2 Is 3 Are 4 Are 5 Is 6 Are 7 Is 8 Is

b) Students do the exercise in pairs. Remind students to use the correct short answers.

Get ready ... Get it right!

9 Put students into new pairs, student A and student B. Student As turn to SB p87 and student Bs turn to SB p93. Check they are all looking at the correct exercise.

a) Focus students on the six photos. Tell the class that the people are all friends of Ben (the man in the photo on SB p17).

Students work on their own and write *yes/no* questions to check the information in blue, as in the example. Students are not allowed to look at each other's books at any stage of the activity. While they are working, monitor and check their questions for accuracy.

— EXTRA IDEA —
- Ask students to check their *yes/no* questions with another student from the same group before they work with their partner in **b)**.

b) Check students understand that some of the information in blue is correct and some is incorrect. Students work with their partners. Student A in each pair asks his/her questions from **a)** and either ticks the correct information or changes the incorrect information for each person. Encourage student Bs to use the correct short answers during the activity. While they are working, monitor and check students are doing the activity correctly.

c) Students swap roles and student B in each pair asks his/her questions from **a)**.

d) Put students in pairs with another student of the same group. Students compare answers by saying sentences about the people, as in the example.

Finally, ask students to tell the class about each person in turn.

— EXTRA PRACTICE AND HOMEWORK —
[Ph] **Class Activity** 2B New identities p115 (Instructions p101)
2 Review Exercises 3, 4 and 5 SB p21
CD-ROM Lesson 2B
Workbook Lesson 2B p9

2C Personal information

Vocabulary titles; greetings
Real World email addresses; personal information questions
Review jobs; *be* (singular): questions

QUICK REVIEW ●●●

This activity reviews jobs. Students work on their own and write four jobs. Pre-teach *mime* by miming a job (for example, a waiter) and asking students what the job is. Put students into pairs. Students take turns to mime the jobs on their list and guess their partner's jobs.

Good morning!

a) Check students remember *married* and *single*. Point out that *Brown*, *King* and *Roberts* are common surnames in the UK.

Students do the exercise on their own. Check answers with the class. Point out that *Ms* can be used for married and single women.

> 1c) 2a) 3b)

b) R2.9 P Focus students on the example. Play the recording (SB p120). Students listen and practise. Highlight the pronunciation of *Mr* /ˈmɪstə/, *Mrs* /ˈmɪsɪz/ and *Ms* /məz/. Repeat the drill if necessary.

a) Focus students on pictures A–D. Ask students who the man is in all four pictures (Mr Brown).

Students do the exercise on their own or in pairs.

> **EXTRA IDEA**
> • If you have a class of complete beginners, teach the words *morning*, *afternoon*, *evening* and *night* before doing **2a)**.

b) R2.10 Play the recording (SB p121). Students listen and check their answers. Check answers with the class.

Point out that *Good morning*, *Good afternoon* and *Good evening* mean *Hello* and that *Good night* means *Goodbye*.

Highlight that *Good morning*, *Good night*, etc. are more formal than *Hello/Hi* and *Goodbye/Bye*. Also point out that we respond to *Good morning*, etc. by repeating the same phrase.

Use picture C to teach *sir* /sɜː/ (a polite way to address a man you don't know) and the female equivalent, *madam* /ˈmædəm/. Use picture D to teach *Thank you very much*.

P Play the recording again, pausing after each sentence or phrase for students to repeat chorally and individually. Check that students sound polite and interested.

> A Good morning   B Good afternoon (x 2)
> C Good evening (x 2)   D Good night (x 2)

c) Students practise the conversations in pairs. Ask a few pairs to role-play their conversations for the class.

Real World Email addresses

Focus students on the email address and the speech bubble. Point out that we say *dot* (.) and *at* (@) in email addresses.

a) Focus students on the business card, mobile phone and email. Students work in pairs and try to say email addresses 1–4.

b) R2.11 Play the recording. Students check their answers.

a) R2.12 P Focus students on the example drill. Play the recording (SB p121). Students listen and practise. Check they say @, .com, .net and .co.uk correctly. Repeat the drill if necessary.

b) Focus students on the speech bubbles. Drill the question *What's your email address?*.

Ask students to write down their email addresses and give them time to work out how to say them in English. If necessary, teach students that we also say *hyphen* (-), *underscore* (_) and *capital a, capital b*, etc. (A, B, etc.) in email addresses. Also check students know how to say the part of their email address that indicates their country (.uk, .es, .ja, etc.).

Students move around the room and ask three people for their email addresses. Alternatively, they can ask three people sitting near them. Students write each person's email address, then check that they have written it correctly.

> **EXTRA IDEA**
> • In some classes it may not be appropriate for students to give each other their real email addresses. If this is the case in your class, write fictitious email addresses on cards and give them to your students before doing **5b)**.

Looking for a job

a) Focus students on the photo of Tony and Amy (from lesson 2B). Pre-teach *employment agency* (a company that helps people find jobs). Tell the class that Tony works for an employment agency called nine2five and that Amy is looking for a job. Give students time to read the form.

R2.13 Play the recording (SB p121). Students listen to the interview and complete the form. Play the recording again if necessary.

b) Students compare answers in pairs. Check answers with the class.

Highlight *M11 6JZ* in Amy's address and teach *a postcode* (US: *a zip code*).

> **surname** Foley **married/single** single **nationality** British **address** 9 Whedon (Road) (Manchester) M11 6JZ **mobile number** 07866 642339 **email address** amy.foley@hotmail.co.uk

Real World Personal information questions

 Students do the exercise on their own, then compare answers in pairs. Check answers with the class.

- **Answers** 2 's 3 Are 4 's 5 's 6 's 7 's
- Point out that we use *Are* in question 3 because it's a *yes/no* question with *you*. All the other questions are *What's your ... ?* followed by a noun.
- Remind students of the question *What's your home number?*. You can also teach *What's your work number?* if you think this will be useful for your students.

— EXTRA IDEA —

- Ask students to look at R2.13, SB p121. Play the recording again. Students listen, read and underline all the personal information questions.

 R2.14 P Play the recording (SB p121). Students listen and practise. Establish that intonation is very important in English and the correct intonation pattern can help students to sound polite.

Play the recording again. Students listen and practise, copying the polite intonation pattern. Drill the language with individual students if necessary.

 a) Put students into pairs. If possible, ask students to work with someone they don't know very well.

Students take turns to interview their partner and fill in the form. Remind students to use the questions in **7** when they are the interviewer, and to begin each conversation with *Good morning. Welcome to the nine2five Employment Agency. My name's ... . Nice to meet you.* etc.

Also remind students of the questions *How do you spell that?* and *Can you repeat that, please?* before they begin.

— EXTRA IDEAS —

- If your students know each other well, or if you feel it is inappropriate for your students to give each other their personal details, use **Class Activity 2C The nine2five Employment Agency** p116 instead of doing **9a)** (see Procedure A, Instructions p101).
- When students have finished **9a)**, put them into new pairs. Students ask questions with *he/his* and *she/her* about the person his/her partner has just interviewed. Alternatively, **Class Activity 2C The nine2five Employment Agency** p116 can also be used to practise *he/his* and *she/her* questions (see Procedure B, Instructions p102).

b) Students work in their pairs and check that all the information on their partner's form is correct.

Finally, you can ask one or two pairs to role-play their conversations for the class.

— EXTRA PRACTICE AND HOMEWORK —

Ph **Class Activity** 2C The nine2five Employment Agency p116 (Instructions p101)
2 Review Exercise 6 SB p21
CD-ROM Lesson 2C
Workbook Lesson 2C p11

How old is she?

QUICK REVIEW ●●●
This activity reviews numbers 0–12. Students do the first part of the activity on their own. Put students into pairs. Students check their partner's spelling and then say the numbers. Students can check spelling in **V1.1** SB p100.

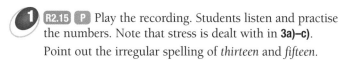

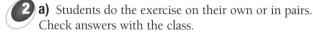

1 R2.15 P Play the recording. Students listen and practise the numbers. Note that stress is dealt with in **3a)–c)**.
Point out the irregular spelling of *thirteen* and *fifteen*.

2 a) Students do the exercise on their own or in pairs. Check answers with the class.
Point out that we can also say *one hundred*, but that *a hundred* is more common.

> **Vocabulary** numbers 13–100
> **Real World** *How old ... ?*
> **Help with Listening** numbers with *-teen* and *-ty*
> **Review** numbers 0–12

> 40 forty 50 fifty 60 sixty 70 seventy
> 80 eighty 90 ninety 100 a hundred

b) Remind students of word stress by writing some multi-syllable words on the board and asking the class which syllable is stressed.
R2.16 P Play the recording. Students listen and practise. Highlight the pronunciation of *thirty* /ˈθɜːti/ and *forty* /ˈfɔːti/.

Help with Listening Numbers with *-teen* and *-ty*

- This Help with Listening section helps students to hear the difference between numbers that end in *-teen* and those that end in *-ty*.

3 **a)** R2.17 Play the recording. Students listen and notice the stress on the numbers. Point out that we usually stress the *-teen* syllable in numbers 13–19 and the first syllable in numbers 20–100.

We appreciate that this stress rule for numbers ending in *-teen* is somewhat simplistic, as there are times when we naturally stress the first syllable (for example, when counting or when the number is followed by a noun). However, we feel that at this level it is more helpful to give students a clear rule that will avoid confusion and be correct most of the time (for example, when talking about ages later in the lesson).

b) Students do the exercise on their own before checking answers in pairs.

c) R2.18 Play the recording. Students listen and check their answers.

If necessary, write the numbers on the board and ask students which syllable is stressed in each number.

> seventeen ninety fifty thirteen
> thirty nineteen seventy fifteen

4 R2.17 R2.18 **P** Play both recordings again. Students listen and practise. Alternatively, model the numbers yourself in order and ask students to repeat chorally and individually. Check that students stress the numbers correctly.

Note that the *th* sound /θ/ (as in *thirty, thirteen*, etc.) is dealt with in the Help with Sounds section at the end of unit 4.

5 **a)** Focus students on the examples. Point out that we use a hyphen (-) in these numbers.

Students do the exercise on their own, then compare answers in pairs.

Check the answers by writing the numbers (23, etc.) on the board and asking students how to write the words (*twenty-three*, etc.).

Point out that we usually stress the final syllable in compound numbers (*twenty-one, twenty-two*, etc.).

Write a few numbers between 31 and 99 on the board and ask students how we say them.

> 23 twenty-three 24 twenty-four 25 twenty-five
> 26 twenty-six 27 twenty-seven 28 twenty-eight
> 29 twenty-nine

b) Students work in pairs and take turns to say the numbers.

Check students' pronunciation by going round the class and asking them to say one number each.

6 **a)** Students work on their own and write four numbers.

b) Students do the exercise in new pairs.

— EXTRA IDEA —
- Use **Class Activity** 2D Hear a number, say a number p117 (Instructions p102).

7 **a)** Focus students on the photo. Ask if students recognise Tony (the interviewer from lesson 2C).

Students do the exercise on their own or in pairs. Check answers with the class.

Model and drill the vocabulary with the class.

> 1 a house 2 a cat 3 a car 4 a dog 5 a girl

b) R2.19 Tell students they are going to listen to five conversations. Play the recording (SB p121). Students listen and fill in the gaps with the correct numbers. Play the recording again if necessary.

Students compare answers in pairs. Check answers with the class.

Note that in the UK and many other countries, we often think of one 'human year' as being equivalent to seven 'dog years'.

> 1 13 2 100 3 9 4 21 5 7 (or 49 'dog years')

8 **a)** Students do the exercise on their own or in pairs. Check answers with the class.

Point out that we use *How old is/are ... ?* to ask about age (not *How many years ... ?* or *What age is/are ... ?*).

Highlight that we use the verb *be* to talk about age, not *have*: *I'm twenty-six.* not *I have twenty-six.*

Also highlight that we don't usually say *years old* for people: *Emily's nine.*, *I'm thirty.*, etc., and we don't say *I'm thirty years*.

Explain that in the UK and other English-speaking countries, asking people how old they are is often considered impolite, particularly if you don't know them very well.

You can also teach the noun *age* /eɪdʒ/, but point out that we don't say *What age are you?*.

> 2 is 3 old 4 are 5 I'm

b) R2.20 **P** Focus students on the speech bubbles in **8a)**. Play the recording. Students listen and practise.

9 Focus students on the photo. Ask them to cover **7** and **8**. Students do the activity in pairs.

— EXTRA IDEA —
- Students move around the room and ask each other how old they are. Students find out if anyone is the same age as them. You can tell your students they don't have to tell the truth!

10 Put students into new pairs. Ask all students to turn to SB p98. Check they are all looking at the correct exercise.

a) Focus students on the photo. You can tell the class that Chris is the author of **face2face** Starter. The photo is of his girlfriend Adela's family and their friends. Note that *Maja* is pronounced /maɪjə/.

Highlight the ages in the boxes and check students understand that these are the correct ages of the girls, women, men and dogs in the photo. Use the speech bubbles to remind students that we say *I think …* when giving our opinion.

Students do the activity in pairs. You can ask students to compare answers in groups of four.

b) Students check their answers on SB p126. Check answers with the class by asking students how old each person in the photo is.

Finally, find out which pair got the most answers correct.

> Maria 45 Mary 76 Christopher 70 John 65
> Chris 46 Stef 43 Martin 38 Adela 41 Alex 37
> Lola 1 Freddie 8 Dagmar 72 Maja 6 Lily 3

EXTRA PRACTICE AND HOMEWORK

Ph **Class Activity** 2D Hear a number, say a number p117 (Instructions p102)

2 Review Exercise 7 SB p21

CD-ROM Lesson 2D

Workbook Lesson 2D p12

Workbook Reading and Writing Portfolio 2 p54

Progress Test 2 p165

Help with Sounds /ɪ/ and /iː/

1 a) R2.21 Focus students on the phonemes /ɪ/ and /iː/, the pictures and the words. Play the recording. Students listen to the sounds and the words. Point out that *i* in *six* is pronounced with an /ɪ/ sound and *ee* in *nineteen* is pronounced with an /iː/ sound.

b) **P** Play the recording again. Students listen and practise. If students are having problems, help them with the mouth position for each sound.

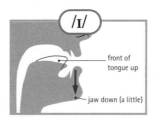 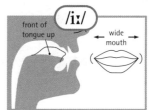

Point out that /ɪ/ is a short sound and /iː/ is a long sound (as indicated by the **ː** symbol). Also highlight that the mouth is wide when saying the /iː/ sound. You can tell students that the letter *e* is also pronounced /iː/.

2 a) R2.22 Focus students on the boxes. Point out that the pink vowels are pronounced /ɪ/ and the blue vowels are pronounced /iː/. Play the recording. Students listen and notice how we say the pink and blue vowels.

b) **P** Play the recording again. Students listen and practise.

3 a) Focus students on the words in the box. Go through the examples with the class. Students do the exercise on their own.

 While students are working, write the words on the board ready for checking in **3c)**.

b) Students compare answers in pairs. Tell students to say the words to each other when comparing answers.

c) R2.23 Play the recording. Students listen and check their answers.

 Check the answers by eliciting the correct sound for each of the vowels in **bold** and writing it on the board under the vowel, as shown in the Answer Key.

P Play the recording again. Students listen and practise the words. Check they pronounce the vowels in **bold** correctly.

Finally, ask students to say the words for the class.

sandwiches	teacher	think	married isn't read
/ɪ/	/iː/	/ɪ/	/ɪ/ /ɪ/ /iː/
musician	assistant	me Spanish Japanese sixteen
/ɪ/	/ɪ/	/iː/ /ɪ/ /iː/ /iː/

2 Review

See p29 for ideas on how to use this section.

1 Mexican Italian Russian German Brazilian American Egyptian Spanish Turkish British Chinese

2 2 isn't, 's 3 'm not, 'm 4 's, isn't 5 aren't, 're

3 actor doctor waitress musician manager taxi driver police officer

4a) 2 Where are you from? 3 What's your job?
4 Where's he from? 5 What's his job? 6 What's her name?
7 What's her job?

4b) a)3 b)4 c)6 d)5 f)7 g)2

5a) 2 Are 3 you 4 Are, your 5 Is 6 your

6a) 2 What's your surname? 3 What's your nationality?
4 What's your address? 5 What's your mobile number?
6 What's your email address?

Progress Portfolio

See p29 for ideas on how to use this section.

3A Two cities

QUICK REVIEW ●●●
This activity reviews numbers 1–100. Students do the activity in pairs. If you have a small class, you can do the activity by asking students to count in threes and fours round the class.

Vocabulary adjectives (1); word order with adjectives; *very*
Grammar *be* (plural): positive, negative, questions and short answers
Help with Listening contractions
Review numbers; *be* (singular)

Adjectives (1)

 a) Pre-teach *adjective*. Focus students on the pictures and the example. Teach *opposite* and tell students that each pair of words in 1–7 are opposites.

Students do the exercise on their own or in pairs. Early finishers can check their answers in Language Summary 3 **V3.1** SB p104. Check answers with the class.

Note that *nice* is a very general positive adjective that can mean *good, friendly, enjoyable, beautiful, delicious,* etc. Its opposite therefore depends on the context.

> 2e) 3c) 4g) 5f) 6b) 7a) 8h)

b) **R3.1** **P** Play the recording. Students listen and practise. Alternatively, model the words yourself and ask students to repeat chorally and individually. Check that students copy the word stress correctly. Repeat the drill if necessary.

— **EXTRA IDEA** —
● After doing **1b)**, students work in pairs and take turns to test each other on the adjectives. One student says an adjective, for example *hot*, and his/her partner says the opposite, for example *cold*.

Help with Vocabulary Word order with adjectives; *very*

 a) ✎ Write the example sentences on the board and go through the rules with the class, highlighting the following points.

● Adjectives go after *be*: *Your watch is nice.* not ~~*Your watch nice is*~~.
● Adjectives go before nouns: *It's a new car.* not ~~*It's a car new*~~.
● Also highlight that the adjective comes after the article *a*, and that we use *an* when the adjective begins with a vowel: *It's an old car.*
● Adjectives are **not** plural with plural nouns. *They're good friends.* not ~~*They're goods friends*~~.
● Also highlight the word order in questions: *Are you cold?, Is he friendly?*, etc.

b) Students do the exercise on their own. Check answers with the class.

> ● **Answers** 1b) 2a)
> ● Highlight that we put *very* before adjectives: *It's **very** hot.*
> ● Point out that we say *It's (very) hot/cold.* to talk about the weather. Highlight *It* at the beginning of the sentence and point out that we say *It's cold.* not ~~*Is cold.*~~, etc.

 Students do the exercise on their own, then compare answers in pairs. Check answers with the class. Highlight the word order in each answer.

> 2 He's a very good actor.
> 3 It's an expensive camera.
> 4 His friends are very nice.
> 5 Your dogs are very friendly.

An email to friends

 a) Pre-teach the vocabulary in the box. Model and drill the words and phrases with the class. Point out that *restaurant* /restrɒnt/ is two syllables, not three.

Also note that although there is usually an accent on *café* in English, we stress the first syllable, not the second.

b) Pre-teach *email* by referring to email A. Point out that the stress is on the first syllable, not the second.

Students read email A and find out where Sally and Dan are (in Moscow).

Teach the new words *and, but, here* and *now* in the email.

Also highlight that *people* is always plural in English: *the people are friendly* not ~~*the people is friendly*~~.

You can also point out that we often end emails to friends or family with *Love* and then our name(s).

 Go through the examples with the class. Students do the exercise on their own before checking in pairs. Check answers with the class.

> 3 It's very **cold** in Moscow. 4 ✓ 5 Sally and Dan are in **a new** hotel. 6 ✓ 7 The rooms are very **big**.

Help with Grammar *be* (plural): positive and negative

6 Students do the exercise on their own or in pairs. Check answers with the class.

- **Answers** We**'re** in a new hotel. They**'re** very big. We **aren't** in the hotel now. They **aren't** very expensive.
- Point out that *are* is the plural form of *be* (as well as the singular *you* form).
- Check students understand *we* and *they*. Point out that we use *they* for people and things.
- Tell students that *you* is singular and plural: *You're a student. You're students.* Also remind students that there is no polite form of *you* in English.
- Highlight that *we're, you're* and *they're* are contracted forms of *we are, you are* and *they are*. Also point out that we don't contract *are* after a name or a noun: *Sally and Dan are in Moscow.* not ~~*Sally and Dan're in Moscow.*~~ and *The rooms are nice.* not ~~*The rooms're nice.*~~
- Check students understand that *aren't* is the contracted form of *are not*.
- Tell students that we can also say *we're not, you're not* and *they're not*.

7 **P** Play the recording. Students listen and practise the sentences in **6**. Check that students pronounce the contractions correctly. Alternatively, model each sentence yourself and ask students to repeat chorally and individually.

You can also point out that the pronunciation of *you're* and *your* is the same /jɔː/.

Help with Listening Contractions

- This Help with Listening section helps students to understand contractions in natural spoken English.

8 **a)** Give students time to read sentences 1–6. Tell the class that they will hear each sentence twice. Play the recording (SB p121). Students listen and fill in the gaps.

Play the recording again if necessary, pausing after each sentence. Students compare answers in pairs.

Check answers with the class by writing the sentences on the board and asking students to tell you the missing words.

1 Spanish 2 good teacher 3 small hotel 4 doctor, married 5 actor, musician 6 very old city

b) Check students understand *contractions* (*aren't, we're,* etc.). Students do the exercise in pairs.

Check the answers by asking students to identify the contractions and underlining them on the board.

Ask students which contractions are negative (*aren't* and *isn't*).

---

1 aren't, we're 2 You're 3 They're
4 He's, isn't 5 I'm, she's 6 It's

c) Play the recording again. Students listen and notice the contractions.

--- EXTRA IDEA ---
- If your students need more pronunciation practice, use R3.3 as a drill. Play the recording again and ask students to repeat each sentence chorally and individually.

Where are they?

9 Focus students on email B. Ask who the people in the photo are (Fiona and Nick). Students do the exercise on their own, then compare answers in pairs. Check answers with the class.

2 're 3 's 4 are 5 aren't 6 're 7 are 8 isn't 9 's

10 Students do the exercise on their own. Check answers with the class.

1b) 2b) 3a)

Help with Grammar *be* (plural): questions and short answers

11 Students do the exercise on their own or in pairs by referring to **10**. Check answers with the class.

- **Answers** See G3.2 SB p105.
- Highlight the inverted word order in *yes/no* questions: *Are they ... ?, Are you ... ?,* etc.
- Point out that we don't usually answer these questions with just *Yes.* or *No.*, as this can sound impolite.
- Highlight that we don't use contractions in positive short answers: *Yes, you are.* not ~~*Yes, you're.*~~, etc.
- Also highlight that we don't use the uncontracted form in negative short answers: *No, you aren't.* not ~~*No, you are not.*~~, etc.
- Point out that we can also say *No, we're not., No, you're not.* and *No, they're not*.
- Highlight the word order in *Wh-* questions. Note that we don't contract *Where are*: *Where are you?* not ~~*Where're you?*~~

--- EXTRA IDEA ---
- Ask students to turn to Language Summary 3, SB p105. Focus students on G3.1 and G3.2. Give students time to study the grammar tables, read the **TIPS!** and ask you any questions.

12 **P** Play the recording. Students listen and practise. Repeat the drill if necessary.

Get ready ... Get it right!

13 Put students into pairs, student A and student B. Student As turn to SB p88 and student Bs turn to SB p94. Check they are all looking at the correct exercise.

a) Students do the exercise on their own. Check answers with the class. Only check the answers so that students don't hear the questions they are about to be asked. Note that the answers are the same for student As and student Bs.

> **Student A/Student B** 2 Are 3 Are 4 's 5 Are 6 Is

b) Students do the exercise on their own. They can make notes of the answers if necessary.

c) Students work with their partners. Student A in each pair asks his/her questions about Sally and Dan from **a)**. Encourage student Bs to use short answers where appropriate (*Yes, they are.*, etc.). Student A then tells his/her partner how many of his/her answers are correct.

d) Students swap roles so that student Bs ask their questions about Fiona and Nick from **a)**.

Finally, ask the class how many students answered all the questions correctly.

┌─ **EXTRA IDEA** ─────────────────────────
* Ask your students to bring in photos of their family to the next class, so that they can be used during the Get ready ... Get it right! speaking activity in lesson 3B.
└──

─ **EXTRA PRACTICE AND HOMEWORK** ─────────
Ph **Class Activity** 3A Where are they? p118 (Instructions p102)
3 Review Exercises 1 and 2 SB p29
CD-ROM Lesson 3A
Workbook Lesson 3A p13

3B Brothers and sisters

QUICK REVIEW ●●●
This activity reviews adjectives. Students work on their own and write four adjectives. Tell students to choose adjectives they learned in lesson 3A. Students complete the activity in pairs, as shown in the examples. Ask each pair to tell the class one or two things for the adjectives they chose.

> **Vocabulary** family
> **Grammar** possessive *'s*; subject pronouns (*I, you*, etc.) and possessive adjectives (*my, your*, etc.)
> **Review** adjectives; jobs; *How old ... ?*

Our family

1 Focus students on the photo of the Cooper family. Point out that Nick and Fiona were the married couple in New York in lesson 3A.

R3.5 Play the recording. Students listen and read speech bubbles 1–4. Play the recording again if necessary.

Note that students are often asked to 'listen and read' in the Student's Book. At this level we feel it is very useful for students to listen and read at the same time, as this helps them to 'tune in' to English, and to connect what they hear with how it is written.

2 a) Focus students on the table. Go through the headings with the class. Check they understand the male ♂ and female ♀ symbols in the column headings and teach the meaning of *both*.

Students do the exercise on their own or in pairs.
✐ While they are working, draw the table (including the examples) on the board.

Check answers with the class by eliciting the missing words and writing them in the correct places in the table.

Point out that your *parents* are your mother and father only, and that other family members are called *relatives*.

Also point out that *dad* and *mum* are informal words for *father* and *mother*. You can also teach *kids*, which is an informal word for *children*, and *a boyfriend/a girlfriend*.

Point out that the singular form of *parents* is *a parent* and that the plural of *wife* is *wives*, not ~~wifes~~. Also highlight that the plural of *child* is irregular (*children*).

men/boys ♂	women/girls ♀	both ♂♀
father (dad)	mother (mum)	parents
son	daughter	children (singular: child)
husband	wife	
brother	sister	

b) **R3.6** **P** Play the recording. Students listen and practise the words. Highlight the pronunciation of *parents* /ˈpeərənts/. Point out that the stress on all the two-syllable words in the table is always on the first syllable. Also highlight the /ʌ/ sound in *mother* /ˈmʌðə/, *mum* /mʌm/, *son* /sʌn/, *husband* /ˈhʌzbənd/ and *brother* /ˈbrʌðə/. Note that this sound is practised further in the Help with Sounds section in this unit.

- If you have a class of complete beginners, consider teaching the family vocabulary yourself at the beginning of the lesson. ✍ Draw the Cooper family tree on the board (father: Nick, mother: Fiona, son: Kevin, daughter: Anne). Then use the relationships between the people to teach the vocabulary in **bold** in the speech bubbles. You can then use **2** for practice.
- Alternatively, draw your own family tree and use this to teach the family vocabulary. You can also bring in photos of your family to show the class.

3 Students do the exercise on their own before comparing answers in pairs. Check answers with the class.

> 2 son 3 mother 4 daughter 5 father 6 sister 7 parents

Help with Grammar   Possessive 's

4 Go through the rule with the class. Highlight the following points.

- We use a name or a noun for a person + 's for the possessive. For example, we say *Fiona is Nick's wife.* not ~~*Fiona is the wife of Nick.*~~, and *It's my sister's car.* not ~~*It's the car of my sister.*~~ Use the second example to highlight that we use 's for things we have, as well as for family relationships.
- Check students understand that we can use 's with other nouns for people: *It's my **teacher's** car. He's the **doctor's** son. It's his **friend's** camera.*, etc.
- Point out that 's can mean *is* or the possessive: *She's my sister.* ('s = is); *Kevin is Nick's son.* ('s = possessive).
- Also highlight that when there are two names, the 's goes after the second name only: *They're Kevin and Anne's parents.* not ~~*They're Kevin's and Anne's parents*~~.
- You can tell students that when a name ends in an /s/ sound, the 's is pronounced as an extra syllable /ɪz/, for example *Chris's* /ˈkrɪsɪz/, *Luis's* /luːˈiːsɪz/, etc.
- Note that for plural nouns, the apostrophe (') is **after** the s: *It's my parents' house.*

5 R3.7 **P** Play the recording (SB p121). Students listen and practise the sentences in **3**. Check that students pronounce the possessive 's in each sentence correctly.

Students might ask why we don't contract *is* in these sentences (*Nick's Fiona's son.*, etc.). You can point out that writing 's twice in short sentences such as these looks rather unnatural, but is still correct.

6 Focus students on the example. Students do the exercise on their own. Check answers with the class.

> 2 Fiona is Nick's wife. 3 Kevin is Fiona's son.
> 4 Anne is Nick's daughter. 5 Kevin is Anne's brother.
> 6 Anne and Kevin are Nick and Fiona's children.

Our grandchildren

7 a) Focus students on the photo of Sid and Mary. Tell the class that they are Kevin and Anne's grandparents.

Students work on their own and complete the table with the words in the box. Check answers with the class.

Point out that the singular of *grandchildren* is *a grandchild*.

♂	grandfather	**grandson**
♀	**grandmother**	granddaughter
♂♀	**grandparents**	grandchildren

b) R3.8 **P** Play the recording. Students listen and practise. Point out that the stress on these words is always on the first syllable, and that we don't pronounce the *d* in *grand-*: *grandfather* /ˈɡrænˌfɑːðə/, etc.

8 a) R3.9 Tell the class they are going to listen to Mary talk about her family. Play the recording (SB p121). Students listen and put the people in the order she talks about them. Check answers with the class.

> 2 Fiona 3 Nick 4 Anne 5 Kevin

b) Give students time to read questions 1–6. Play the recording again. Students listen and answer the questions. Check answers with the class.

> 2 She's a teacher. 3 She's 43. 4 He's a doctor.
> 5 Yes, she is. 6 He's 12.

Help with Grammar   Subject pronouns (*I, you,* etc.) and possessive adjectives (*my, your,* etc.)

9 a) Focus students on the four example sentences from the recording. Point out the words in blue and pink in these sentences. Students complete the table on their own or in pairs.

✍ While students are working, draw the table on the board so that you are ready to check their answers. Check answers with the class.

- subject pronouns: **I**, you, **he**, she, **it**, we, they
- possessive adjectives: **my**, your, his, **her**, its, **our**, **their**

b) Focus students on the box. Use the examples to check students understand the difference between *a verb* and *a noun*. Do the exercise with the class (*listen* and *read* are verbs, *family* and *dog* are nouns).

c) Go through the rules with the class. Use the examples to highlight that we use subject pronouns with verbs (***I'm***, etc.) and possessive adjectives with nouns (***my*** *sister*, etc.).

Point out that *you* and *your* are both singular and plural.

Also point out that verbs in English always need a subject: *It's my bag.* not ~~*Is my bag.*~~, etc.

10 Students do the exercise on their own, then compare answers in pairs. Check answers with the class.

You can also highlight that *their* is pronounced the same as *they're* /ðeə/.

> **2** They, their **3** our, His **4** My, your **5** you, his **6** Her, she

Get ready … Get it right!

 11 Students write a list of people in their family. Tell students to only write the names of family members that have been taught in the lesson (not uncles, aunts, cousins, etc.).

— **EXTRA IDEAS** —

- If you asked your students to bring in photos of their family at the end of the previous lesson, they can use these photos instead of writing the names of their family. Teach students to say *This is …* when they point to a person in the photo (*This is Lucas. He's my brother.*, etc.).

- Students can draw their family tree instead of writing a list of names in **11**.

 12 a) Use the speech bubbles to remind students of the questions *How old is he?*, *What's his job?* and *Is he married?*. Elicit the corresponding questions with *she* (*How old is she?*, etc.).

Put students into pairs. If possible, ask students to work with someone they don't know very well.

Students take turns to tell their partner who the people are on their list. Their partner asks questions about each person, as in the speech bubbles. While students are working, monitor and correct any mistakes you hear.

b) Finally, ask each student to tell the class about one person in their partner's family, as shown in the speech bubble.

— **EXTRA PRACTICE AND HOMEWORK** —

Ph **Class Activity** 3B Barry and Wendy's family p119–p120 (Instructions p102)

3 Review Exercises 3, 4 and 5 SB p29

CD-ROM Lesson 3B

Workbook Lesson 3B p14

 ## 3C Eat in or take away?

QUICK REVIEW ●●●
This activity reviews family vocabulary. Students do the first part of the activity on their own. Put students into pairs. Students take turns to tell their partner about their friends and family. Encourage students to ask questions about the people if possible.

Vocabulary food and drink (1)
Real World money and prices; *How much … ?*; in a café
Review family; numbers

Money and prices

 1 a) Pre-teach *money* /ˈmʌni/ and *price* /praɪs/. Drill these words with the class.

Students do the exercise on their own, then compare answers in pairs. Check answers with the class.

Check students understand the symbols £, $, €, p and c.

Point out that in the UK it is much more common to say *ten p* than *ten pence*, although both are correct.

Also point out that we often miss out the currency words (*pounds, euros*, etc.) in prices with both pounds and pence or euros/dollars and cents if the context is clear (*ten fifty, five ninety-nine*, etc.). However, we always say the currency with round numbers (*ten pounds, fifty euros, twelve dollars*, etc.).

Also teach students how to say the currency from their country/countries in English if appropriate.

> **2**b) **3**e) **4**c) **5**a) **6**d)

b) R3.10 **P** Play the recording. Students listen and practise the prices. Check that students pronounce *p* /piː/, *euros* /ˈjʊərəʊz/ and *cents* /sents/ correctly. Repeat the drill if necessary.

 2 a) Students do the exercise in pairs.

b) R3.11 Play the recording (SB p121). Students listen and check their answers.

P Play the recording again. Students listen and practise the prices.

> **a)** seventeen pounds **b)** seventy p **c)** a hundred dollars **d)** twenty-one euros **e)** thirty-five cents **f)** twenty-one dollars **g)** three euros seventy-five **h)** seven pounds sixty

3 a) R3.12 Tell students that they are going to listen to five conversations. Play the recording (SB p121). Students listen and write the prices. Play again if necessary.

b) Students compare answers in pairs. Check answers with the class.

> **1** £25 **2** $64 **3** 70p **4** £48.50 **5** €95

Real World *How much ... ?*

4 Students do the exercise on their own, then compare answers in pairs. Check answers with the class.

> **Answers** 1 is 2 is 3 are 4 are

Point out that we use *How much is ... ?* for singular nouns and *it*, and *How much are ... ?* for plural nouns and *they*.

You can teach students *this* (in question 1). Note that *this, that, these* and *those* are taught in lesson 4C.

5 R3.13 P Play the recording. Students listen and practise the questions in **4**. Alternatively, model and drill the questions yourself.

Can I help you?

6 a) Focus students on the Café Pronto price list. Teach *food* and *drink*.

Students work on their own or in pairs and match the food and drink on the price list to photos 1–10. Check answers with the class.

Point out that the Italian words *cappuccino* and *espresso*, and the French word *croissant*, are also very common in English, particularly in coffee shops and cafés.

Also teach students that we can say *a white coffee* (with milk) and *a black coffee* (without milk).

Point out that we can say *a mineral water* or *a bottle of mineral water*.

Also teach students that we can say *a coffee/tea* or *a cup of coffee/tea*.

> **EXTRA IDEAS**
> - If you have a monolingual class and speak the students' language, ask them what they usually buy in cafés and tell them how to say these items in English.
> - Give students one minute to remember all the things on the Café Pronto price list. Ask students to close their books. Students work in pairs and write down all the food and drink items they can remember.

b) R3.14 P Play the recording (SB p121). Students listen and practise the food and drink on the price list. Highlight the pronunciation of *cappuccino* /ˌkæpʊˈtʃiːnəʊ/, *orange juice* /ˈɒrɪndʒ dʒuːs/, *croissant* /ˈkwæsɒ/ and *sandwich* /ˈsænwɪdʒ/. Play the recording again, pausing after each word so that students can repeat individually.

c) Ask students to cover the price list. Students do the exercise in pairs, as shown in the speech bubbles.

7 Focus students on the speech bubbles and drill these examples with the class.

Students do the exercise in new pairs. While they are working, monitor and correct students' pronunciation if necessary.

8 a) Focus students on the photo of Café Pronto on SB p27. Use the people in the photo to teach *customer* and *assistant*.

R3.15 Play the recording (SB p121). Students listen and tick what the two customers order on the price list. Students compare answers in pairs. Check answers with the class.

> 1 two cappuccinos and a croissant
> 2 an espresso and an egg sandwich

b) Play the recording again. Students listen and write how much each customer spends. Check the answers with the class.

> 1 £5.85 2 £3.75

> **EXTRA IDEA**
> - If you have a class of complete beginners, deal with the two conversations separately. Play conversation 1, check the answers with the whole class, then repeat the procedure for conversation 2.

Real World In a café

9 Focus students on the flow chart. Check they understand that the assistant says the sentences in the green boxes and the customer says the sentences in the pink boxes. Point out that the language in brackets can change, depending on what the customer orders.

Note that the language that students need to learn for **productive** use is always in the **pink** boxes in these flow charts.

Students do the exercise on their own, then compare answers in pairs. Check answers with the class.

> - **Answers** 2 please 3 away 4 in 5 very
> - Check students understand all the sentences in the conversation. Highlight the difference between *eat in* and *take away*.
> - You can point out that we say *take away* in British English and *to go* in American English.
> - You can also teach *Of course.* as an alternative to *Sure*.

10 a) R3.16 P Play the recording (SB p122). Students listen and practise the sentences in **9**. Encourage students to copy the polite intonation.

Play the recording again, pausing after each sentence for students to repeat chorally and individually.

b) Put students into pairs, student A and student B. Student As are assistants and student Bs are customers. Students practise the conversation in **9** with their partner. After students have practised the conversation a few times, ask them to change roles. While students are working, monitor and correct their pronunciation if necessary.

EXTRA IDEA

- Before asking students to work in pairs, practise the conversation in 'open pairs'. See tips on drilling on p20.

 a) Put students into new pairs. Focus students on the Café Pronto price list on SB p26.

Students take turns to be the customer and order food and drink. The assistant must work out how much to charge the customer. You can ask students to cover the conversation in **9** before they begin.

While students are working, monitor and correct any language and pronunciation mistakes you hear.

b) Finally, ask a few pairs to role-play a conversation in Café Pronto for the class.

EXTRA PRACTICE AND HOMEWORK

3 Review Exercise 6 SB p29
CD-ROM Lesson 3C
Workbook Lesson 3C p16

 # Bread and cheese

QUICK REVIEW ●●●
This activity reviews money and prices. Students work on their own and write four prices, as in the examples. Students complete the activity in pairs.

Vocabulary food and drink (2); *love, like, eat, drink, a lot of*
Review money and prices; food and drink (1)

 a) Focus students on the photo. Students do the exercise on their own or in pairs. Check answers with the class.

Note that many of these words (*milk, tea, rice, fruit,* etc.) are uncountable nouns. However, we feel that asking Starter students to differentiate between countable and uncountable nouns would be unnecessarily complicated at Starter level. Note that countable and uncountable nouns are dealt with thoroughly in **face2face** Elementary.

1 fruit 2 tea 3 coffee 4 vegetables 5 orange juice
6 milk 7 bread 8 water 9 fish 10 rice 11 meat
12 cheese 13 eggs 14 sugar 15 pasta 16 chocolate

b) **R3.17** **P** Play the recording. Students listen and practise. Alternatively, model the words yourself and ask students to repeat chorally and individually. Highlight the pronunciation of *orange juice* /'ɒrɪndʒ dʒuːs/, *vegetables* /'vedʒtəbəlz/, *fruit* /fruːt/ and *chocolate* /'tʃɒklət/. Point out that *vegetables* is three syllables, not four, and *chocolate* is two syllables, not three.

EXTRA IDEAS

- If you have a class of complete beginners, consider teaching this vocabulary yourself at the beginning of the lesson. Prepare flashcards of the food and drink items and teach the words one by one. You can then use **1** for practice.
- If you have a strong class, use **Vocabulary Plus 3 Food and drink** p153 (Instructions p147) in this lesson or give this worksheet to students for homework.

 a) Give students one minute to remember all the words for food and drink in the photo. Students are not allowed to write anything down.

b) Ask students to close their books. Put students into pairs. Students say all the words for food and drink in the photo they can remember. Alternatively, ask them to write down the words in their pairs.

Ask one pair to tell you all the words for food and drink they can remember and write them on the board. Ask other students to tell you any missing words until you have all 16 words from **1a)**.

Focus students on pictures A–D. Students do the exercise on their own, then compare answers in pairs. Check answers with the class.

Check students understand the new verbs *like, love, eat* and *drink*. We suggest you treat these verbs as lexical items at this stage and avoid eliciting any negative sentences during the lesson. Note that the Present Simple is taught in units 4 and 5.

Also check students understand *a lot of: I eat a lot of rice.,* etc.

2A 3D 4C

 R3.18 **P** Play the recording. Students listen and practise the sentences in **3**. Highlight the vowel sound in *love* /lʌv/.

 a) Ask students to look at the photo of Fiona and her family in lesson 3B on SB p24. Ask the class what they remember about Fiona and her family.

R3.19 Focus students on the vocabulary box in **1a)**. Play the recording (SB p122). Students listen and tick the food and drink that Fiona talks about. Students can compare answers in pairs. Check answers with the class.

coffee tea meat fish eggs pasta chocolate

b) Give students time to read sentences 1–5. Play the recording again. Students listen and choose the correct words. Play the recording again if necessary. Check answers with the class.

Use the recording to remind students that we say *black coffee* (without milk) and *white coffee* (with milk).

| 2 tea 3 fish 4 eggs 5 chocolate |

 6 a) Students do the exercise on their own. They can use vocabulary from **1a)** or their own ideas. Point out that they can use any of the new verbs in sentences 5 and 6. While students are working, check their sentences for accuracy and help with any new vocabulary.

b) Teach the phrase *Me too*. Students compare sentences in groups. Students say which of their partners' sentences are also true for them, for example: A *I love bread and cheese.* B *Me too!*.

Finally, ask each group to tell the class about food and drink they love, like, etc., for example: *Jan and I love bread and cheese.*

┌─ EXTRA PRACTICE AND HOMEWORK ─────────

  Ph Class Activity 3D From start to finish p121 (Instructions p103)

  Ph Vocabulary Plus 3 Food and drink p153 (Instructions p147)

  CD-ROM Lesson 3D

  Workbook Lesson 3D p17

  Workbook Reading and Writing Portfolio 3 p56

  Progress Test 3 p166
└──────────────────────────────────────

Help with Sounds /ɒ/ and /ʌ/

 1 a) R3.20 Focus students on the phonemes /ɒ/ and /ʌ/, the pictures and the words. Play the recording. Students listen to the sounds and the words. Point out that *o* in *coffee* is pronounced with an /ɒ/ sound and *u* in *umbrella* is pronounced with an /ʌ/ sound.

b) P Play the recording again. Students listen and practise. If students are having problems producing the sounds, help them with the mouth position for each sound.

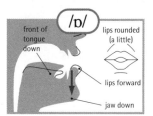 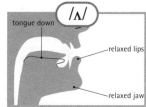

Point out that we round the lips when we say /ɒ/. Also highlight that the lips are relaxed when we say /ʌ/.

 2 a) Focus students on the boxes. Point out that the pink vowels are pronounced /ɒ/ and the blue vowels are pronounced /ʌ/.

R3.21 Play the recording. Students listen and notice how we say the pink and blue vowels.

b) P Play the recording again. Students listen and practise.

 3 a) Go through the example with the class. Students do the exercise on their own.

b) Students compare answers in pairs. Encourage students to say all the words when comparing answers.

c) R3.22 Play the recording. Students listen and check their answers.

Note that all the words with an /ɒ/ sound are said by a man and all the words with an /ʌ/ sound are said by a woman.

P Play the recording again. Students listen and practise the words. Check they say the vowels in **bold** correctly.

Finally, ask students to say each group of three words for the class. If necessary, correct their pronunciation and ask them to say the words again.

┌─ EXTRA IDEA ──────────────────────────
• Remind students that there is a chart of the phonemic symbols on SB p126 and that they can practise the Help with Sounds drills at home on the CD-ROM/Audio CD.
└──────────────────────────────────────

3 Review

See p29 for ideas on how to use this section.

1a) 2 big 3 new 4 cheap 5 ugly 6 cold

1b) 2 small 3 old 4 expensive 5 beautiful 6 hot

2a) 2 's 3 isn't 4 's 5 are 6 're 7 are 8 aren't

2b) 2 Is the school cheap? 3 Is the teacher good? 4 Are the students friendly? 5 Where's the hotel? 6 Are the rooms very big?

2c) 1 In London. 2 No, it isn't. 3 Yes, he/she is. 4 Yes, they are. 5 Near the school. 6 No, they aren't.

3 2 wife 3 daughter 4 son 5 sister 6 brother 7 father 8 mother

4 2 possessive 3 is 4 is 5 is, possessive 6 is, possessive

5 2 your 3 his 4 her 5 its 6 our 7 their

6a) 3d) 4i) 5c) 6h) 7a) 8f) 9e)

Progress Portfolio

See p29 for ideas on how to use this section.

4 My world

Student's Book p30–p37

4A I like it!

Vocabulary phrases with *like, have, live, work, study*
Grammar Present Simple (*I, you, we, they*): positive and negative
Review food and drink (1) and (2); family; *be*

QUICK REVIEW ●●●

This activity reviews food and drink vocabulary. Check students remember *like*. Students work on their own and write a list of ten words for food and drink. Students then complete the activity in pairs. Ask a few students to tell the class which things they like on their partner's list.

Life in Peru

 a) Check students know where Peru is (in South America). Focus students on the photo of Ricardo and the speech bubble.

R4.2 Play the recording. Students listen, read and find out who Cecilia, Carlos and Diego are.

Check answers with the class.

> Cecilia is Ricardo's wife.
> Carlos and Diego are Ricardo and Cecilia's sons.

b) Students do the exercise on their own.

c) Check students understand *homework* /'həʊmwɜːk/. Students compare answers in pairs. Check answers with the class.

> 2 married
> 3 is
> 4 nine
> 5 are
> 6 Chinese

Phrases with *like, have, live, work, study*

 a) Students do the exercise on their own or in pairs. Early finishers can check their answers in Language Summary 4 **V4.1** SB p106.

Check answers with the class. Check students understand all the new vocabulary, referring to the pictures if necessary.

Point out that we can say *in the centre of the city* or *in the city centre*. However, when we use the name of the city, we say *I live in the centre of London.* not ~~*I live in London centre*~~.

Also highlight that we say *a flat* in British English and *an apartment* in American English.

You can also teach students *live in a (big/small) house* and *work at home* (not ~~*work in my house*~~).

Highlight that we use *a house* to refer to the type of building, whereas we use *home* to refer to the place where you live.

> b) like **rock music** c) have **two children** d) have **a car**
> e) live **in a flat** f) live **in the centre of the city**
> g) work **for a Spanish company** h) work **in an office**
> i) study **English** j) study **languages**

b) **R4.1** **P** Play the recording. Students listen and practise the phrases. Highlight the pronunciation of *work* /wɜːk/, *company* /'kʌmpəni/, *office* /'ɒfɪs/ and *languages* /'læŋgwɪdʒɪz/. Repeat the drill if necessary.

--- **EXTRA IDEAS** ---

- Students work in pairs and take turns to test each other on the collocations. One student says a word or phrase from the box in **1a)**, for example *football*, and his/her partner says the whole collocation, for example *like football*.
- Students work in pairs and write one more word or phrase for each of the verbs in **1a)** (*like chocolate, have a cat, live in London, work for a computer company, study German*, etc.). Write correct collocations on the board for students to copy.

Help with Grammar Present Simple (*I, you, we, they*): positive and negative

 a) Students do the exercise on their own. Check answers with the class.

- **Answers** You <u>study</u> English. We <u>live</u> in a very nice flat. They <u>like</u> football.
- Point out that these verbs are in the Present Simple.
- Use the four example sentences to highlight that the Present Simple positive is the same for *I, you, we* and *they*.

b) Draw the table on the board and write in the example sentences. Note that in grammar tables the auxiliary verbs are shown in blue and the main verbs are shown in pink. This approach helps visual learners to understand the word order of positive sentences, negatives and question forms in English. Go through the following points with the class.

- Use the examples to highlight the word order: *I/you/we/they* + *don't* + verb + ...
- Point out that *don't* is the contracted form of *do not* and that we usually use this form when writing and speaking.
- Establish that the auxiliary *do* has no meaning, but is used to make the negative form of the Present Simple with *I/you/we/they*.
- Also point out that we use *don't* in negatives with *I, you, we, they* for all verbs except *be*. If necessary, write these sentences on the board for comparison: *I'm not a teacher. You aren't French. We aren't in this class. They aren't from the USA.*
- With a strong class you can teach students that *I, you, we* and *they* in the example sentences are called 'the subject', and that in positive sentences the subject always comes before the verb. However, we suggest you simply call the infinitive 'the verb' at this level to avoid overloading students with grammatical terms.

c) Students do the exercise on their own. Check answers with the class.

- ✏️ Focus students on the table on the board. Elicit which words in sentences 1 and 2 from **3c)** go in each column and complete the table (see the table in **G4.1** SB p107).
- Use the sentences in the table to check students understand the word order in Present Simple negatives.

4 **R4.3** **P** Play the recording. Students listen and practise. Check that students pronounce *don't* /dəʊnt/ correctly in each sentence. Repeat the drill if necessary.

Life in Australia

5 **a)** Focus students on the photo of Sandra and the speech bubble. Students do the exercise on their own before checking in pairs. Check students understand that a (+) sign indicates a positive sentence and a (–) sign indicates a negative sentence before they begin.

b) **R4.4** Play the recording. Students listen and check their answers. Check answers with the class.

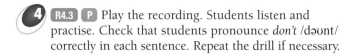

2 live
3 have
4 don't have
5 don't live
6 work
7 study
8 like

EXTRA IDEA

- Put students into pairs, A and B. Ask student As to look at the text about Ricardo and student Bs to look at the text about Sandra. Students underline all the phrases from **1a)** they can find in their texts. Students then work with their partner, swap books and check their partner's answers.

6 **a)** Check students understand what to do by focusing on the example and asking individual students which sentence is true for them.
Students do the exercise on their own.

b) Students work in pairs and say their sentences to each other. Students also decide how many of their sentences are the same.
Ask each pair to tell the class two sentences that are true for both students, for example, *We don't work in an office., We like Italian food.*, etc.

Get ready ... Get it right!

7 Focus students on the examples and check they remember *false*.
Students do the exercise on their own. While they are working, check their sentences for accuracy and help with any new vocabulary.

EXTRA IDEA

- ✏️ Demonstrate the activity by writing three true and three false sentences about you on the board using language from **1a)**. Students work in pairs and guess which sentences are false. Students can then do **7** on their own.

8 Drill the sentences in the speech bubbles to remind students of the language they need to do the exercise.
Put students into new pairs, A and B. Student As say their sentences from **7**. Student Bs decide if they are true or false.
When they have finished, students change roles.
Finally, ask each student to tell the class one of their partner's true sentences.

EXTRA PRACTICE AND HOMEWORK
4 Review Exercises 1 and 2 SB p37
CD-ROM Lesson 4A
Workbook Lesson 4A p18

4B My free time

Vocabulary free time activities
Grammar Present Simple (*I, you, we, they*): questions and short answers
Help with Listening questions with *do you*
Review phrases with *like, have, live, work, study*

Free time activities

1 a) Teach the phrase *free time activities* (things you do when you're not working or studying). Point out that the singular of *activities* is *an activity*.

Students do the exercise on their own or in pairs. Alternatively, use the pictures to teach the vocabulary yourself, then use the matching activity for practice. Check answers with the class.

Highlight the different phrases with *go*: **go to** *concerts*, **go to** *the cinema*, **go** *shopping*, **go out** *with friends*. Point out *the* in *go to **the** cinema* (not ~~go to cinema~~).

Also highlight the capital letters in *TV* and *DVD* and point out that *TV* stands for *television*.

You can also tell students that we can say *eat out* or *go out to eat*.

> **1** watch TV or DVDs **2** go shopping **3** go to the cinema
> **4** go out with friends **5** eat out **6** play tennis
> **7** go to concerts **8** play computer games

b) R4.5 P Play the recording. Students listen and practise. Check that students stress the phrases correctly. Note that only the main stress in words and phrases is shown in vocabulary boxes and the Language Summary. Play the recording again, pausing after each phrase for students to repeat individually.

> — EXTRA IDEA —
> • If you have a strong class, consider using **Vocabulary Plus 4** Free time activities p154 (Instructions p148) at this stage of the lesson.

2 a) Focus students on the example sentences. Point out the preposition in the first sentence (*I play tennis **in** my free time.*).

Use the second sentence to teach the meaning of *a lot* (*I watch TV **a lot**.*).

Also highlight the negative form of the Present Simple in the third sentence (*I **don't go** to concerts.*).

Students work on their own and write four sentences about their free time using phrases from the lesson.

b) Students compare sentences in pairs.

Ask a few students to tell the class their sentences.

An online interview

3 a) Focus students on the web page on SB p33 and the photo of rock stars Mike and Kim Black. Ask what their band is called (Bad Day) and what type of music they play (rock music).

R4.6 Play the recording. Students listen, read and find three things that Mike and Kim do in their free time. Check answers with the class.

> listen to (a lot of rock) music, go out with friends, watch TV (a lot), go to concerts, eat out (a lot)

b) Students do the exercise on their own, then compare answers in pairs. Check answers with the class.

> 2T 3F 4F 5F 6T 7F

> — EXTRA IDEA —
> • With a strong class, teach the following new words and phrases in the interview: *rock star, also, fantastic, listen to (rock music), of course, Have a nice day!*.

Help with Grammar Present Simple (*I, you, we, they*): questions and short answers

4 a) Draw the table on the board and write in the example questions. Go through the following points with the class.

> • Use the examples to highlight the word order: question word + *do* + *I/you/we/they* + verb + ...
> • Establish that the auxiliary *do* has no meaning, but is used to make the question form of the Present Simple with *I, you, we, they*.
> • Also point out that we use the auxiliary *do* with all verbs except *be*. If necessary, write the following questions with *be* on the board for comparison: *Where am I? Where are you from? Where are we? Where are they from?*.

b) Students do the exercise on their own. Check answers with the class.

> • Focus students on the table on the board. Elicit which words in questions 1 and 2 from **4b)** go in each column and complete the table (see the table in G4.2 SB p107).

- Use these questions to further highlight the word order in *Wh*- questions. Point out that Present Simple questions are the same for *I, you, we* and *they*.
- Use question 2 to highlight that we sometimes use a noun after *What ...* : **What food** do you like?, **What music** do you like?, etc.
- You can also teach students the question *What do you do?* = *What's your job?*.

c) Students do the exercise on their own or in pairs. Check answers with the class.

- **Answers Do** you like London? Yes, I do. No, I **don't**. **Do** you go to concerts? Yes, we **do**. No, we don't. **Do** they like Mexican food? Yes, they **do**. No, they **don't**.
- Highlight the word order in the *yes/no* questions: *Do + I/you/we/they + verb + ...*
- Point out that we use *do* or *don't* in the short answers, but we don't repeat the verb: *Yes, I do.* not ~~Yes, I like.~~ or ~~Yes, I do like.~~

5 a) Go through the example with the class. Point out that all the questions are about Mike and Kim Black.

Students do the exercise on their own. Check answers with the class.

You can point out that in question 3 *do* is both the auxiliary and the main verb.

2 Do, have 3 do, do 4 Do, go 5 Do, eat 6 Do, like

b) Students do the exercise in pairs. Remind students to use the correct short answers where appropriate. They can check their answers on the web page about Mike and Kim Black if necessary.

Help with Listening Questions with *do you*

- This Help with Listening helps students understand Present Simple questions with *do you ... ?*.

6 a) R4.7 Focus students on sentences 1–4. Play the recording. Students listen, read and notice how we say *do you* in Present Simple questions.

Highlight the pronunciation of *do you* /djə/ and point out that these words are often pronounced in this 'weak form' in natural spoken English. While it is not essential for students at this level to use the weak form themselves, it is important that they understand it when they are asked questions in the Present Simple.

Note that *do you* can also be pronounced /dʒə/, but we rarely use the strong form /du juː/. The alternative weak form /dʒə/ is practised in **face2face** Elementary.

b) R4.8 Play the recording (SB p122). Students listen and write the questions. Before you begin, point out that students will hear each question twice. Play the recording again if necessary.

c) Students compare sentences in pairs.

Check answers by eliciting each question and writing it on the board. You can leave these questions on the board so that they can be used in **7b)**.

Encourage students to use weak forms when speaking and highlight them when appropriate in future classes.

1 Do you go to the cinema? 2 What food do you like?
3 Where do you go shopping? 4 Do you play computer games?

7 a) R4.9 Play the recording (SB p122). Students listen and practise. Encourage students to copy the pronunciation of *do you* in the questions. Play the recording again, pausing after each question and short answer for students to repeat individually.

b) Put students into pairs, student A and student B. Student As ask the questions in **6a)**. Student Bs ask the questions in **6b)** that are on the board. Remind students to give their own answers.

Avoid doing any whole-class feedback at the end of the activity, as this would require *he* and *she* forms of the Present Simple. These forms are taught in unit 5.

Get ready ... Get it right!

8 Put students into new pairs, student A and student B. If possible, put students in pairs with somebody they don't know very well.

Student As turn to SB p86 and student Bs turn to SB p92. Check they are all looking at the correct exercise.

a) Focus students on the questions in column A of the table. Students do the exercise on their own.

Avoid checking the questions with the whole class so that students don't hear the questions that they are about to be asked.

Student A 2 Do you watch DVDs? 3 Do you live in a house or a flat? 4 Do you like Italian food? 5 Do you have a computer?
Student B b) Do you play tennis or football? c) Do you work in an office? d) Do you like Chinese food? e) Do you have a dog or a cat?

b) Students work on their own and guess their partner's answers to the questions in column A of the table. Students should put a tick or a cross in column B of the table. Students are not allowed to talk to their partner at this stage of the activity.

c) Students work with their partner. Student As ask questions 1–5 and put a tick or a cross for each of their partner's answers in column C of the table. Remind student Bs to use *Yes, I do.* or *No, I don't.* when answering the questions. When student A has finished asking the questions, he/she tells his/her partner how many of his/her guesses were correct.

d) Students swap roles so that student B asks questions a)–e).

Finally, students tell the class how many of their guesses were correct. Again, avoid doing any class feedback on the answers themselves, as this would require students to use *he* and *she* forms of the Present Simple.

┌─ EXTRA PRACTICE AND HOMEWORK ─
Ph **Class Activity** 4B Find two people p122
(Instructions p103)
Ph **Vocabulary Plus** 4 Free time activities p154
(Instructions p148)
4 Review Exercises 3 and 4 SB p37
CD-ROM Lesson 4B
Workbook Lesson 4B p19
└─

4C Buying things

QUICK REVIEW ●●●

This activity reviews free time activities and Present Simple *yes/no* questions with *you*. Check students remember the meaning of *both*. Students do the activity in pairs, as shown in the examples. Then ask each pair to tell the class one or two things they both do.

Vocabulary things to buy; *this, that, these, those*
Real World in a shop
Review free time activities; money and prices; *How much ... ?*

Things to buy

1 a) Focus students on pictures 1–10. Students do the exercise on their own or in pairs. Check answers with the class.

Check students understand *birthday* and teach the phrase *Happy birthday* as shown on the card (picture 6).

> 2 tissues 3 a map 4 a newspaper 5 a postcard
> 6 a birthday card 7 batteries 8 chewing gum
> 9 sweets 10 a box of chocolates

─ EXTRA IDEA ─
• If you have a class of complete beginners, consider teaching these words yourself by bringing the items to the class. Hold up each item in turn and tell students the word in English. You can then use **1a)** for practice.

b) **R4.10** **P** Play the recording. Students listen and practise. Check they stress the words correctly and highlight the pronunciation of *birthday* /ˈbɜːθdeɪ/, *chocolates* /ˈtʃɒkləts/ and *tissues* /ˈtɪʃuːz/. Point out that *batteries* /ˈbætrɪz/ is usually pronounced as two syllables, not three. Note that the stress on *magazine* can also be on the first syllable.

Point out that the plural of *box* is *boxes* and that the singular of *batteries* is *a battery*.

c) Students do the activity in pairs.

2 Focus students on photos A–D. Ask where the people are (in a shop). Check students remember *customer* and *shop assistant*.

R4.11 Play the recording. Students listen and fill in the gaps with the correct prices. Play the recording again if necessary.

Students compare answers in pairs. Check answers with the class.

> A £4.75
> B 50p
> C £6.95
> D £3.59

Help with Vocabulary *this, that, these, those*

3 Students do the exercise on their own. ✏ While they are working, draw the blank table on the board. Check answers with the class and highlight the following points.

• Focus students on the table on the board. Check students understand *here* and *there*. Elicit which words go in each column and complete the table (see the table in **V4.4** SB p106).
• Point out that we use *this/these* for something close to us and *that/those* for something further away.
• Check students understand that we use *this/that* for singular nouns and *these/those* for plural nouns.
• Point out that *this, that, these, those* go **before** *be* in sentences: **Those** are nice.
• Also highlight that *this, that, these, those* go **after** *be* in questions: How much are **these**?.

4 **R4.12** **P** Focus students on the example drill. Play the recording (SB p122). Students listen and practise. Highlight the /ɪ/ sound in *this* /ðɪs/ and the /iː/ sound in *these* /ðiːz/, which students studied in the Help with Sounds section in unit 2. Repeat the drill if necessary.

5 Students do the exercise on their own, then compare answers in pairs. Check answers with the class.

> 1 these
> 2 That
> 3 those
> 4 this

Anything else?

 6 a) Focus students on photos A and B. Give students time to read the conversations. Avoid dealing with any new language at this stage.

R4.13 Play the recording. Students listen and fill in the gaps.

b) Students compare answers in pairs. Check answers with the class.

> 2 tissues
> 3 £5.45
> 4 postcards
> 5 two
> 6 £10.65

Real World In a shop

 7 a) Focus students on the flow chart. Point out that the language in brackets can change, depending on what the customer wants to buy.

Students do the exercise on their own by referring to the conversations in **6a)**. Check answers with the class.

- **Answers** 2 much 3 have 4 else 5 are 6 lot
- Check students understand the new words/phrases: *Yes, they're over there.*, *They're (50p) each.* and *Here you are.*
- Point out that we say *Thanks a lot.* or *Thanks very much.* Also remind students of other ways to say thank you: *Thanks.*, *Thank you.* and *Thank you very much.* You can point out that *Thanks.* is more informal than *Thank you.*

b) Students do the exercise on their own. Check answers with the class.

- **Answers** 1 Do you have any (maps of London)? 2 Can I have (that box of chocolates), please? 3 How much is (this map)? How much are (these postcards)?
- Check students understand the phrases *Do you have ... ?*, *Can I have ... ?* and *How much ... ?*. Point out that we use *Can I have ... ?* to ask for things.
- We suggest you teach *any* as part of the phrase *Do you have any ... ?* and point out that this phrase is followed by a plural noun (*maps*, etc.). Note that *a/an*, *some* and *any* are studied in unit 6.

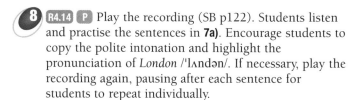 **8** R4.14 P Play the recording (SB p122). Students listen and practise the sentences in **7a)**. Encourage students to copy the polite intonation and highlight the pronunciation of *London* /ˈlʌndən/. If necessary, play the recording again, pausing after each sentence for students to repeat individually.

 9 Students practise the conversations in **6a)** in pairs, taking turns to be the customer. Encourage the customers to use polite intonation when asking for things.

— EXTRA IDEA —
- Ask each pair to choose conversation A or B from **6a)**. Students decide who is the customer and who is the shop assistant. Students practise the conversation until they can remember it. Ask students to close their books and practise the conversation again. Ask two or three pairs to role-play their conversations for the class.

 10 Students work in the same pairs. Student As turn to SB p88 and student Bs turn to SB p94. Check they are all looking at the correct exercise.

a) Pre-teach *spend (money)*. Ask students to look at photos a)–d). Allow students time to read the information about their roles and point out the prompts in the box.

Students role-play the conversation in their pairs. Student A in each pair starts the conversation by saying *Excuse me. Do you have any batteries?*.

b) Students swap roles so that student B is the customer and student A is the shop assistant in each pair. Again, draw students' attention to the prompts in the box before they begin.

At the end of the activity, ask students how much they spent (student A: £17.90, student B: £12.50).

 11 a) Students do the activity in new pairs. While they are working, check their conversations for accuracy and correct any mistakes.

b) Students practise their conversations until they have memorised them.

c) Put two pairs together so that they are working in groups of four. Pairs then take turns to role-play their conversations. Students listen to the other pair's conversation and find out what the customer buys and how much he/she spends. Students can ask the other pair to repeat the conversation if necessary.

Finally, ask two or three pairs to role-play their conversations for the class.

— EXTRA PRACTICE AND HOMEWORK —
Ph **Class Activity** 4C Shopping bingo p123 (Instructions p104)
4 Review Exercise 5 SB p37
CD-ROM Lesson 4C
Workbook Lesson 4C p21

4D Days and times

Vocabulary days of the week; time words
Real World telling the time; talking about the time
Review things to buy; numbers 0–100

QUICK REVIEW ●●●

This activity reviews things to buy. Ask students to close their books. Students work in pairs and write a list of things in the shop in lesson 4C. Students check their ideas in **1a)** on SB p34. Students then discuss which of these things they have with them.

EXTRA IDEA

- If you have a class of complete beginners, consider teaching the time yourself first by using a large clock with movable hands. ✍ Alternatively, you can draw clock faces on the board. You can then use **3** and **4** for practice.

1 a) **R4.15** **P** Focus students on the days of the week. Play the recording. Students listen and practise. Alternatively, model and drill the days yourself. Point out that *Wednesday* /ˈwenzdeɪ/ is two syllables, not three. Point out that the stress on each day is on the first syllable.

b) Students do the exercise in pairs.

c) Students do the exercise in the same pairs. Check answers with the class. Teach and drill *today*, *tomorrow* and *the weekend*. Note that *weekend* can be stressed on either the first or the second syllable.

2 a) Students do the exercise in pairs. Alternatively, teach the words yourself first and use this exercise for practice.

b) **R4.16** Play the recording. Students listen and check their answers.

P Play the recording again. Students listen and practise. Highlight the pronunciation of *minute* /ˈmɪnɪt/ and the silent h in *hour* /aʊə/.

Teach students that 30 minutes = *half an hour*, 15 minutes = *quarter of an hour* and 18 months = *a year and a half*.

You can also point out that we say *two and a half hours* not ~~two hours and a half~~.

> 2 a minute 3 an hour 4 a day 5 a week 6 a month

c) Students do the exercise on their own before checking in pairs. Check answers with the class.

> b) minutes c) hours d) week e) year f) months

3 a) Pre-teach *time* and highlight the difference between *a clock* and *a watch*.

Students do the exercise on their own or in pairs. Check answers with the class. Point out that we can say *quarter past/to ...* or *a quarter past/to ...* .

> A six o'clock B quarter past six D quarter to seven

b) Tell students that we can say times in two ways. Students do the exercise on their own or in pairs. Check answers with the class.

Also highlight that we can say *(a) quarter past (six)* or *six fifteen*, but not ~~fifteen past (six)~~.

> six thirty C six forty-five D six fifteen B

4 Students do the exercise on their own or in pairs. Check answers with the class.

Tell students that we can also say these times as *six ten*, *six twenty-five*, etc. Although this alternative form is probably easier for students to use than the *past/to* form, it is important that they understand both ways of telling the time when they hear them.

Point out that we say *six oh five* for 6.05, not ~~six five~~ or ~~six zero five~~.

You can also highlight that in American English 6.05 = *five after six*, 6.10 = *ten after six*, etc.

> 2a) 3h) 4b) 5g) 6f) 7e) 8d)

5 **R4.17** **P** Play the recording. Students listen and practise the times in **3a)** and **4**. Note that the times are recorded in logical order (*six o'clock, five past six*, etc.).

Highlight the pronunciation of *quarter* /ˈkɔːtə/ and *half* /hɑːf/. Also highlight that we don't pronounce the t in *five past* /pɑːs/ *six*, etc., and that we use the weak form of *to* in *five to* /tə/ *six*, etc. Repeat the drill if necessary.

6 a) **R4.18** Tell students that they are going to listen to five conversations. Play the recording (SB p122). Students listen and write the times.

b) Students compare answers in pairs. Play the recording again, pausing after each conversation to check students' answers.

> 1 twenty to three 2 half past eight
> 3 six o'clock 4 quarter to twelve 5 two thirty

7 a) Focus students on pictures 1 and 2. Students do the exercise on their own.

b) **R4.19** Play the recording. Students listen and check their answers.

P Play the recording again, pausing after each sentence and asking students to repeat individually. Encourage students to copy the polite intonation in the questions.

Check students understand that we use *What time is it, please?* to ask the time. You can also teach and drill the alternative question *What's the time, please?*.

Also point out that we use *at* for times: *It's **at** half past eight.*

Teach students that we use *a.m.* for times 0.00–12.00 and *p.m.* for times 12.00–24.00.

> 1 WOMAN Excuse me. **What** time is **it**, please?
>   MAN It's twenty **to** three.
> 2 WOMAN What **time** is your English class?
>   MAN It's at **half** past eight.

 Put students into new pairs, student A and student B. Student As turn to SB p89 and student Bs turn to SB p95. Check they are all looking at the correct exercise.

a) Focus students on the film times. Use the speech bubbles to teach *What time is ... on?* and the response *It's on at ...* . You can point out that we also use these phrases to talk about TV programmes.

Students take turns to ask the times of the films and fill in the gaps on the timetable. Students are not allowed to look at their partner's book.

b) Students compare times with their partner and check that they are correct.

> ┌─ EXTRA PRACTICE AND HOMEWORK ─────
> **Ph** **Class Activity** 4D Time dominoes p124
> (Instructions p104)
> **CD-ROM** Lesson 4D
> **Workbook** Lesson 4D p22
> **Workbook** Reading and Writing Portfolio 4 p58
> **Progress Test 4** p167

Help with Sounds /θ/ and /ð/

1 **a)** Tell students that there are two different ways to pronounce *th*. Focus students on the phonemes /θ/ and /ð/, the pictures and the words.

R4.20 Play the recording. Students listen to the sounds and the words. Point out that *th* in *three* is pronounced with a /θ/ sound and *th* in *mother* is pronounced with a /ð/ sound.

b) **P** Play the recording again. Students listen and practise. If students are having problems producing the sounds, help them with the mouth position for each sound.

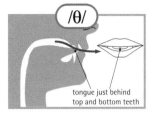 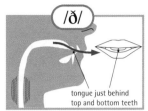

Point out that the mouth position is the same for both sounds, with the tongue just behind the top and bottom teeth. However, when we say the /θ/ sound, there is no voice from the throat and you can feel the air from your mouth on your hand. When we say the /ð/ sound, there is voice from the throat.

You can ask your students to place their fingers and thumb on their throats. When they say the /ð/ sound, they will feel vibration in the throat.

Another useful tip is to ask them to place their index finger on their lips, as if they were making a *shhh* sound. When saying both *th* sounds, the tip of the tongue should touch the side of the finger.

2 **a)** **R4.21** Focus students on the boxes. Play the recording. Students listen and notice how we say *th* in both sets of words.

b) **P** Play the recording again. Students listen and practise.

3 **a)** **R4.22** Play the recording. Students listen and read the sentences.
P Play the recording again. Students listen and practise. Repeat the drill if necessary.

b) Students practise the sentences in pairs.
Finally, ask students to say the sentences for the class. If necessary, correct their pronunciation and ask them to say the sentences again.

4 Review

See p29 for ideas on how to use this section.

1 2 study 3 work 4 have 5 like 6 live 7 study 8 live 9 have 10 work

3 go shopping, watch DVDs, play computer games, eat out, watch TV, go to the cinema, go out with friends, play tennis

4a) 2 Where do they live in the UK? 3 Do they have a house in the USA? 4 What music do they like? 5 What do they do in their free time? 6 Do they go to concerts? 7 What food do they like? 8 Do they go to the cinema?

4b) See web page on SB p33.

5a) 2 sweets 3 batteries 4 postcard 5 newspaper 6 magazine 7 birthday card 8 chewing gum 9 tissues 10 box of chocolates

Progress Portfolio

See p29 for ideas on how to use this section.

5 Day-to-day life

5A   A typical day

QUICK REVIEW ●●●

This activity reviews ways of telling the time. Students work on their own and write six times. Students complete the activity in pairs. Ask students to say the times with *past* or *to* if possible. Early finishers can take turns to say each time in two ways.

> **Vocabulary** daily routines
> **Grammar** Present Simple (*he, she, it*): positive and negative
> **Review** telling the time; Present Simple (*I, you, we, they*); free time activities

> **morning** have breakfast, leave home, start work
> **afternoon** have lunch, finish work, (get home)
> **evening** get home, have dinner, (go to bed)
> **night** go to bed, sleep

Daily routines

 1 **a)** Focus students on pictures 1–10 of Carol's routine. Teach the phrase *daily routine* /ˌdeɪli ruːˈtiːn/.

Students do the exercise on their own or in pairs. Early finishers can check their answers in Language Summary 5 **V5.1** SB p108. Check answers with the class.

Point out that we usually say *have breakfast/lunch/dinner* not *eat breakfast/lunch/dinner*. Also point out that *get home* means *arrive home*, and that we say *go to bed* not ~~*go to the bed*~~.

Highlight that *work* is a noun in *start work* and *finish work*, not a verb.

If your students are at school or university, teach them the phrases *start/finish school, start/finish university* and *start/finish classes* as alternatives to *start/finish work*.

> 2 have breakfast 3 leave home 4 start work
> 5 have lunch 6 finish work 7 get home
> 8 have dinner 9 go to bed 10 sleep

─── **EXTRA IDEA** ───
- Teach the words/phrases in **1a)** yourself first by telling the students about your daily routine. You can then use **1a)** for practice.

b) **R5.1** **P** Play the recording. Students listen and practise. Alternatively, model the sentences yourself and ask students to repeat chorally and individually. Highlight the pronunciation of *breakfast* /ˈbrekfəst/, *lunch* /lʌnʃ/ and *work* /wɜːk/. You can also compare the vowel sounds in *leave* /liːv/ and *live* /lɪv/, which students studied in the Help with Sounds section in unit 2. Repeat the drill if necessary.

Note that only the main stress in each phrase is shown in vocabulary boxes and in the Language Summaries.

c) Check students remember *morning, afternoon, evening* and *night*.

Students do the exercise on their own or in pairs.

Check answers with the class. Note that some phrases may match with more than one time of day.

 2 **a)** Focus students on the speech bubbles. Remind students that we use *at* with times. Check students understand *at the same time*. Tell students to talk about their routine in the week, not at the weekend.

Students do the activity in pairs. Before students begin, tell them to make a note of things they both do at the same time.

b) Students tell the class things that they and their partner do at the same time, as in the speech bubble.

Carol's routine

 3 **a)** Pre-teach the vocabulary in the box. Model and drill the words with the class. Highlight the pronunciation of *university* /ˌjuːnɪˈvɜːsəti/ and point out the different stress patterns in *midday* and *midnight*.

b) Focus students on pictures 1–10 on SB p38 and the photo of Carol on SB p39. Check students understand that the pictures are of Carol's routine.

Students read the text and fill in the gaps with the correct times. Tell students to write the times in numbers, not words, as shown in the example.

c) **R5.2** Play the recording. Students listen and check their answers. Check answers with the class.

> b) 7.45 c) 8.15 d) 9.00 e) 12.45
> f) 5.30 g) 6.15 h) 7.30

Help with Grammar Present Simple (*he, she, it*): positive and negative

 4 **a)** Focus students on the example sentences in the Student's Book or write them on the board. Point out that the verbs in blue are in the Present Simple. Ask students to complete the rule.

Check students understand that in Present Simple positive sentences with *he, she* and *it* we add **-s** or **-es** to the verb.

b) Focus students on the table. Point out that the first column of the table shows the spelling rules for the *he, she, it* positive form of the Present Simple, and that the second column gives some examples.

Students do the exercise on their own by referring back to the verbs in **bold** in the text about Carol. While students are working, draw the table from **4b)** on the board. Check answers with the class.

- Focus students on the table on the board. Elicit which verbs go in each row and complete the table (see the table in `G5.1` SB p109).
- Go through the spelling rules with the class by asking students to tell you the endings on each verb in the second column. Underline these endings on the board.
- Point out that *have* is irregular and that we say *has*, not ~~haves~~.
- Use the examples and the context to highlight that we use the Present Simple to talk about daily routines.
- Note that verbs ending in *-ss, -sh, -x* or *-zz* (*miss, wish, fix, buzz,* etc.) also add *-es* in the *he, she, it* form of the Present Simple. However, as students haven't met any of these verbs yet, we suggest that you highlight these *he, she, it* forms in future lessons as and when they occur.

c) Focus students on the sentences in the table. Go through the following points with the class.

- Use the sentences to highlight the word order: *he/she/it + doesn't + verb + … .*
- Point out that *doesn't* is the contracted form of *does not* and that we usually use this form when writing and speaking.
- Also highlight that there is no *-s* or *-es* on the main verb in Present Simple negatives: *She doesn't like mornings.* not ~~She doesn't likes mornings~~.
- Use the **TIP!** to highlight that the negative is the same for *he, she* and *it: He doesn't have a car. It doesn't start today.*
- Also point out that we use *doesn't* in negatives with *he, she, it* for all verbs except *be*. If necessary, write these sentences on the board for comparison: *He isn't a doctor. She isn't Italian. It isn't expensive.*

5 `R5.3` `P` Play the recording. Students listen and practise. Check that students pronounce *doesn't* /ˈdʌzənt/ correctly. Repeat the drill if necessary.

6 **a)** Students do the exercise on their own, then compare answers in pairs.
 Check the answers by writing each verb on the board and then writing the *he, she, it* form next to it.

2 plays 3 starts 4 finishes 5 has 6 studies 7 loves
8 goes 9 eats 10 watches 11 drinks 12 reads

b) `R5.4` `P` Play the recording (SB p122). Students listen and practise. Note that students should repeat both the verb and its *he, she, it* form together (*like, likes,* etc.), not separately.

Ask students which *he, she, it* forms have the sound /ɪz/ at the end (*finishes* /ˈfɪnɪʃɪz/, *studies* /ˈstʌdɪz/, *watches* /ˈwɒtʃɪz/). Highlight the endings of these words on the board. Repeat the drill if necessary.

Tom's routine

7 **a)** Focus students on the photo of Tom. Ask the class who he is (Carol's brother). Students do the exercise on their own.

b) Students compare answers in pairs. Check answers with the class. Highlight that answers 14, 15 and 16 are plural forms and therefore do not end in *-s* or *-es*.

2 doesn't work 3 gets up 4 doesn't have 5 has 6 goes
7 leaves 8 starts 9 finishes 10 doesn't eat 11 has
12 gets 13 watches 14 don't work 15 have 16 talk

— EXTRA IDEA —
- Put students into pairs, student A and student B. Student As write two true and two false sentences about Carol. Student Bs write two true and two false sentences about Tom. Ask students to close their books. Students take turns to say their sentences to each other. Students say if their partner's sentences are true or false.

Get ready … Get it right!

8 Put students into new pairs, student A and student B. Student As turn to SB p89 and student Bs turn to SB p95. Check they are all looking at the correct exercise.

a) Focus students on column A of the table. Students do the exercise on their own, as in the example.

If necessary, check the answers with the class. Only check the words they need to fill in the gaps, so that students don't hear the questions they are about to be asked.

Student A 2 Do, watch 3 Do, have 4 Do, drink
5 Do, sleep
Student B b) Do, have c) Do, go d) Do, work
e) Do, eat

b) Students work with their partners. Student As ask questions 1–5 and put a tick or a cross in column B of the table. Remind student Bs to use short answers (*Yes, I do.* and *No, I don't.*). Student Bs can give more information if possible.

c) Students swap roles so that student B in each pair is asking his/her partner questions a)–e). Remind student Bs to put ticks and crosses in column B of the table.

d) Student As work in pairs with another student A and student Bs work in pairs with another student B. Students take turns to tell their new partner about their partner in **b)** and **c)**. Check that students use the *he, she* forms of the verbs.

Finally, ask each student to tell the class one or two things about their first partner.

> ┌─ EXTRA PRACTICE AND HOMEWORK ──────────
> │ **Ph** **Class Activity** 5A My partner's life p125
> │ (Instructions p104)
> │ **5 Review** Exercises 1 and 2 SB p45
> │ **CD-ROM** Lesson 5A
> │ **Workbook** Lesson 5A p23

 5B **Where does she work?**

QUICK REVIEW ●●●

This activity reviews daily routines and the Present Simple. Put students into pairs. Students do the activity in their pairs, as shown in the examples. Ask a few students to tell the class one or two things about their partner.

> **Vocabulary** time phrases with *on, in, at*
> **Grammar** Present Simple (*he, she, it*): questions and short answers
> **Help with Listening** sentence stress (1)
> **Review** daily routines

Time phrases with *on, in, at*

 a) Focus students on the tables. Point out the prepositions *on, in, at* and the examples.

Students do the exercise on their own or in pairs. Early finishers can check their answers in **V5.2** SB p108.

✎ While students are working, draw the tables on the board. Check answers with the class by saying each phrase in the box and asking students which column of the table it goes in.

Use the tables to highlight the following patterns: we use *on* with days of the week (*Sunday*, etc.) and parts of particular days (*Tuesday morning*, etc.); we use *in* with *the morning, the afternoon* and *the evening* (but we say *at night* not ~~in the night~~); we use *at* with times (*six o'clock, midday*, etc.). Also point out that we say *in the week* and *at the weekend*.

You can also highlight that in American and Australian English we say *on the weekend*.

Remind students that *midday* = 12.00 and *midnight* = 24.00.

Tell the class that when we talk about our routines, we can use the singular or plural form of days, parts of days and *the weekend*: *I play football on Friday/Fridays. He goes to the cinema on Wednesday evening/evenings. They eat out at the weekend/weekends.*

b) **R5.5** **P** Play the recording. Students listen and practise. Point out that we say the weak form of *at* /ət/ with time phrases. Repeat the drill if necessary.

> ── EXTRA IDEA ──────────────
> * Students work in pairs and test each other on the prepositions. One student says a word or phrase from the box in **1a)**, for example *Monday,* and his/her partner says the phrase with the correct preposition, for example *on Monday.*

2 a) Students do the exercise on their own before checking in pairs. Check answers with the class.

> 1 at 2 at, in 3 on 4 at, on 5 in 6 on

b) Students do the exercise on their own.

c) Students do the exercise in pairs. Before they begin, remind students of the phrase *Me too.*

Ask each pair to tell the class sentences that are true for both of them.

Lunch on Monday

 a) Focus students on the photo. Ask students what they remember about Carol and Tom from lesson 5A. Don't tell students anything about Nadine /næ'diːn/ at this stage.

Give students time to read sentences 1–5. Check students understand *other people* in question 5.

R5.6 Play the recording (SB p122). Students listen and choose the correct words in the sentences. Students compare answers in pairs. Check answers with the class.

> 2 doesn't work 3 Italian 4 Germany 5 two

b) Give students time to read questions 1–6. Play the recording again. Students listen and answer the questions.

c) Students compare answers in pairs. Check answers with the class.

> 2 In the mobile phone shop with Carol.
> 3 She's a student at the university.
> 4 She lives near the university.
> 5 Yes, she does.
> 6 She plays tennis and she goes to the cinema a lot.

Help with Grammar Present Simple (*he, she, it*): questions and short answers

4 a) Draw the table on the board and write in the example questions. Highlight the following points.

- Use the example questions to highlight the word order: question word + *does* + *he/she/it* + verb + ...
- Highlight that the auxiliary *does* has no meaning, but is used to make the question form of the Present Simple with *he, she* and *it*.
- Point out that there is no *-s* on the main verb in Present Simple questions: *Where does Nadine work ... ?* not *Where does Nadine works ... ?*.
- Also point out that Present Simple questions are the same for *he, she* and *it*.
- Highlight that we use the auxiliary *does* with all verbs except *be*: *Where is he?*, etc.

b) Students do the exercise on their own. Check answers with the class.

- Focus students on the table on the board. Elicit which words in questions 1 and 2 from **4b)** go in each column and complete the table (see the table in **G5.2** SB p109).
- Use these example questions to further highlight the word order.
- You can also teach the question *What does he/she do? = What's his/her job?*.

c) Students do the exercise on their own or in pairs. Check answers with the class.

- **Answers Does** he know Nadine? Yes, he **does**. No, he doesn't. **Does** she like Manchester? Yes, she does. No, she **doesn't**.
- Highlight the word order in the *yes/no* questions: *Does + he/she/it + verb + ...* .
- Point out that there is no *-s* or *-es* on the main verb in Present Simple questions: *Does she work at home?* not *Does she works at home?*.
- Also point out that we use *does* or *doesn't* in the short answers, but we don't repeat the verb: *Yes, she does.* not *Yes, she likes.* or *Yes, she does like.*

d) Students do the exercise on their own. Check answers with the class.

- We use *does* in questions with *he, she* and *it*.
- We use *do* in questions with *I, you, we* and *they*.

— EXTRA IDEA —

- If you have a class of false beginners, ask students to do **4a)–d)** in pairs. Students can then check their answers in **G5.2** SB p109. Check answers with the class and highlight the bullet points in **4a)–d)** above.

5 **R5.7** **P** Play the recording. Students listen and practise. Check that students pronounce *does* /dʌz/ correctly in the questions. Play the recording again if necessary, pausing after each question or short answer for students to repeat individually.

Help with Listening Sentence stress (1)

- This Help with Listening section introduces students to sentence stress and highlights that we stress the important words.

6 a) **R5.8** Play the recording. Students listen and notice the sentence stress. Point out that we stress the important words (the words that carry the meaning).

b) Play the recording again. Students listen and read the sentences. Ask the class if *does* is stressed in questions (it isn't).

Note that students whose languages have different stress patterns from English can often find it difficult to tune in to the way words are stressed. We suggest you use every opportunity to work on sentence stress with your class when drilling and doing listening activities.

— EXTRA IDEA —

- With a strong class, use the questions in **6a)** to point out what types of word we usually stress, such as question words (*Where*, etc.), names (*Tom*, etc.), verbs (*live*, etc.) and nouns (*week*, etc.). You can also highlight grammatical words such as articles (*the, a/an*), prepositions (*with*, etc.) and pronouns (*she*, etc.) that are usually unstressed in natural spoken English.

7 a) **R5.8** **P** Play the recording again. Students listen and practise. Check they copy the sentence stress correctly. Repeat the drill if necessary.

b) Students do the exercise in pairs, as shown in the speech bubbles. While students are working, monitor and check they are saying the questions with the correct stress.

8 Students work in the same pairs, student A and student B. Student As turn to SB p89 and student Bs turn to SB p95. Check they are all looking at the correct exercise.

a) Check students understand that the woman in the pictures is Nadine. Students do the exercise on their own.

Check answers with the class if necessary. Only check the words they need to fill in the gaps, so that the students don't hear the questions they are about to be asked. Note that the answers are the same for student A and student B.

Student A/Student B 2 does/Does she, on
3 Does/does she, on 4 Does/does she, at 5 Does she, on

b) Students work with their partner. Student A in each pair asks questions 1–5. Student B looks at pictures a)–e) and answers his/her partner's questions. Remind students to use short answers (*Yes, she does., No, she doesn't.*) where appropriate.

> **Student A** 1 8.45 2 She plays tennis. 3 No, she doesn't.
> 4 Yes, she does. 5 Yes, she does.

c) Students swap roles so that student B in each pair asks questions 1–5. Student A looks at pictures a)–e) and answers his/her partner's questions.

> **Student B** 1 11.30 2 Yes, she does. 3 She goes to the cinema. 4 8.00 5 No, she doesn't.

Get ready … Get it right!

9 **a)** Put students into new pairs, student A and student B. If possible, ask students to work with someone they don't know very well.

Pre-teach *best friend*. Students tell their partner their best friend's name and if this friend is male or female. Note that this stage is included so that students will know whether to write questions with *he* or *she* in **9b)**.

b) Students do the exercise on their own. Before they begin, point out that they can write questions about the topics in the box and the things in the photos, or use their own ideas.

10 **a)** Students work with their partner. Student A in each pair asks all his/her questions about his/her partner's best friend. Encourage students to ask more questions if possible. When he/she has finished, students swap roles so that student B asks all his/her questions.

b) Finally, ask each student to tell the class two things about their partner's best friend.

EXTRA IDEAS

- Bring in a photo of your best friend and show it to the class. Students work in pairs and write five questions to ask you about him/her. Students then take turns to ask you questions about your best friend.

- Students write a profile of their best friend for homework. These can be collected in next class and displayed around the classroom for other students to read.

EXTRA PRACTICE AND HOMEWORK

Ph **Class Activity** 5B A writer's week p126–p127 (Instructions p105)
Ph **Vocabulary Plus** 5 Jobs p155 (Instructions p148)
5 Review Exercises 3 and 4 SB p45
CD-ROM Lesson 5B
Workbook Lesson 5B p24

5C The New Moon

QUICK REVIEW ●●●
This activity reviews the Present Simple and ways of telling the time. Go through the instructions and the examples with the class. Students do the activity in pairs. At the end of the activity, ask a few pairs to tell the class three things they both do at the same time of the day.

Vocabulary food and drink (3)
Real World in a restaurant
Help with Listening sentence stress (2)
Review Present Simple; telling the time; money and prices; *How much … ?*

What's on the menu?

1 **a)** Focus students on the New Moon restaurant menu. Teach students the meaning of *menu* /ˈmenjuː/ and *moon*, and check they remember *restaurant* /ˈrestrɒnt/. Model and drill these words with the class. Point out that *restaurant* is two syllables, not three.

Students work on their own or in pairs and match the food and drink on the menu to photos 1–10. Early finishers can check their answers in **V5.3** SB p108. Check answers with the class.

Check students understand all the new vocabulary.

Use the menu to teach *main course* /ˈmeɪn kɔːs/ and *dessert* /dɪˈzɜːt/. You can also teach *starter*, which is eaten before the main course.

Highlight the difference between *still mineral water* (without bubbles) and *sparkling mineral water* (with bubbles). In restaurants in the UK it is also very common to ask for *tap water*, which is always clean, drinkable and free!

1 burger and chips 2 mushroom pizza 3 vegetable lasagne 4 chicken salad 5 fruit salad 6 chocolate ice cream, strawberry ice cream, vanilla ice cream 7 apple pie and cream 8 Coke, orange juice 9 a bottle of still mineral water, a bottle of sparkling mineral water
10 coffee, tea

b) **R5.9** **P** Play the recording (SB p122). Students listen and practise. Highlight the pronunciation of *chicken* /ˈtʃɪkɪn/, *vegetable* /ˈvedʒtəbəl/, *lasagne* /ləˈzænjə/, *burger* /ˈbɜːgə/, *chocolate* /ˈtʃɒklət/ and *orange juice* /ˈɒrɪndʒ dʒuːs/. Also point out that we can stress either word in *ice cream*. Repeat the drill if necessary.

— EXTRA IDEA ————————————

- If you have a monolingual class, teach students how to say common main courses, desserts and drinks that are found in restaurants in the students' country.

 Use the speech bubbles to remind students that we use *How much ... ?* to ask about prices.

Students do the activity in pairs. Tell students to ask about three different combinations of food and drink.

Are you ready to order?

3 a) Focus students on the restaurant photo. Ask students who the waiter is (Tom, from lessons 5A and 5B) and what they know about him. Check students remember *customer*.

R5.10 Focus students on the menu. Play the recording. Students listen and tick the food and drink the customers order. Play the recording again if necessary.

Note that the conversation is reproduced in the Real World section in **4a)** SB p43. However, we suggest you don't draw students' attention to this and treat this stage as a 'pure' listening. Alternatively, you can ask students to cover **4** before playing the recording.

Note that students listen to this conversation again in **5**, when they focus on sentence stress.

b) Pre-teach *the bill*. Students compare answers in pairs and then work out the customers' bill.

Check answers with the class. You can also teach *(leave) a tip* at this point in the lesson.

> **The customers ordered** the chicken salad, the vegetable lasagne, a Coke, a bottle of sparkling mineral water, the apple pie and two coffees. **The bill** is £23.40.

Real World In a restaurant

4 a) Focus students on the flow chart. Students do the exercise on their own. Check answers with the class.

- **Answers** chicken salad, vegetable lasagne, a Coke, a bottle of (sparkling) mineral water, apple pie, coffees
- Point out that we can use *the* or *a* when we order food: *Can I have **the/a** chicken salad, please?*.

b) Students do the exercise on their own before checking in pairs. Check answers with the class.

- **Answers** 1 Can I have (the chicken salad), please? And can I have (the vegetable lasagne)? 2 And can we have (a bottle of mineral water)? Can we have the bill, please? 3 What would you like to drink? Would you like a dessert?
- Check students understand that we use *Can I/we have ... ?* to ask for things and *Would you like ... ?* to ask people what they want.
- At this level, we suggest you teach *Can I/we have ... ?* and *Would you like ... ?* as fixed phrases, rather than explore the grammar of *can* and *would*.

Help with Listening Sentence stress (2)

- This Help with Listening section reviews sentence stress in the context of a real-life conversation.

5 **R5.10** Focus students on the conversation in **4a)**. Play the recording again. Students listen and notice the sentence stress. Remind students that we stress the important words (the words that carry the meaning).

Note that while 'listening and noticing' might seem a rather passive activity, we feel this type of task helps students to tune in to the rhythm of the language, which will increase students' confidence and their ability to understand natural spoken English.

6 a) **R5.11** **P** Play the recording. Students listen and practise. Check that students copy the sentence stress correctly and that they sound polite when practising questions with *Can I/we have ... ?* and *Would you like ... ?*. Play the recording again if necessary, pausing after each sentence for students to repeat individually.

b) Put students into groups of three. If you have extra students, have one or two pairs and ask one student in each pair to play both customers.

Students practise the conversation in **4a)** in their groups. Students take turns to be the waiter/waitress.

7 a) Students do the activity in the same groups. Before they begin, remind students to use language from **4a)** and the food and drink on the menu. Also ensure that both customers speak in each conversation.

b) Students in each group decide who is the waiter/waitress and who are the customers. Students practise their conversation until they remember it.

c) Each group role-plays their conversation for the class. Students listen to the other groups' conversations and find out what they order. Finally, the class can decide which group's conversation was the best.

— EXTRA PRACTICE AND HOMEWORK ————

5 Review Exercise 5 SB p45

CD-ROM Lesson 5C

Workbook Lesson 5C p26

5D A day off

Vocabulary frequency adverbs and phrases with *every*
Review food and drink (3); Present Simple;
time phrases with *on, in, at*

QUICK REVIEW ●●●

This activity reviews food and drink vocabulary. Ask students to close their books. Check students remember the New Moon restaurant in lesson 5C. Students work in pairs and make a list of all the food and drink on the menu they can remember. Students compare lists with another pair, then check on SB p42. Ask if any pairs remembered all the food and drink on the menu.

1 a) Focus students on the diagram and point out the 100% and 0% at each end. Use the diagram to teach the meaning of *always, sometimes* and *never*. Point out that *never* has a negative meaning.

Students write *usually* and *not usually* on the line.

Check answers with the class. Note that the word order of frequency adverbs is dealt with in **4**.

always **usually** sometimes **not usually** never

b) Teach students the meaning of *every day* by using an example about yourself, for example, *I watch TV every day*. Students do the exercise on their own. Check answers with the class.

Point out that we use *every* with time words: *every day, every week*, etc. Highlight that we say *every day* not *every days*.

Establish that we can also use *every* in other phrases, for example, *every morning, every afternoon, every evening, every night, every Monday, every Friday evening, every six weeks, every four years*, etc.

2 every week 3 every month 4 every year

c) R5.12 P Play the recording. Students listen and practise. Highlight the pronunciation of *usually* /ˈjuːʒəli/ and point out that *every* is two syllables, not three.

2 a) Teach the words in the vocabulary box. Model and drill the new words with the class, highlighting the pronunciation of *early* /ˈɜːli/, *tired* /taɪəd/ and *busy* /ˈbɪzi/.

b) Focus students on the photos of Pete and Maggie and the speech bubbles. Tell the class that they are going to read and listen to Pete and Maggie's Sunday routines. Teach the phrase *a day off* (= a day when you don't work or study), which is the title of the lesson.

R5.13 Play the recording. Students read, listen and find out what Pete and Maggie always do together on Sundays. Check the answer with the class (Pete and Maggie always have dinner at the New Moon restaurant on Sundays).

Point out that Pete and Maggie are the customers in the photo in lesson 5C (SB p42).

3 a) Students do the exercise on their own.

b) Students compare answers in pairs. Check answers with the class.

Some students may include sentences with *every* as examples of things that Pete and Maggie always do. If so, praise students for their understanding of the language, and check that the rest of the class understands that *I play football every Sunday morning. = I always play football on Sunday morning.*

Pete always gets up early. He never has breakfast. He sometimes sleeps for an hour or two (in the afternoon). He usually watches football on TV.
Maggie always has breakfast in bed. She never gets up before midday. She usually phones her friends in the afternoon. She sometimes goes and sees her parents. (She and Pete always have dinner at the New Moon restaurant.)

Help with Vocabulary Frequency adverbs and phrases with *every*

4 While students are doing **3b)**, write the examples from the rules in **4** on the board and highlight the words in blue and pink. Alternatively, focus students on the rules in the Student's Book. Go through the following points with the class.

- Frequency adverbs go after the verb *be*: *I'm always tired on Sundays. It's not usually very busy.*
- Frequency adverbs go before other verbs: *I never have breakfast. I don't usually go out.*
- Highlight that with other verbs we say *I don't usually ... , He doesn't usually ... ,* etc. not *I not usually ... , He not usually ... ,* etc.
- Phrases with *every* are usually at the end of the sentence: *I work every Saturday., I play football every Sunday morning*.
- Also point out that we can use the plural form of days, parts of days or *the weekend* when we are talking about daily routines and habits:
  I'm always tired on Sunday/Sundays.
  I play tennis in the afternoon/afternoons.
  I go out a lot at the weekend/weekends., etc.
- Remind students we don't use a plural noun after *every*: *every Saturday,* etc. not *every Saturdays,* etc.
- Also note that there is a lot of flexibility regarding the position of these adverbs (for example, *sometimes* can go at the beginning of a sentence, but *always* can't). However, at this level we feel that students only need the simplified rules given in the Student's Book.

EXTRA IDEA

- Students look at the texts about Pete and Maggie again and underline all the examples of frequency adverbs and phrases with *every*. Students work in pairs, compare answers and notice the word order.

5 a) Students do the exercise on their own, as shown in the example. While they are working, monitor and check the word order in students' sentences.

b) Students compare sentences in pairs. Ask students to tell the class one or two of their sentences.

6 a) Students do the exercise on their own. Remind students to write about their Sunday routine only.

b) Put students into pairs. Students take turns to say their sentences. Their partner guesses if the sentences are true or false.

Finally, ask students to tell the class one or two of their partner's true sentences.

EXTRA IDEA

- Demonstrate this activity first by writing two true sentences and two false sentences about your Sunday routine on the board in random order. Students guess which sentences are true and which are false.

EXTRA PRACTICE AND HOMEWORK

Ph **Class Activity** 5D Always, sometimes, never p128 (Instructions p105)
CD-ROM Lesson 5D
Workbook Lesson 5D p27
Workbook Reading and Writing Portfolio 5 p60
Progress Test 5 p168–p169 (note that this is a two-page test with a listening section)

Help with Sounds /w/ and /v/

1 a) Focus students on the phonemes /w/ and /v/, the pictures and the words.
R5.14 Play the recording. Students listen to the sounds and the words.

b) **P** Play the recording again. Students listen and practise. If students are having problems, help them with the mouth position for each sound.

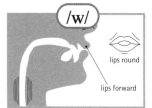 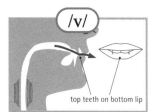

Highlight that we round the lips to make the /w/ sound, then relax and open them as we push air out of the mouth.

Point out that we make the /v/ sound by placing the top teeth on the bottom lip and pushing air through the space. Also highlight that both of these sounds are voiced (there is vibration in the throat).

2 a) **R5.15** Focus students on the boxes. Play the recording. Students listen and notice how we say *w* and *v* in these words.

b) **P** Play the recording again. Students listen and practise.

3 a) **R5.16** Play the recording. Students listen and read the conversation.

P Play the recording again, pausing after each sentence for students to repeat chorally and individually.

b) Students practise the conversation in pairs.

Finally, ask a few pairs to role-play the conversation for the class.

5 Review

See p29 for ideas on how to use this section.

1a) 2 have 3 leave 4 start 5 have 6 finish 7 get 8 have 9 go

2a) 2 works 3 doesn't like 4 goes 5 studies 6 watches 7 doesn't have 8 has

3a) 2 Where does he work?
3 Does he like his job?
4 What does he do in his free time?
5 Does he have any children?
6 Does his wife like cats?

4 2 in 3 on 4 at 5 in 6 at 7 in 8 at 9 in 10 on 11 at 12 at

5a) 1 Are you **ready** to **order**? 2 **What** would you like to **drink**? 3 **Would** you **like** a dessert? a) **Not** for me, **thanks**. b) A Coke **for** me, **please**. c) Yes. **Can I have** the lasagne, please?

5b) 1c) 2b) 3a)

Progress Portfolio

See p29 for ideas on how to use this section.

6 Towns and cities

6A   My home town

QUICK REVIEW ●●●

This activity reviews frequency adverbs and the Present Simple. Students do the first part of the activity on their own. Put students into pairs. Students take turns to say their sentences. At the end of the activity, ask students to tell the class two things about their partner's Saturday routine.

> **Vocabulary** places in a town or city (1)
> **Grammar** *a, some, a lot of*; *there is/there are*: positive
> **Review** frequency adverbs; Present Simple; adjectives (1)

Places in a town or city (1)

1 a) Teach *a town* and check students remember *a city*. Highlight the title of the lesson and teach the phrase *my home town*. Point out that we use this phrase to talk about the place where we live, even if we live in a city.

Students do the exercise on their own or in pairs. Check answers with the class. Check students understand all the new vocabulary.

Point out that we use *a station* to mean *a train station*.

Teach students that we say *go to museums* but *go to **the** theatre*. You can compare these phrases to *go to concerts* and *go to **the** cinema* from lesson 4B.

You can also teach students that *a shopping centre* is called *a mall* /mɔːl/ in American English.

> 1 a park 2 a station 3 a theatre 4 a building
> 5 a river 6 an airport 7 a bus station
> 8 a museum 9 a shopping centre

— EXTRA IDEAS —

- When students have finished the matching activity in **1a)**, they can check their answers in Language Summary 6 **V6.1** SB p110. Alternatively, ask early finishers to check in the Language Summary before you check the answers with the class.
- If you have a strong class, teach other words for places in a town or city, for example, *a bridge, a mosque, a church, a temple, an underground station, a pub, an art gallery, a department store, a car park, a library, a hospital*, etc.

b) **R6.1** **P** Play the recording. Students listen and practise. Alternatively, model and drill the words yourself and ask students to repeat chorally and individually. Highlight the pronunciation of *building* /ˈbɪldɪŋ/, *museum* /mjuːˈziːəm/ and *theatre* /ˈθɪətə/. Highlight that the main stress on *shopping centre* and *bus station* is on the first word, not the second. Repeat the drill if necessary. For tips on drilling, see p20.

Note that only the **main** stress is shown in the vocabulary boxes and Language Summaries.

My city

2 a) Pre-teach the vocabulary in the box. Tell students that *great = very good*, and that *hot springs* are places where hot water flows naturally from the ground. Model and drill the words with the class, highlighting the pronunciation of *famous* /ˈfeɪməs/ and *mile* /maɪl/.

Note that the aim of these boxes is to highlight which words you need to pre-teach in order to help students understand the exercise or text that follows. The vocabulary in these boxes is not included in the Language Summaries in the Student's Book.

b) Focus students on the photos of Bath, a famous city in England. Drill *Bath* /bɑːθ/ and *England* /ˈɪŋglənd/ with the class. Students do the exercise on their own or in pairs. Check answers with the class.

Note that the photo on SB p47 is of the Roman Baths Museum in Bath.

> buildings, a park, a river, a museum (with hot springs)

3 a) Focus students on the photo of Susan and the speech bubble.

R6.2 Play the recording. Students listen and read. Ask students if Susan likes living in Bath. (Yes, she does.)

b) Students do the exercise on their own before comparing answers in pairs. Check answers with the class. Note that *Thermae* is pronounced /ˈθɜːmeɪ/.

> 3 F Susan goes to the Thermae Bath Spa every **Sunday**.
> 4 F The Jane Austen Centre is a **museum**.
> 5 ✓
> 6 ✓

Help with Grammar *a, some, a lot of*; *there is/there are*: positive

4 a) Focus students on pictures A–C. Students do the exercise on their own. Check answers with the class.

- **Answers** 1C 2A 3B
- Check students understand the difference between *some* (more than one, but not a large number) and *a lot of* (a large number).

- Point out that we use *a* or *an* with singular nouns (*a person*, *an airport*, etc.). We use *some* and *a lot of* with plural nouns (*some people*, *some museums*, *a lot of restaurants*, etc.).
- Also point out that we use *some* and *a lot of* in positive sentences.
- Teach the alternative form *lots of* and tell students that we often use this form when speaking or in informal writing: *There are **lots of** people in the park.*

b) Students do the exercise on their own. Check answers with the class.

- **Answers SINGULAR** There<u>'s</u> **an** airport in Bristol. **PLURAL** There <u>are</u> **five** theatres. There <u>are</u> **some** very nice parks. There <u>are</u> **a lot of** old buildings.
- Use the words in **bold** in the example sentences to highlight that we use *there's* with *a* or *an* and *there are* with *some*, *a lot of* or a number (*five*, etc.).
- Point out that *there's* is the contracted form of *there is*.
- Also highlight that we write *there are* not ~~there're~~.
- We use *there is/there are* to say that things exist in a place. Students often confuse *there is/there are* with *it is/they are*. If this is a problem for your students, write *There's a park. It's very big.* and *There are two restaurants. They're expensive.* on the board to highlight the difference.
- You can also highlight that *there*, *they're* and *their* all have the same pronunciation /ðeə/.
- Note that the negative and question forms of *there is/there are* are taught in lesson 6B.

┌─ **EXTRA IDEA** ─────────────────────
- Students read about Bath again and underline all the examples of *there's* and *there are* in the text. Students compare answers in pairs and notice if these phrases are followed by *a*, *an*, *some*, *a lot of* or a number.
└────────────────────────────────────

5 **a)** Point out that sentences 1–8 are also about Bath. Pre-teach *a five-star hotel*.

Students do the exercise on their own.

b) **R6.3** Play the recording. Students listen and check their answers. Check answers with the class.

Play the recording again. Students listen and notice how we say *there's* /ðeəz/ and *there are* /ðeərə/, as shown in the examples.

Also point out that *there's* and *there are* aren't usually stressed.

> 2 are 3 's 4 are 5 's 6 are 7 's 8 are

c) **P** Play the recording again, pausing after each sentence for students to repeat chorally and individually. Repeat the drill if necessary.

6 **a)** Students do the exercise on their own.

b) Students compare answers in pairs. Check answers with the class.

Students then work with their partner and discuss which sentences are true for the town or city they are in now.

Ask students to tell the class some of their true sentences.

> 2 three 3 some 4 a 5 some 6 an 7 a lot of 8 some

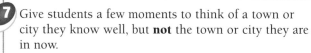
Get ready … Get it right!

7 Give students a few moments to think of a town or city they know well, but **not** the town or city they are in now.

If you have a monolingual class, encourage students to think of towns or cities in other countries or regions if possible.

Students do the exercise on their own, as shown in the examples. Tell students to write at least six sentences if possible.

While they are working, check their sentences for accuracy and help students with any new vocabulary.

Tell students to memorise their sentences so that they can do **8a)** without referring to their written work.

8 **a)** Put students into pairs. If possible, students should work with someone who doesn't know their town or city.

Students take turns to tell their partner about the town or city they chose in **7**.

b) Students tell the class two things about their partner's town or city.

Finally, ask students if they would like to visit their partner's town or city. Ask them to give reasons for their answers if possible.

┌─ **EXTRA IDEA** ─────────────────────
- If your students haven't visited any other towns or cities, ask them to write three true sentences and three false sentences with *there's/there are* about the town or city they are in now. Students take turns to say their sentences to each other. Students say if their partner's sentences are true or false.
└────────────────────────────────────

┌─ **EXTRA PRACTICE AND HOMEWORK** ──────
6 Review Exercises 1 and 2 SB p53
CD-ROM Lesson 6A
Workbook Lesson 6A p28
└────────────────────────────────────

Vocabulary places in a town or city (2)
Grammar *there is/there are*: negative, *yes/no* questions and short answers; *any*
Help with Listening linking (1)
Review *a, some, a lot of; there is/there are*: positive

 QUICK REVIEW ●●●

This activity reviews *a, some, a lot of, there is/there are* and places in a town or city. Write these prompts on the board: *There's a/an ... , There are some ... , There are a lot of ... , There are (three) ...* . Students do the activity in pairs. Tell students to say at least five sentences each. At the end of the activity, ask students to tell the class one or two of their sentences.

Places in a town or city (2)

1 a) Students do the exercise on their own or in pairs. Early finishers can check their answers in **V6.2** SB p110. Check answers with the class.

Point out the possessive *'s* in *chemist's* and tell students that the person is called *a chemist*. Also point out that we say *a pharmacy* /ˈfɑːməsi/ in American English.

Check students understand the difference between *a bus stop* and *a bus station*.

Highlight that we say *in* or *at* with shops: *You buy food in/at a supermarket.*, etc.

> 1 a bank 2 a chemist's 3 a road 4 a cashpoint/an ATM
> 5 a bus stop 6 a supermarket 7 a square 8 a market
> 9 a post office

b) **R6.4** **P** Play the recording. Students listen and practise. Highlight the pronunciation of *chemist's* /ˈkemɪsts/ and *square* /skweə/. Also highlight that the main stress on *post office* and *bus stop* is on the first word, not the second. Repeat the drill if necessary.

c) Students do the exercise in pairs, as shown in the speech bubbles.

— EXTRA IDEA —

• If you have a strong class, teach other words for shops, for example, *a baker's, a butcher's, a bookshop, a department store, a newsagent's, a kiosk*, etc. Then ask students to work in pairs and discuss what people buy at each place: *You buy bread in a baker's.*, etc.

Welcome to my home

2 a) Focus students on the photo of Susan and Isabel. Ask students where Susan lives (in Bath). Tell the class that Susan's friend Isabel has come to stay with her.

R6.5 Play the recording (SB p122). Students listen and put the things in the order that Susan and Isabel talk about them. Check answers with the class.

> 2 shops 3 banks 4 trains and buses 5 restaurants

b) Give students time to read sentences 1–6 and check students remember *a mile*. Play the recording again. Students listen and choose the correct words.

c) Students compare answers in pairs. Check answers with the class.

> 2 some 3 post office 4 two miles 5 ten 6 in the centre

Help with Grammar *there is/there are*: negative, *yes/no* questions and short answers; *any*

3 a) Students do the exercise on their own. Check answers with the class.

• **Answers** 1 isn't 2 aren't
• Use the examples to highlight that we make singular negatives with *there isn't* and plural negatives with *there aren't*.

b) Students do the exercise on their own before checking in pairs. Check answers with the class.

• **Answers Is** there a bank? Yes, there **is**. No, there **isn't**. **Are** there any shops? Yes, there are. No, there **aren't**.
• Highlight the inverted word order in the questions: *Is there ... ?/Are there ... ?*.
• Also point out that we don't contract *there is* in short answers: *Yes, there is.* not ~~Yes, there's.~~
• Note that *Wh-* questions with *there is/there are* are not very common, and are therefore not taught at this level.

c) Students do the exercise on their own. Check answers with the class.

• We use *any* in negatives and questions with *there are*.
• Elicit the sentences with *any* from **3a)** and **3b)**, and write them on the board: *There aren't **any** good restaurants near here. Are there **any** shops?.* Highlight the position of *any* in these sentences.
• Also remind students that we can use *some* in positive sentences with *there are*.
• Note that it is also possible to use *some* in questions with *there is/there are*. However, at this level we feel it is important to give students a simple rule that always results in correct sentences.
• Also note that students don't study the use of *some* and *any* with uncountable nouns at this level. This is dealt with in **face2face** Elementary.

Help with Listening Linking (1)

- This Help with Listening section introduces consonant-vowel linking in sentences.

4 Focus students on sentences 1–6. Point out the consonants in blue and the vowels in pink.

R6.6 Play the recording. Students listen and notice the linking between the consonant sounds and the vowel sounds. Play the recording again if necessary.

Use the examples to highlight that when a word ends in a consonant sound and the next word begins with a vowel sound, we usually link them together so that they sound like one word. Point out that it is the initial and final sounds that are important, not the spelling. For example, *there are* links together, even though *there* ends in the letter *e*.

5 **R6.7** **P** Play the recording (SB p123). Students listen and practise the sentences in **4** and the short answers. Check students copy the stress and linking correctly.

Play the recording again, pausing after each sentence for students to repeat individually.

6 a) Tell students that prompts 1–8 are about places near Susan's flat. Use the examples to point out that a tick means students must write a positive sentence and a cross means they must write a negative sentence.

Students do the exercise on their own.

b) Students compare answers in pairs. Check answers with the class.

> **3** There's a market. **4** There aren't any museums.
> **5** There's a park. **6** There isn't a square. **7** There aren't any nice cafés. **8** There are a lot of old houses.

7 Students work in the same pairs, student A and student B. Student As turn to SB p86 and student Bs turn to SB p92. Check they are all looking at the correct exercise.

a) Students do the exercise on their own. Check answers with the class. Only check the words they need to fill in the gaps, so that students don't hear the questions they are about to be asked. Note that these answers are the same for student As and student Bs.

> **Student A/Student B** **2** Are, any **3** Is, a **4** Are, any **5** Is, a

b) Students work with their partners. Student A in each pair asks questions 1–5 from **a)**. Student Bs answer the questions without looking at the Student's Book. When student A has asked all five questions, he/she says how many answers were correct. Point out that the answers to student A's questions are in brackets in **a)** before they begin.

c) Students swap roles so that student Bs are asking their questions 1–5 from **a)**.

At the end of the activity, find out how many students answered all five questions correctly.

Get ready ... Get it right!

8 Focus students on the picture and point out the places in the bubbles above and below the house. Students do the exercise on their own. Remind students to use *Is there a ... ?*, *Are there any ... ?* and the places in the bubbles in their questions.

9 a) Focus students on the speech bubbles and teach the phrase *It's (five) minutes away.* = It's (five) minutes from my home.

Put students into pairs. If possible, ask students to work with someone they don't know very well. Students take turns to ask their questions from **8**. Remind students to make notes on their partner's answers, as they will need this information in **9b)**. Students can put ticks and crosses next to each question to indicate a positive or negative answer, and write down any other interesting information they hear.

Tell students to begin each conversation with *Where do you live?* before asking their questions from **8**. Remind students to use correct short answers (*Yes, there is.*, *No, there isn't.*, etc.) where appropriate and to give more information if possible.

Early finishers can ask each other about the other places on the picture they haven't already talked about.

b) Put students into new pairs. Students take turns to tell their new partner about places near their first partner's home. Remind students to refer to their notes from **9a)**. Tell students to begin each conversation by saying where their first partner lives.

Finally, ask students to tell the class one or two sentences about places near their first partner's home.

EXTRA IDEAS

- Students write a description of where they live and places near their home for homework. These descriptions can be collected in next class and displayed around the classroom for other students to read.
- Use **Vocabulary Plus** 6 Rooms and furniture p156 (Instructions p149) in class or give it to students for homework. Note that this worksheet also practises *there is/there are*.

EXTRA PRACTICE AND HOMEWORK

Ph **Class Activity** 6B London Road p129–p130 (Instructions p106)
Ph **Vocabulary Plus** 6 Rooms and furniture p156 (Instructions p149)
6 Review Exercises 3 and 4 SB p53
CD-ROM Lesson 6B
Workbook Lesson 6B p29

6C Tourist information

Vocabulary things in your bag (2)
Real World at the tourist information centre
Review places in a town or city; telling the time

Things in your bag (2)

a) Focus students on photo A. Students do the exercise on their own or in pairs. Early finishers can check in **V6.3** SB p110. Check answers with the class.

Point out that men usually have *wallets* and women usually have *purses*. Also check students understand that the singular of *keys* is *a key*.

> 1 a map 2 a purse 3 a camera 4 keys 5 a laptop
> 6 a passport 7 a guide book 8 a wallet
> 9 an ID card 10 a credit card 11 money

b) **R6.8** **P** Play the recording. Students listen and practise. Alternatively, model the words yourself and ask students to repeat chorally and individually. Check that students stress the words correctly and highlight the pronunciation of *purse* /pɜːs/, *money* /'mʌni/ and *guide book* /'gaɪd bʊk/. Repeat the drill if necessary.

c) Use the speech bubbles to teach the phrase *I have ... with me*. Students do the exercise in pairs.

┌─ **EXTRA IDEAS** ─────────────────
● Before students do **1c)**, ask your class what else they have in their bags and teach them how to say any new words in English. Words that students might find useful are *glasses, a driving licence, a handheld computer, a debit card, make-up*, etc.
● Use **Class Activity** 6C What's in your bag? p131 (Instructions p106) to practise the new vocabulary from **1a)** and the vocabulary from lesson 1C.
└──────────────────────────────────

When is it open?

a) Pre-teach the vocabulary in the box. Point out that *open* is an adjective and a verb: *That shop is* **open**., *The school* **opens** *at half past seven*. Also highlight that *closed* is an adjective (*That shop is* **closed**.) and the verb is *close* /kləʊz/: *What time does the school* **close**?.

Model and drill the new vocabulary, highlighting the pronunciation of *tourist* /'tʊərɪst/. Point out that *closed* /kləʊzd/ is one syllable, not two.

b) Focus students on photo B. Tell the class that this is the tourist information centre in Bath. Point out Isabel, Susan's friend from lesson 6B, and check students remember *assistant*.

Students work on their own or in pairs and find things from **1a)** in the photo. You can give students a time limit of one minute. Check answers with the class.

> **from left to right** maps (on the counter),
> a purse (in Isabel's hand), a camera,
> a guide book, money, a wallet, keys

a) Tell the class that they are going to listen to three conversations in the tourist information centre in Bath. **R6.9** Play the recording (SB p123). Students listen and match conversations 1–3 to a)–c).

Check answers with the class.

> 1b) 2a) 3c)

b) Give students time to read sentences 1–6. Play the recording again. Students listen and choose the correct answers. Students compare answers in pairs. Check answers with the class.

> 2 a pound 3 9, 5 4 open 5 Hot Bath Street 6 five

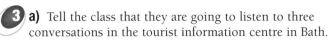

Real World At the tourist information centre

Focus students on the flow chart. Check students understand that the tourists say the sentences in the pink boxes and the assistant says the sentences in the green boxes.

Students do the exercise on their own. Check answers with the class.

● **Answers** 2 have 3 much 4 open 5 day 6 map 7 minutes
● Check students understand *show* in *Can you show me on this map?*. Point out that we use *Can you + verb ... ?* to ask people to do things for us.
● Also check they understand *It's about (five) minutes away*. = *It's about (five) minutes from here*.
● Also point out the difference between *Here you are*. (which we use when we give something to someone) and *Here it is*. (when we show someone where something is on a map).
● Highlight that we use *Where's the ... ?* to ask where a place is (*Where's the Thermae Bath Spa?*, etc.).

- Also point out that we use *in* with names of streets or roads (*It's **in** Hot Bath Street.*).
- Note that the question *When is the (Roman Baths Museum) open?* asks about both opening and closing times. The question *When/What time does the (Roman Baths Museum) open?* only asks about the opening time.

5 **a)** R6.10 P Play the recording (SB p123). Students listen and practise the sentences in **4**. Check they copy the polite intonation in the questions. Point out the importance of sounding polite in these types of situation, and that a flat intonation pattern will make students sound bored or rude.

Play the recording again, pausing after each sentence for students to repeat individually.

— EXTRA IDEA —
- Ask students to turn to R6.10, SB p123. Play the recording again. Students listen and practise, copying the sentence stress as shown in their books.

b) Put students into pairs. Students practise the conversations in **4**, taking turns to be the tourist. Ask students to practise the conversations two or three times before they change roles.

Ask a few confident pairs to role-play the conversations for the class. Students don't have to leave their seats.

— EXTRA IDEA —
- Before students practise the conversations in pairs, ask students to practise in 'open pairs' (see tips on drilling on p20).

6 **a)** Ask students to cover the conversations in **4**. Students do the exercise on their own.

b) R6.11 Play the recording. Students listen and check. Check answers with the class.

> 2 of 3 Here you are. 4 is it 5 It's 6 afternoon 7 is
> 8 from 9 to 10 Is it 11 day 12 help 13 Where's 14 in
> 15 map 16 Here it is.

c) Students practise the conversations in pairs, taking turns to be the tourist.

7 Put students into new pairs, student A and student B. Student As turn to SB p90 and student Bs turn to SB p96. Check they are all looking at the correct exercise.

a) Focus students on the questions about Bath in column A of the table. Students work on their own and fill in the gaps. Students are not allowed to look at each other's books.

Check answers with the class. Only check the words they need to fill in the gaps, so that students don't hear the questions they are about to be asked. Note that these answers are the same for student As and student Bs.

> **Student A/Student B**
> 1b) much 2a) open 2b) on 3a) Where's 3b) show

b) Tell student As that they are tourists in Bath. Tell student Bs that they work at Bath tourist information centre. Student A in each pair asks his/her questions from column A of the table in **a)** and writes the answers in column B and on the map. Student B in each pair answers the questions by referring to the information in the Student's Book.

While students are working, monitor and help them with any problems. Don't check answers with the class at this stage.

c) Students swap roles so that student Bs are tourists in Bath and student As work at Bath tourist information centre. Student Bs ask their questions from column A of the table in **a)** and write their answers in column B and on the map. Student As answer the questions by referring to the information in their books. Again, don't check answers with the class at this stage.

d) Students check their partner's answers to see if they are correct.

Finally, check answers with the class if necessary.

> **Student A**
> 1a) yes 1b) £4.50 2a) from 12.00 to 5.00 p.m.
> 2b) Yes, it is. 3a) It's in James Street West.
> 3b) See map on SB p96.
> **Student B**
> 1a) yes 1b) £4.99 2a) from 10.30 a.m. to 5.00 p.m.
> 2b) Yes, it is. 3a) It's in Manvers Street. 3b) See map on SB p90.

— EXTRA PRACTICE AND HOMEWORK —
Ph **Class Activity** 6C What's in your bag? p131 (Instructions p106)
CD-ROM Lesson 6C
Workbook Lesson 6C p31

Vocabulary clothes, colours, *favourite*
Review things in your bag (1) and (2); frequency adverbs; Present Simple

QUICK REVIEW ●●●
This activity reviews vocabulary for things in your bag. Students do the activity in pairs, as shown in the examples. ✎ Write *We both have ...* on the board and then ask each pair to tell the class one or two things they both have with them.

1 **a)** Pre-teach and drill *clothes* /kləʊðz/. Point out that *clothes* is one syllable, not two. You can also point out that many native speakers pronounce this word the same as *close* /kləʊz/.

Focus students on the photos. Students do the exercise on their own or in pairs. Early finishers can check in **V6.4** SB p110. Check answers with the class.

Point out that *trousers* and *jeans* are always plural and we can't say *a trouser* or *a jean*.

Also point out that *shoes*, *trainers* and *boots* are usually plural, but that we can say *a shoe*, *a trainer* and *a boot* when we refer to only one.

Teach students *a pair of ...* , which we often use with plural nouns: *a pair of trousers*, *a pair of boots*, etc.

Also highlight that *clothes* is always plural. When we want to use the singular, we can say *an item of clothing*.

> 1 a shirt 2 a tie 3 a suit 4 trousers 5 a jumper
> 6 a skirt 7 boots 8 a jacket 9 a T-shirt 10 jeans
> 11 trainers 12 a dress 13 a coat 14 shoes

b) **R6.12** **P** Play the recording. Students listen and practise. Alternatively, model the words yourself and ask students to repeat chorally and individually. Highlight the pronunciation of *suit* /suːt/, *shirt* /ʃɜːt/, *jumper* /'dʒʌmpə/, *jacket* /'dʒækɪt/, *trousers* /'traʊzəz/ and *jeans* /dʒiːnz/. Elicit and drill the plural of *dress* (*dresses* /'dresɪz/). Repeat the drill if necessary.

Note that the /dʒ/ sound in *jumper, jacket* and *jeans* etc. is practised in the Help with Sounds section on SB p53.

c) Students do the activity in pairs.

— **EXTRA IDEA** —
- If you don't think your class will know any of the words in **1a)**, teach the vocabulary yourself first by using flashcards or examples from your or students' own clothes. You can then use **1a)** for practice.

2 **R6.13** **P** Focus students on the words for colours. Play the recording. Students listen and practise. Repeat the drill if necessary.

3 **a)** Focus students on the photos. Allow students two minutes to memorise the people's names, their clothes and the colour of each item of clothing.

b) Use the speech bubbles to teach *What colour ... ?*. Point out that we say *What colour **are** (Lisa's shoes)?* for plural words, and *What colour **is** (Wayne's shirt)?* for singular words. Also highlight the possessive *'s* in *Lisa's*.

Put students into pairs, student A and student B. Ask student Bs to close their books. Student A in each pair asks his/her partner what colour the people's clothes are. After a minute or two, students change roles.

4 **a)** **R6.14** Focus students on the photos. Play the recording (SB p123). Students listen and put the people in the order they hear them. Check answers with the class. Ask students to give reasons for their answers.

> 1 Lisa 2 Brad 3 Wayne 4 Monica

b) Pre-teach *wear* by using an example about yourself in the Present Simple, for example, *I wear jeans every day.* Avoid using the Present Continuous (*I'm wearing a green shirt.*, etc.) as students don't study this verb form until **face2face** Elementary.

Play the recording again. Students listen and write what the people never wear. Check answers with the class.

> **Lisa** never wears trainers. **Brad** never wears brown.
> **Wayne** never wears jeans. **Monica** never wears dresses.

5 **a)** Check students remember *usually, sometimes* and *never*. Students do the exercise on their own.

b) Students compare lists in groups. Ask each student to tell the class one thing they usually, sometimes or never wear.

Help with Vocabulary *favourite*

6 **a)** Teach *favourite* by telling students your favourite colour, singer, etc. Tell students that your *favourite* is the thing or person you like best. Students do the exercise on their own. Check answers with the class.

- **Answers** 1 My 2 This 3 These 4 What 5 Who
- Highlight the word order in sentence 1 and teach the phrase *My favourite (colour, singer, etc.) is ...* .
- Use sentences 2 and 3 to show that we use *This is my favourite ...* for singular nouns and *These are my favourite ...* for plural nouns. Point out that we say *favourite* in sentence 3, not *favourites*.
- Use sentences 4 and 5 to teach the phrases *What's your favourite ... ?* and *Who's your favourite ... ?*. Point out that *What* = a thing and *Who* = a person.

b) Play the recording (SB p123). Students listen and practise the sentences in **6a)**. Check that students pronounce *favourite* /ˈfeɪvrət/ correctly in each sentence.

7 Put students into pairs. Ask all students to turn to SB p99. Check they are all looking at the exercise with four cartoons in the right-hand column.

a) Use the examples to remind students that we use *What's your favourite ... ?* to ask about things and *Who's your favourite ... ?* to ask about people.
Students do the exercise on their own, using the words in the box or their own ideas.

b) Students work with their partners and take turns to ask their questions. Students should make a note of their partner's answers. They only need to write the colour, actor, etc., not complete sentences.

c) Put students into new pairs. Students tell their new partner about the person they spoke to in **b)**.

d) Finally, ask each student to tell the class two things about their first partner.

EXTRA PRACTICE AND HOMEWORK

Ph Class Activity 6D Review snakes and ladders p132 (Instructions p106)
6 Review Exercise 5 SB p53
CD-ROM Lesson 6D
Workbook Lesson 6D p32
Workbook Reading and Writing Portfolio 6 p62
Progress Test 6 p170

Help with Sounds /tʃ/ **and** /dʒ/

1 **a)** Focus students on the phonemes /tʃ/ and /dʒ/, the pictures and the words.

 Play the recording. Students listen to the sounds and the words. Point out that *ch* in *cheese* is pronounced with a /tʃ/ sound and both *ge* and *j* in *orange juice* are pronounced with a /dʒ/ sound.

b) **P** Play the recording again. Students listen and practise. If students are having problems, help them with the mouth position for each sound.

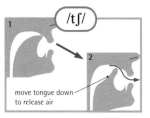 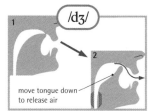

Point out that we make the /tʃ/ sound by placing the tongue on the top of the mouth behind the teeth, then moving the tongue down to release air. Highlight that this is an unvoiced sound (there is no vibration in the throat).

Also highlight that we use the same mouth position to make the /dʒ/ sound, but that this sound is voiced (there is vibration from the throat).

2 **a)** Focus students on the boxes. Play the recording. Students listen and notice how we say the pink and blue letters.

b) **P** Play the recording again. Students listen and practise.

3 **a)** Tell the class that many common English first names start with the /dʒ/ sound. Put students into pairs. Students work with their partner and try to say the names using a /dʒ/ sound.

b) Play the recording. Students listen and check.
P Play the recording again. Students listen and practise. Finally, ask students to say the names around the class.

6 Review

See p29 for ideas on how to use this section.

1 2 shopping centre 3 theatre 4 station 5 river 6 airport 7 building 8 bus station 9 museum

2a) 2 some 3 are 4 a lot of 5 's 6 an

2b) 1T 2T 3F 4T 5T 6F

3 2 bus stop 3 bank 4 market 5 supermarket 6 post office 7 square

4a) 2 isn't 3 's 4 aren't 5 isn't 6 are 7 aren't

4b) 2 Is, a 3 Is, a 4 Are, any 5 Is, a 6 Is, a 7 Are, any 8 Are, any

4c) 1 Yes, there are. 2 No, there isn't. 3 Yes, there is. 4 No, there aren't. 5 Yes, there is. 6 No, there isn't. 7 Yes, there are. 8 No, there aren't.

5a) → suit, T-shirt, trousers, tie, shirt
↓ jeans, dress, boots, jumper, trainers, skirt, coat, shoes

Progress Portfolio

See p29 for ideas on how to use this section.

7 Love it, like it, hate it!

Student's Book p54–p61

7A We're twins

QUICK REVIEW ●●●

This activity reviews phrases with *favourite*. Students do the first part of the activity on their own. They can write film and book titles in their own language. Put students into groups of three. Students take turns to say what their favourite things are, as shown in the examples. Students make a note of any that are the same. At the end of the activity, ask each group to tell the class about any favourite things that are the same for more than one student.

A I love …
B I like …
C I don't like …
D I hate …

Help with Vocabulary *love, like, hate*

Things you like and don't like

1 a) Focus students on pictures 1–9. Students do the activity on their own or in pairs. Early finishers can check answers in Language Summary 7 **V7.1** SB p112. Check answers with the class.

Point out that *visiting new places, flying, dancing, watching sport on TV* and *shopping for clothes* are all activities. You can also teach the corresponding verbs *visit, fly, dance* and *shop*. (Note that students learned the verb *watch* in lesson 4B.)

Check that students don't confuse *a soap opera* (a type of TV programme) with *opera* (a type of music).

Highlight the preposition in *watching sport **on** TV*. Check students remember that *TV* stands for *television*.

Also point out that we say *a film* in British English and *a movie* in American English.

> 1 animals
> 2 classical music
> 3 visiting new places
> 4 horror films
> 5 watching sport on TV
> 6 shopping for clothes
> 7 soap operas
> 8 dancing
> 9 flying

b) **R7.1** **P** Play the recording. Students listen and practise. Highlight the pronunciation of *horror* /ˈhɒrə/ and *clothes* /kləʊðz/. Also check students stress the phrases correctly. Point out that the stress in *soap opera* is on the first word, not the second. Note that only the **main** stress is shown in the vocabulary boxes and Language Summaries. Repeat the drill if necessary.

2 Focus students on pictures A–D. Students do the exercise on their own before checking in pairs. Check answers with the class. Model and drill the phrases with the class.

3 a) Focus students on the example sentences. Point out the nouns in blue and the verb+*ing* forms in pink. Go through the following points with the class.

- Highlight that after *love, like* and *hate* we can use a noun or verb+*ing*.
- Also point out that we use the plural form of most nouns after *love, like* and *hate* (*animals, soap operas*, etc.) because we are talking about things in general.
- You can also highlight that we don't use *the* when we talk about things we like or don't like in general: *I like dogs*. (= all dogs), etc.
- Students may ask why we don't say ~~I like classical musics~~. We suggest you simply tell the class that some nouns don't have a plural form. This will probably be enough explanation without introducing the difference between countable and uncountable nouns, which may overload students. Note that all the phrases in **1a)** are already in the correct form to be used with *love, like* and *hate*.

b) Students do the exercise on their own. Check answers with the class.

- **Answers** visiting, flying, dancing, watching, shopping
- For the spelling rules for verb+*ing* forms, see **V7.2** SB p112.

4 a) Students do the exercise on their own, as shown in the examples. While they are working, monitor and check their sentences for accuracy.

b) Students do the exercise in pairs.

Ask students to tell the class one or two of their (or their partner's) true sentences.

- If you have a strong class, ask students to turn to the **SPELLING OF VERB+*ING* FORMS** section in V7.2 SB p112. Go through the spelling rules with the class. ✍ Write these phrases on the board: *go to the cinema, play computer games, eat out, live in this town/city, study English, get up early, have breakfast in bed, sleep in the afternoon.* Students work on their own and write sentences about themselves with *love, like* and *hate* and the phrases on the board. Students compare sentences in pairs.

We're very different

5 a) Pre-teach the words in the box. Note that in English we use *twins* to refer to two people who were born at the same time, whether they are identical twins or not.

Point out that *different* and *the same* are opposites. Model and drill the words with the class. Highlight that *different* is two syllables, not three.

b) Ask students if they know any twins. If so, ask students to tell the class about them. If you know any twins, you can tell the class about them before asking students to do the same.

6 a) Focus students on the photo of Jack and Jenny, and the speech bubbles. You can highlight the /dʒ/ sound in *Jack* /dʒæk/ and *Jenny* /ˈdʒeni/, which students studied in the Help with Sounds section in unit 6.

R7.2 Play the recording. Students listen, read and find two things that Jack and Jenny both like.

Check answers with the class.

> They both like watching TV. They both like having a twin.

b) Students do the exercise on their own before checking in pairs. Check answers with the class.

> 2 Jenny 3 Jenny 4 Jack 5 Jack 6 Jenny

Help with Grammar Object pronouns

7 a) ✍ Draw the table on the board and write in the example sentences. Go through the following points with the class.

- Use the example sentences to highlight the typical word order in sentences: subject + verb + object.
- Highlight *I* in pink in the first sentence and remind students that this is a subject pronoun.
- Highlight *them* in blue in the second sentence. Teach students that this is called an object pronoun.
- Point out that subject pronouns go before the verb and object pronouns go after the verb in sentences. If possible, compare this structure to that of your students' own language(s).
- Drill *subject* /ˈsʌbdʒekt/ and *object* /ˈɒbdʒekt/ with the class, highlighting the /dʒ/ sound in both words.

b) Focus students on the texts about Jack and Jenny and point out the object pronouns in blue. Students do the exercise on their own or in pairs.

✍ While they are working, draw the table from **7b)** on the board. Check answers with the class.

- **Object pronouns** me, (you), him, her, it, us, them

8 a) Students do the exercise on their own.

b) R7.3 Play the recording (SB p123). Students listen and check their answers. Check answers with the class. Highlight that we usually use *Do you like … ?* to ask for people's opinions, not *Do you love … ?* or *Do you hate … ?*.

You can point out that when we say that we like or hate famous people, we usually mean that we like or hate their music, acting, etc., not the people themselves.

Also use question 3 to highlight that we use *it* to refer to a word/phrase with verb+*ing* (*shopping for clothes*, etc.).

Note that while *Yes, I do.* and *No, I don't.* are also correct answers to *Do you like … ?* questions, they are not as common as you might expect. This exercise therefore aims to provide students with a variety of more common ways to respond to these types of question.

P Play the recording again, pausing after each question and answer for students to repeat chorally and individually. Students can also turn to R7.3, SB p123 and follow the stress patterns as they practise. Repeat the drill if necessary.

> 2 her
> 3 it
> 4 him
> 5 them
> 6 me

c) Students do the exercise in pairs. Remind students to give their own answers before they begin.

9 a) Students do the exercise on their own, as shown in the example.

✍ While they are working, write the following possible answers on the board: *Yes, he/she loves it/them., No, he/she hates it/them., Yes, he/she does.,* and *No, he/she doesn't.*

b) Students work in pairs and ask their questions. Remind students to answer the questions with one of the short answer forms on the board.

- Students do **9a)** in pairs. Ask students to make a note of the answers to their questions. Put two pairs together in groups of four and ask them to close their books. Each pair takes turns to ask their questions. The pair who answers more questions correctly wins.

Get ready … Get it right!

10 Put students into new pairs, student A and student B. Student As turn to SB p90 and student Bs turn to SB p96. Check they are all looking at the correct exercise.

a) Students do the exercise on their own, as shown in the example. Note that some of the pictures represent vocabulary from **1a)**, while other pictures represent vocabulary taught in earlier lessons.

> **Student A**
> 2 Do you like horror films?
> 3 Do you like playing tennis?
> 4 Do you like flying?
> 5 Do you like rock music?/
>   Do you like going to concerts?
> 6 Do you like strawberry ice cream?
> **Student B**
> b) Do you like visiting new places?
> c) Do you like cats?
> d) Do you like watching sport on TV?
> e) Do you like classical music?
> f) Do you like coffee?

b) Students do the exercise on their own. They are not allowed to talk to their partners during this stage of the activity.

c) Students work with their partners. Student A in each pair asks his/her questions from **a)** and puts a tick or a cross in column C of the table.

After student As have asked their questions, they tell their partners how many of their guesses in column B of the table are correct.

d) Students swap roles and repeat the activity, with student B in each pair asking his/her questions from **a)**.

e) Finally, ask each student to tell the class two things about his/her partner. Check students use the *he*, *she* forms *likes*, *doesn't like*, *loves* and *hates* in their sentences.

--- EXTRA PRACTICE AND HOMEWORK ---

Ph **Class Activity** 7A I like dominoes p133 (Instructions p107)
7 Review Exercises 1, 2 and 3 SB p61
CD-ROM Lesson 7A
Workbook Lesson 7A p33

 Can you drive?

QUICK REVIEW ●●●
This activity reviews things you like and don't like. Students do the activity in pairs. Remind students that they can also answer *Do you like … ?* questions with *Yes, I love it.*, *No, I hate them.*, etc. At the end of the activity, ask each pair to tell the class one or two of the things they both like.

Vocabulary abilities
Grammar *can* for ability
Help with Listening *can* or *can't*
Review things you like and don't like; Present Simple questions

Abilities

 a) Focus students on pictures 1–10. Students do the exercise on their own or in pairs. Early finishers can check their answers in **V7.3** SB p112. Check answers with the class.

Point out that we can say *ride a bike* or *ride a bicycle*.

Note that we say *play basketball* not ~~play basket~~. Also highlight that we say *play basketball* but *play **the** piano* and *play **the** guitar*.

> 1 ski
> 2 ride a bike
> 3 drive
> 4 swim
> 5 speak German
> 6 play the piano
> 7 sing
> 8 play the guitar
> 9 play basketball
> 10 cook

--- EXTRA IDEA ---

- If you have a strong class, teach other sports that are played with a ball (*play volleyball*, etc.) and other musical instruments (*play the violin*, etc.).

b) **R7.4** **P** Play the recording. Students listen and practise. Repeat the drill if necessary.

c) Pre-teach *mime* by miming one of the activities from **1a)**.

Put students into pairs. Students take turns to mime activities from **1a)** for their partner to guess.

I can't swim!

 Focus students on pictures A–D. Students do the exercise on their own before checking in pairs. Check answers with the class. Use picture C to teach *Help!*.

> 1C
> 2A
> 3B
> 4D

Help with Grammar *can: positive and negative*

 3 Focus students on the tables in the Student's Book or draw them on the board. Go through the following points with the class.

- We use *can* or *can't* to talk about ability.
- Use the first table to highlight the word order in **positive** sentences: subject + *can* + verb + ...
- Use the second table to highlight the word order in **negative** sentences: subject + *can't* + verb + ...
- Point out that *can* and *can't* are the same for *I, you, he, she, it, we* and *they*.
- We sometimes use *(very) well* with *can*: *They can ski* **(very) well**. not ~~They can ski (very) good~~.
- We say *She* **can play** *the piano*. not ~~She can to play the piano~~.
- Remind students that we also use *can* for offers (*Can I help you?*) and requests (*Can I have the bill, please?, Can you show me on this map?*).

Help with Listening *can or can't*

- This Help with Listening section focuses on how we say *can* and *can't* in sentences.

 4 a) R7.5 Focus students on the four sentences and highlight the sentence stress. Play the recording. Students listen and notice how we say *can* /kən/ and *can't* /kɑːnt/.

Ask students if *can* is stressed (it isn't). Point out that *can* is usually pronounced in its weak form in positive sentences and that the vowel sound is a schwa /ə/.

Ask if *can't* is stressed (it is). Point out that *can't* is stressed because it is negative.

Play the recording again if necessary.

You can also teach students that *can't* is pronounced /kænt/ in American English.

b) R7.6 Play the recording (SB p123). Students listen and decide if they hear *can* or *can't*. Tell students to write their answers for each question as they listen.

Play the recording again, pausing after each sentence to check students' answers.

1 can 2 can't 3 can 4 can't 5 can't 6 can

 5 R7.6 P Play the recording again. Students listen and practise. Check that students pronounce *can* and *can't* correctly. Repeat the drill if necessary, pausing after each sentence for students to practise individually.

 6 a) Students do the exercise on their own. Students can use words and phrases from **1a)** or their own ideas.

b) Students do the exercise in pairs. Ask each student to tell the class one or two of their true sentences.

Help with the children

 7 a) Pre-teach *au pair* /ˌəʊ ˈpeə/. Focus students on the photo. Explain that Mrs Jones is going to interview Maria because she wants an au pair to help her with her two children, Ella and Daniel.

R7.7 Play the recording (SB p123). Students listen to the interview. Ask students if Maria gets the job (she does).

b) Give students time to read prompts 1–9. Play the recording again. Students listen and tick the things Maria can do and put a cross next to the things she can't do.

c) Students compare answers in pairs. Check answers with the class.

2 ✓ 3 ✗ 4 ✓ 5 ✓ 6 ✗ 7 ✗ 8 ✓ 9 ✓

--- EXTRA IDEA ---

- Ask students to look at R7.7, SB p123. Play the recording again. Students listen, read and underline all the examples of *can* and *can't* in the conversation.

Help with Grammar *can: yes/no questions and short answers*

 8 Students do the exercise on their own, then compare answers in pairs. Check answers with the class and go through the following points.

- Focus students on the first column of the table. Highlight the inverted word order of *yes/no* questions: *Can* + subject + verb + ...
- Point out that we don't use *do* or *does* in questions with *can*: *Can you cook?* not ~~Do you can cook?~~.
- Focus students on the second column of the table. Check that students have completed the short answers correctly: *Yes, I* **can**. *No, I* **can't**. *Yes, he* **can**. *No, she* **can't**.
- Remind students that *can* and *can't* are the same for all subjects (*I, you, he,* etc.) in *yes/no* questions and short answers.
- Note that we also make *Wh-* questions with *can*: *How many languages can you speak?, Which instrument can you play?,* etc. However, these are less common than *yes/no* questions with *can* and are therefore taught in **face2face** Elementary.

 9 Focus students on the examples. Highlight that we usually use the weak form of *can* /kən/ in *yes/no* questions and that we always use the strong form of *can* /kæn/ in short answers.

Note that we can also use the strong form of *can* in *yes/no* questions: *Can* /kæn/ *you cook?*.

P Play the recording. Students listen and practise the questions and short answers in **8**. Encourage them to copy the weak and strong forms of *can* and remind students that *can't* is always stressed. Repeat the drill if necessary.

10 Put students into pairs, student A and student B. Student As turn to SB p91 and student Bs turn to SB p97. Check they are all looking at the correct exercise.

a) Focus students on the photos of Ella and Daniel. Check students understand that they are Mrs Jones's children.

Students do the exercise on their own, as shown in the example. Point out that all the pictures correspond to vocabulary in **1a)**.

If necessary, check answers with the class. Note that all the answers are the same for student As and student Bs, apart from the person's name.

> 2 Can Ella/Daniel play the piano? 3 Can Ella/Daniel play the guitar? 4 Can Ella/Daniel ride a bike? 5 Can Ella/Daniel ski? 6 Can Ella/Daniel swim? 7 Can Ella/Daniel play tennis? 8 Can Ella/Daniel play basketball?

b) Students do the activity in their pairs. Remind students to use the correct short answers (*Yes, he/she can.* and *No, he/she can't.*) when answering their partner's questions. Students are not allowed to look at their partner's book.

c) Students compare tables with their partner and find out what both children can do. Check answers with the class. (They can both ride a bike and swim.)

Get ready ... Get it right!

11 Students work on their own and make a list of things they can do. Students should just write the things, not complete sentences, as in the example. While students are working, monitor and help them with any new vocabulary they might need.

12 a) Put students into new pairs. Students take turns to ask questions about the things on their list in **11**, as shown in the example. Each student must find out how many things on their list they can both do.

b) Finally, ask students to tell the class some of the things they can both do, using *We can both ... .*

EXTRA PRACTICE AND HOMEWORK

 Class Activity 7B What can the class do? p134 (Instructions p107)

 Vocabulary Plus 7 Parts of the body p157 (Instructions p149)

7 Review Exercise 4 SB p61

CD-ROM Lesson 7B

Workbook Lesson 7B p34

7C Directions

QUICK REVIEW ●●●

This activity reviews abilities and *can*. Put students into pairs, if possible with someone that they don't know very well. Students do the activity in their pairs, as shown in the examples. Then ask students to tell the class some things they can do, but their partner can't do.

> **Vocabulary** prepositions of place
> **Real World** asking for and giving directions
> **Review** abilities; *can*; places in a town or city (1) and (2)

Where's the café?

1 a) Ask students to close their books. Students work on their own and write down ten places in a town or city (*a restaurant, a café,* etc.).

b) Put students into groups of three or four. Students compare lists to find out if they have the same places.

 Ask one group to tell you their words and write them on the board. Ask other groups to tell you any other words they have and add them to the list on the board.

Check that students have remembered all the vocabulary in **V6.1** and **V6.2** SB p110. Drill all the words chorally with the class.

Help with Vocabulary Prepositions of place

2 Focus students on pictures a)–f). Check students understand that the building with the cup and saucer is a café and the building with a pound sign is a bank.

Students do the exercise on their own or in pairs. Check answers with the class.

Point out that we can say *in* or *on* with streets and roads (*The café is in/on King Street.,* etc.).

Use pictures e) and f) to highlight the difference between *next to* and *near*.

Also check students understand *left* and *right*, and highlight that we say *It's on **the** left/right.* not ~~*It's on left/right*~~.

> 2f) 3e) 4d) 5a) 6b)

3 **a)** R7.9 P Play the recording. Students listen and practise. Highlight the pronunciation of *opposite* /ˈɒpəzɪt/ and the weak form of *to* /tə/ in *next to*.

b) Drill the sentences in the speech bubbles. Students do the exercise in pairs.

It's over there

4 **a)** Focus students on the photo and ask who the woman is (Maria, from lesson 7B).

Ask what Maria's job is now (she's an au pair) and tell students that she now lives with the Jones family in a small town called Hampton.

Focus students on the map of Hampton on SB p59. Students work in pairs and decide what places 1–12 are on the map. Check answers with the class.

> 1 a museum 2 a theatre 3 a café 4 a hotel
> 5 a supermarket 6 a chemist's 7 a bank
> 8 a park 9 a cinema 10 a post office
> 11 a restaurant 12 a station

b) Students do the exercise in the same pairs, as shown in the speech bubbles. Remind students to use the prepositions of place in **2** in their sentences. Ask students to say at least five sentences each.

— EXTRA IDEA —
- Ask students to write down four sentences describing where places on the map are before they do the speaking activity in **4b)** in their pairs.

5 **a)** Focus students on the photo of Maria asking for directions. Tell students that she is at the ✱ on the map.

Point out that the answers to both gaps in conversations B and C are the same.

Students do the exercise on their own before comparing answers in pairs.

b) R7.10 Play the recording. Students listen and check their answers. Check answers with the class.

You can also use the conversations to teach the phrases *Oh, yes. I can see it.* and *You're welcome.* Also highlight three different ways to say thank you in the conversations: *Thanks. Thank you very much.* and *Thanks a lot.* (not ~~Thank you a lot.~~).

> 2 museum 3 museum 4 bank 5 bank

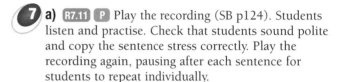

6 Check students understand the headings **ASKING FOR DIRECTIONS** and **GIVING DIRECTIONS** by referring students to conversations A–C in **5a)**.

Students do the exercise on their own before checking in pairs. Check answers with the class.

- **Answers** 2 here 3 road 4 turn 5 to 6 on 7 over
- Point out the use of *the* and *a* in the questions *Where's the (museum)?* and *Is there a (bank) near here?*. This is because in the first question, we know there is only one museum in the town and we only want to know its location. In the second question we want to know if there is a bank near here or not (i.e. if a bank exists). However, at this level it is probably easier just to teach *Where's the ... ?* and *Is there a ... (near here)?* as fixed phrases.
- Check students understand the new phrases *go along*, *turn left/right* and *It's over there*.
- Point out that we can say *on **the** right/left* or *on **your** right/left* when giving directions.
- Note that native speakers say *go along*, *go up* or *go down* to mean the same thing. If your students are studying in an English-speaking country, you can teach these alternatives.

7 **a)** R7.11 P Play the recording (SB p124). Students listen and practise. Check that students sound polite and copy the sentence stress correctly. Play the recording again, pausing after each sentence for students to repeat individually.

b) Students do the exercise in pairs. Make sure that all students take turns to be Maria.

While students are working, check they are sounding polite and help them with any pronunciation problems.

You can ask one or two pairs to role-play their conversations for the class. Students don't have to leave their seats.

8 **a)** Students do the exercise on their own. Remind them to refer to the map when choosing the correct words.

b) R7.12 Play the recording. Students listen and check their answers. Check answers with the class.

> 2 here 3 right 4 on 5 near 6 Where's 7 over
> 8 next to 9 near 10 along 11 right 12 hotel

c) Students practise the conversations in pairs, taking turns to ask for directions.

9 Put students into new pairs. Students take turns to ask for directions to places on the map. When students are listening to their partner's directions, they should follow the route and make sure the directions are correct.

Before they begin, remind students that they must start every conversation from ✱ on the map.

Finally, ask a few pairs to role-play one of their conversations for the class.

— EXTRA PRACTICE AND HOMEWORK —
Ph **Class Activity** 7C It's on the left p135–p136 (Instructions p108)
CD-ROM Lesson 7C
Workbook Lesson 7C p36

Vocabulary things people do online
Review *there is/there are; can;* Present Simple questions

QUICK REVIEW ●●●
This activity reviews *there is/there are* and places in a town or city. Students work on their own and write sentences with *there is/there are* about places near their school (or near the building you are in now). Students compare sentences in pairs and decide if they know their partner's places, as shown in the examples. At the end of the activity ask students to tell the class about any interesting places they talked about.

1 a) Use the lesson title to teach *the Internet*. Focus students on the Internet questionnaire. Students do the exercise on their own or in pairs. Check answers with the class.

Go through the new vocabulary with the class and teach any words students don't know. You can use the pictures in **V7.5** SB p113 to help convey meaning.

Point out that we can say *receive emails* or *get emails*, and that *receive* is more formal than *get*. Note that we always use *receive* in the phrase *send and receive emails*, but we usually use *get* in conversation, for example, *I **get** lots of emails every day.*, etc.

Highlight the prepositions in *listen **to** the radio* and *chat **to** friends and family*.

Also teach students that *online* = connected to the Internet.

> 2 theatre 3 watch 4 listen 5 friends
> 6 sell 7 holidays 8 music

b) **R7.13** **P** Play the recording (SB p124). Students listen and practise. Note that each phrase is said separately on the recording (*send emails, receive emails,* etc.). Highlight the pronunciation of *receive* /rɪˈsiːv/, *videos* /ˈvɪdiəʊz/, *listen* /ˈlɪsən/ and *flights* /flaɪts/. Point out the silent *t* in *listen*. Repeat the drill if necessary.

2 Pre-teach *website*. Focus students on the website logos. Check students remember how to say . (= *dot*) in website addresses. Highlight the phrase *You can ...* in the speech bubble. Students do the activity in pairs.

Check students' ideas with the class. Point out that we can use *at* with most websites, but we say **on** *eBay* not ~~at eBay~~. We can also say we *download music **from*** or *buy tickets **from*** a particular website.

> **Possible answers** You can book flights or holidays and buy concert or theatre tickets at **lastminute.com**. You can watch TV programmes at **itv.com**. You can listen to the radio at **realradio**. You can send and receive emails, chat to friends and family and watch videos at **Yahoo!**. You can book flights or holidays at **Cheapflights.co.uk**. You can buy and sell things on **eBay**. You can buy concert or theatre tickets at **ticketmaster**.

3 a) Focus students on the examples. Point out that we say *listen to **the** radio* but *listen to music*.

Students do the activity in new pairs. While students are working, monitor and help them with any new vocabulary.

b) Students compare lists with another pair to find out if they have the same things.

 Check students' ideas by eliciting phrases from the class and writing correct phrases on the board for other students to copy.

> **Possible answers**
> send and receive photos
> buy cinema tickets
> buy clothes
> buy food
> buy DVDs and CDs
> book a restaurant
> download videos
> meet new people
> play computer games
> read the news
> bank online
> search for information

— **EXTRA IDEA** —
* Ask students to write down their three favourite websites. Students compare their ideas in groups and say what they do at each website.

4 a) Focus students on the photo. Tell students that the interviewer is asking Alice about things she does online. **R7.14** Focus students on the Internet questionnaire. Play the recording (SB p124). Students listen and put a tick or a cross in column B of the questionnaire. Students compare answers in pairs. Check answers with the class.

> 1 ✓ 2 ✓ 3 ✓ 4 ✗ 5 ✓ 6 ✓ 7 ✗ 8 ✗

b) Give students time to read questions 1–6. Check that students know the websites YouTube and Amazon and that they remember what *an iPod* is.

Play the recording again. Students listen and answer the questions. Students compare answers in pairs. Check answers with the class.

> 1 Yes, she does. (About a hundred.) 2 YouTube.
> 3 In New York. 4 DVDs. 5 Yes, she is. 6 No, she doesn't.

a) Focus students on the speech bubbles. Use the first answer to highlight that we usually say *get emails* in spoken English, not *receive emails*.

Point out the question form *Do you ... online?* in the second question. Note that students can use this question 'formula' for phrases 2–7 on the questionnaire, but that for phrase 8 we would simply say *Do you download music?* not ~~Do you download music online?~~.

 Elicit the questions students need to ask for phrases 1–8 on the questionnaire and write them on the board. Drill these questions chorally and individually.

Put students into pairs. If possible, ask students to work with someone they don't know very well. Students take turns to interview their partner. Students put a tick or a cross for each of their partner's answers in column C on the questionnaire.

b) Students work in new pairs and take turns to tell each other about their partners in **5a)**. Before they begin, remind students to use *he, she* forms of the verbs: *Gloria sends and receives a lot of emails. She doesn't buy concert or theatre tickets.*, etc.

c) Finally, ask students to tell the class two things about their first partner.

```
EXTRA PRACTICE AND HOMEWORK
7 Review  Exercise 5 SB p61
CD-ROM  Lesson 7D
Workbook  Lesson 7D p37
Workbook  Reading and Writing Portfolio 7 p64
Progress Test 7  p171
```

Help with Sounds /s/ and /ʃ/

1 a) Focus students on the phonemes /s/ and /ʃ/, the pictures and the words.

R7.15 Play the recording. Students listen to the sounds and the words. Point out that *s* in *suit* is pronounced with a /s/ sound and *sh* in *shirt* is pronounced with a /ʃ/ sound.

b) **P** Play the recording again. Students listen and practise. If students are having problems, help them with the mouth position for each sound.

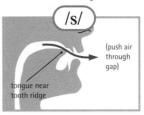
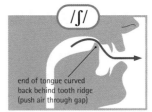

Point out that when we make the /s/ sound, the lips are relaxed, the tongue is near the back of the teeth, and there is some contact between the tongue and the teeth at the sides of the mouth. Also highlight that /s/ is an unvoiced sound (there is no vibration in the throat).

Also point out that when we make the /ʃ/ sound, the lips are more rounded and pushed forward slightly. The end of the tongue is curved back behind the teeth and we push air through the gap. Highlight that /ʃ/ is also an unvoiced sound.

You can also tell students that /ssss/ is the sound a snake makes, and that /ʃʃʃʃ/ is the sound people make when they want someone to be quiet.

2 a) **R7.16** Focus students on the boxes. Play the recording. Students listen and notice how we say the pink and blue consonants.

b) **P** Play the recording again. Students listen and practise.

3 a) Give students time to read the poem and help students with any vocabulary problems.

R7.17 Play the recording. Students listen and read the poem. Highlight that the pink consonants are pronounced /s/ and the blue consonants are pronounced /ʃ/.

P Play the recording again, pausing after each line for students to practise chorally and individually.

b) Students work in pairs and take turns to say lines of the poem.

Finally, ask one or two students to say the poem for the class.

7 Review

See p29 for ideas on how to use this section.

1a) 2 animals 3 horror films 4 dancing 5 flying
6 classical music 7 watching sport on TV
8 visiting new places 9 shopping for clothes

2 2 don't like 3 doesn't like 4 hates 5 likes 6 hate 7 loves
8 love

3 2 She, us 3 he, me 4 I, her 5 We, them 6 him

5a) 2 ~~friends~~ 3 ~~radio~~ 4 ~~the radio~~ 5 ~~friends~~ 6 ~~emails~~
7 ~~flights~~ 8 ~~chat~~

Progress Portfolio

See p29 for ideas on how to use this section.

8 Days to remember

Student's Book p62–p69

Vocabulary adjectives (2)
Grammar Past Simple of *be*: positive and negative
Review adjectives (1); *favourite*

Adjectives (2)

1 a) Focus students on pictures a)–h). Students do the exercise on their own or in pairs. Early finishers can check their answers in **V8.1** SB p114. Check answers with the class.

Point out that we can use *short* or *long* for amount of time (*It's a short/long film.*, etc.) and for physical length (*It's a short/long dress.*, etc.).

Use the pictures in e) to point out that the book (which is arrowed in each picture) is *interesting* or *boring*, not the person. Note that *bored* is taught in lesson 10C.

Point out that we use *old/young* for people or animals, and *old/new* for things, buildings, etc.

With a strong class you can also teach *sad* (= *unhappy*), *hard* (= *difficult*) and *wonderful* (= *fantastic*).

> 2f) 3e) 4h) 5d) 6c) 7g) 8b)

b) **R8.1** **P** Play the recording. Students listen and practise. Alternatively, model and drill the adjectives yourself. Highlight the pronunciation of *awful* /ˈɔːfəl/ and *great* /greɪt/. Also point out that *interesting* is three syllables, not four. Repeat the drill if necessary.

Three amazing days

2 a) Pre-teach the vocabulary in the box. Note that *a match* refers to *a football match*. You can also teach *New Year's Day*. Model and drill these words chorally and individually with the class.

b) Focus students on the photos and speech bubbles at the bottom of SB p62–p63.

R8.2 Play the recording. Students listen, read and decide what the people's amazing days were.

Check answers with the class. If students ask you about the meaning of *was* or *were* at this stage, simply say they are the past of the verb *be*. Note that these verb forms are studied in **3**.

If necessary, teach students how to say the years in the texts (1966, 1999 and 1998). Note that years are practised in lesson 8B.

Melanie the Beatles' last concert in San Francisco in 1966 **Tania** New Year's Eve in Sydney in 1999 **Pascal** the World Cup Final in Paris in 1998

c) Students read the texts in the speech bubbles again and choose the correct words in sentences 1–6. Check answers with the class.

> 2 half an hour 3 parents 4 fantastic 5 Brazil 6 three

Help with Grammar Past Simple of *be*: positive and negative

3 a) Give students time to read the sentences. Ask students if the sentences are in the present or the past (the past). Check students understand that *was, were, wasn't* and *weren't* are all past forms of the verb *be*.

b) Students do the exercise on their own before checking in pairs. While they are working, draw the table from **3b)** on the board. Check answers with the class.

- Focus students on the table on the board. Elicit which words go in each column and complete the table (see the table in **G8.1** SB p115).
- Point out that *wasn't* = *was not* and *weren't* = *were not*. Remind students that we usually use contracted forms when speaking and writing.
- Highlight that we use *was* or *wasn't* with *I, he, she* and *it*, and *were* or *weren't* with *you, we* and *they*.
- Also point out that the past of *there is/there are* is *there was/there were*. Elicit the negative forms (*there wasn't* and *there weren't*).

> — EXTRA IDEA —
> - Students read the texts in the speech bubbles again and underline all the examples of *was, were, wasn't* or *weren't*. Students compare answers in pairs.

4 **R8.3** **P** Play the recording (SB p124). Students listen and practise. Use the examples to highlight how we say *was* /wəz/ and *were* /wə/ in positive sentences. Point out that *was* and *were* are not usually stressed, but that *wasn't* and *weren't* are always stressed because they are negative words.

Play the recording again, pausing after each sentence for students to repeat individually. Alternatively, ask students to turn to R8.3, SB p124, which has the stress marked on all sentences. Play the recording again. Students listen and practise.

 a) Students do the exercise on their own.

b) Put students into pairs. Students compare answers and decide who says each sentence, Melanie, Tania or Pascal. Check answers with the class.

> 2 weren't (Melanie) 3 were (Tania) 4 was (Melanie)
> 5 were (Tania) 6 was (Pascal) 7 weren't (Pascal)
> 8 were, wasn't (Tania) 9 wasn't, was (Melanie)

Get ready … Get it right!

 Put students into groups of three. Ask all students to turn to SB p99. Check they are all looking at the correct exercise.

a) Ask students to think about their lives when they were ten. Go through the words and phrases in the box. Check students remember *favourite* and point out the phrase *good at* (*sports, languages,* etc.).

Students work on their own and write six sentences about their lives when they were ten, using *was*, *were* and ideas from the box or their own. While students are working, check their sentences for accuracy and help them with any new vocabulary they need.

─── **EXTRA IDEA** ───
- ✍ Introduce this activity by writing sentences about your own life when you were ten on the board as examples.

b) Students work in their groups and take turns to say their sentences, as shown in the speech bubbles. Students decide if any of the other students' sentences are true for them.

c) Finally, ask students to tell the class two interesting things about other students in their group.

─── **EXTRA PRACTICE AND HOMEWORK** ───
Ph **Class Activity** 8A Opposite adjectives p137 (Instructions p108)
8 Review Exercises 1 and 2 SB p69
CD-ROM Lesson 8A
Workbook Lesson 8A p38

8B Happy anniversary!

QUICK REVIEW ●●●
This activity reviews adjectives from lessons 3A and 8A. Students work on their own and write six adjectives and their opposites. Put students into pairs to complete the activity, as shown in the examples.

> **Vocabulary** years and past time phrases
> **Grammar** Past Simple of *be*: questions and short answers; *was born/were born*
> **Review** adjectives; Past Simple of *be*: positive and negative

Years and past time phrases

 a) Students do the exercise on their own or in pairs. Check answers with the class.
Point out that for the years 2000–2009, we usually say *two thousand, two thousand and one,* etc. For the years 2010–2099, we usually say *twenty ten, twenty eleven,* etc. Also highlight that we use *in* with years: *in 1980,* etc.

> 2e) 3a) 4f) 5d) 6b)

b) R8.4 P Play the recording. Students listen and practise. Check students stress the years correctly. Repeat the drill if necessary.

c) Students do the exercise in pairs. Check answers with the class.

> 2012 twenty twelve, 1977 nineteen seventy-seven,
> 2018 twenty eighteen, 1815 eighteen fifteen,
> 1990 nineteen ninety, 2003 two thousand and three

 a) Focus students on pictures A–D of Joe. Students do the exercise on their own. Check answers with the class.
Point out that we say *last night, last week, last weekend, last month, last year, last Monday, last Tuesday,* etc.
Also highlight that we say *yesterday morning, yesterday afternoon, yesterday evening,* but *last night,* not ~~yesterday night~~.
Teach students that *ago* means 'before now'. Check students' understanding by asking them what time it was three hours ago, what day it was four days ago, etc.
Use the example sentences to highlight that we usually put past time phrases (*last week, four hours ago, yesterday afternoon,* etc.) at the end of the sentence.

> 2D 3C 4B

b) R8.5 P Play the recording. Students listen and practise sentences 1–4. Point out that we don't usually pronounce the *t* in *last week* /lɑːs wiːk/, etc. and that the stress on *yesterday* is on the first syllable, not the last.

3 Students do the exercise on their own before checking answers in pairs. Check answers with the class.

> 2 last 3 in 4 yesterday 5 last 6 ago

— EXTRA IDEA —
- Students tick the sentences in **3** that are true for them. Put students in pairs to compare sentences.

An Indian wedding

 4 **a)** Pre-teach the vocabulary in the box. Drill the words with the class. You can also teach the phrase *Happy anniversary!* (the title of the lesson).

b) Pre-teach the adjective *Indian* and the country *India*. Focus students on the photos of an Indian wedding. Ask students who is the bride (the woman in red and green sitting down) and who is the groom (the man in white sitting next to her).

Note that the other photos show other aspects of a traditional Indian wedding, such as a woman's hennaed hands, bangles and sweets.

c) Tell the class they are going to listen to Rajeet, the groom in the photo, talk to a friend about his wedding anniversary. Give students time to read sentences 1–5.

R8.6 Play the recording (SB p124). Students listen and choose the correct words. Students compare answers in pairs. Check answers with the class.

> 2 ten 3 India 4 were 5 was

d) Give students time to read questions 1–6. Play the recording again. Students listen and answer the questions. Students compare answers in pairs. Check answers with the class.

Note that Mumbai used to be called Bombay.

> 2 Rajeet was 34 and Gita was 27.
> 3 There were 300 people there. 4 He was in Australia.
> 5 Yes, they were. 6 Three days.

Help with Grammar Past Simple of *be*: questions and short answers; *was born/were born*

5 **a)–b)** Students do the exercise on their own. While they are working, draw the table from **5a)** on the board. Check answers with the class and highlight the following points.

- Focus students on the table on the board. Elicit which words in questions 1 and 2 from **5b)** go in each column and complete the table (see the table in G8.2 SB p115).
- Use the example sentences to highlight the word order: question word + *was/were* + subject + … .
- Remind students that we use *was* or *wasn't* with *I, he, she* and *it*, and *were* or *weren't* with *you, we* and *they*.

- Use question 1 to highlight that we sometimes use a noun after *How many* … : **How many people** *were at the wedding?*, etc.
- You can compare the questions in the table to questions with *be* in the present: *Where are you from?, What's your name?*, etc.

c) Students do the exercise on their own, then compare answers in pairs. Check answers with the class.

- **Answers Was** I/he/she/it at the wedding? Yes, I/he/she/it was. No, I/he/she/it **wasn't**. **Were** you/we/they at the wedding? Yes, you/we/they **were**. No, you/we/they **weren't**.
- Use the questions in the first column of the table to highlight the word order in *yes/no* questions with *was* and *were*.
- Point out that we use contractions (*No, I wasn't., No, you weren't.*, etc.) in the negative short answers.
- Check students understand that the short answers to *Was I at the wedding?* are *Yes, you were./No, you weren't.* Also highlight that the short answers to *Were you at the wedding?* are *Yes, I was./No, I wasn't.* if *you* in the question is singular, and *Yes, we were./No, we weren't.* if it's plural.
- Also point out that we can also make questions with *Was there* … ? and *Were there* … ?.

d) Students do the exercise on their own. Check answers with the class.

- **Answers** 1 was 2 were, was
- Point out that we say *I was born in 1987.* not *I borned in 1987.*, etc.
- Establish that we often answer these questions with short forms, for example, *In the UK.* and *In 1987.*

 6 R8.7 P Play the recording (SB p124). Students listen and practise. Point out that we don't stress *was* and *were* in questions, but that these words are stressed in short answers. Play the recording again, pausing after each sentence for students to practise individually. You can also ask students to turn to R8.7, SB p124 and follow the stress as they listen and practise.

 7 **a)** Check students understand the phrase *the same age*. Students do the exercise on their own. Check answers with the class.

> 2 Were 3 was 4 Were 5 was 6 was

b) Students ask and answer the questions in pairs. Check answers with the class.

> 1 Rajeet and Gita. 2 No, they weren't. 3 Ten years ago.
> 4 Yes, they were. 5 Rajeet's brother.
> 6 (She was born) in the UK.

a) Students do the exercise on their own, then compare answers in pairs. Check answers with the class.

> 2 Where were you yesterday evening?
> 3 Were you on holiday three months ago?
> 4 Where were you on New Year's Eve 1999?
> 5 Were you at work last Monday?
> 6 Where were you born?

b) Students ask and answer the questions in pairs. Alternatively, students can move around the room and talk to as many people as possible.

Ask students to tell the class any interesting things they found out about their partner or classmates.

 a) Students do the exercise on their own. Tell students **not** to write when and where the people were born.

b) Put students into pairs. Students swap papers and ask each other about the people on their partner's paper, as shown in the speech bubbles.

Get ready … Get it right!

 Put students into new pairs, student A and student B. Student As turn to SB p88 and student Bs turn to SB p94. Check they are all looking at the correct exercise.

a) Pre-teach *went* and tell students this is the Past Simple of *go*. Students do the exercise on their own. Note that student As prepare questions about a wedding and student Bs prepare questions about a party.

Check answers with the class. Only check the words they need to fill in the gaps, so that students don't hear the questions they are about to be asked. Note that these answers are the same for student As and student Bs.

> **Student A/Student B** 2 was/Was 3 were/Were
> 4 were 5 Was/was 6 Were 7 Was 8 Was

b) Students work with their partners. Student A in each pair asks his/her questions from **a)** about the last wedding that student B went to. Tell student As to make brief notes on their partner's answers, but not to write complete sentences for each answer.

c) Students swap roles so that student B in each pair asks his/her questions from **a)** about the last party that student A went to. Again, tell student Bs to make brief notes on their partner's answers.

d) Put students into pairs with someone from the same group. Students take turns to talk about the last wedding or party their first partner went to.

Finally, ask students to tell the class about any interesting weddings or parties they or their partners went to.

> ── **EXTRA IDEA** ──
> • Use **Vocabulary Plus** 8 Places with *at*, *in*, *on* p158 (Instructions p149) in class or give this worksheet for homework.

> ── **EXTRA PRACTICE AND HOMEWORK** ──
> **Ph** **Class Activity** 8B Were you or weren't you? p138 (Instructions p108)
> **Ph** **Vocabulary Plus** 8 Places with *at*, *in*, *on* p158 (Instructions p149)
> **8 Review** Exercises 3, 4 and 5 SB p69
> **CD-ROM** Lesson 8B
> **Workbook** Lesson 8B p39

8C When's your birthday?

QUICK REVIEW ●●●

This activity reviews the Past Simple of *be* and past time phrases. Go through the five times (*three hours ago*, etc.) with the class. Also highlight the phrase *Where were you … ?* in the example. Put students into pairs. Students take turns to ask each other their questions.

Months and dates

 a) Focus students on the months in the box. Point out that months always start with a capital letter.

Also highlight that we use *in* with months: *in January*, *in May*, etc.

R8.8 **P** Play the recording. Students listen and practise. Alternatively, model and drill the months yourself.

> **Vocabulary** months and dates
> **Real World** talking about days and dates; making suggestions
> **Help with Listening** linking (2)
> **Review** Past Simple of *be*; past time phrases

Months that students often find hard to pronounce are *January* /ˈdʒænjuəri/, *February* /ˈfebruəri/, *June* /dʒuːn/, *July* /dʒʊˈlaɪ/ and *August* /ˈɔːgəst/. Also check that students stress the months correctly.

> ── **EXTRA IDEA** ──
> • Teach students these abbreviations for months: *Jan, Feb, Mar, Apr, Aug, Sept, Oct, Nov, Dec.* Students will often see these abbreviations on calendars, timetables, etc. Point out that *May, June* and *July* are not usually abbreviated.

b) Students do the activity in pairs, as shown in the examples.

2 a) Focus students on the dates in the box. Point out the letters in pink and highlight the relationship between the last two letters of each word (*first*, *second*, etc.) and the way we write dates (1st, 2nd, etc.).

Also highlight the irregular spelling of these *th* words: *fifth, ninth, twelfth, twentieth* and *thirtieth*.

Point out the hyphen in *twenty-first* and tell students that we also write *twenty-second, twenty-third*, etc.

 R8.9 **P** Play the recording. Students listen and practise the dates.

Students often have difficulty with the 'consonant clusters' at the end of these words (*sixth, twelfth*, etc.). If necessary, play the recording again, pausing after each word so that students can practise individually.

b) Students work in pairs and take turns to say the dates.

c) **R8.10** Play the recording. Students listen and check they said the words correctly. Point out that we usually stress the second syllable in the *-teenth* words (*thirteenth, fourteenth*, etc.).

P Play the recording again. Students listen and practise.

Real World Talking about days and dates

3 Go through the questions and answers with the class and highlight the following points.

- **1** Highlight the question and point out that we can answer with *It's Monday.* or just *Monday.*

- **2** Highlight the question and point out that we say *the* in dates: *(It's) March the seventh.*
- Point out that we write *March 7th* or *7th March.*
- Note that we can also say dates in another way: *the seventh of March*, etc. However, at this level we feel students only need to know one way to say dates. The alternative form is introduced in **face2face** Elementary.
- Also note that dates are often said without *the* in American English: *It's March seventh.*

- **3** Point out that *When's* = *When is* in the question *When's your birthday?*. Also highlight that we use *on* with dates: *(It's on) June the second.* Remind students that we also use *on* with days (*on Monday*, etc.).
- Highlight the difference between these questions: A *When's your birthday?* B *July the twelfth.* (every year); A *When were you born?* B *July the twelfth 1989.* (one specific day in the past).
- You can also point out that dates are written differently in the UK and in the USA. In the UK, 5/6/09 = 5th June 2009 (day/month/year), whereas in the USA, 5/6/09 = 6th May 2009 (month/day/year).

4 **R8.11** **P** Play the recording. Students listen and practise. Repeat the drill if necessary.

5 **R8.12** Give students time to read the dates in 1–4. Play the recording (SB p124). Students listen and circle the dates they hear. Play the recording again if necessary. Students compare answers in pairs. Check answers with the class.

1 June 22nd **2** March 30th **3** October 3rd **4** April 1st

6 a) Use the examples to remind students how we write dates. Students work on their own and write five dates.

b) Students do the activity in pairs.

c) Students move around the room and ask each other when their birthdays are, as shown in the speech bubbles. Students must find out if any other students have birthdays in the same month as them. If students can't move around the room, they should ask as many students as they can sitting near them.

Ask students to tell the class who has a birthday in the same month as them.

Happy birthday!

7 a) Pre-teach the vocabulary in the box and remind students of the phrase *Happy birthday!*. You can also teach *a birthday present* and tell students that we *give someone a present* (not ~~present someone~~).

Model and drill the new words and phrases with the class.

b) Focus students on the photo of Helen and her husband, Sam, on SB p67. Tell the class that it is Helen's birthday today.

R8.13 Play the recording (SB p124). Students listen and write down what Helen and Sam decide to do this evening. Check the answer with the class. (They decide to go to the theatre/see a play.)

8 **R8.13** Give students time to read sentences 1–5. Play the recording again. Students listen and choose the correct words. Students compare answers in pairs. Check answers with the class.

2 a restaurant **3** week **4** museum **5** the theatre, 7.00

Help with Listening Linking (2)

- This Help with Listening section reviews consonant-vowel linking in sentences.

9 a) Focus students on the sentences from the recording. Ask students why we link the words in pink and blue (because the words in pink end in a consonant sound and the words in blue start with a vowel sound).

You can model and drill these sentences yourself with the class, highlighting the linking.

b) `R8.13` Ask students to look at R8.13, SB p124. Play the recording again. Students listen, read and follow the linking as shown in the Student's Book.

Real World Making suggestions

10 Check students understand *a suggestion*. Students do the exercise on their own. Check answers with the class.

- **Answers** 2 idea 3 don't 4 meet 5 time 6 seven
- Point out that we use questions with *shall* to ask for suggestions:
  What shall we do (this evening)?
  Where shall we meet?
  What time shall we meet?
- Also highlight that we use *Why don't we ... ?* and *Let's ...* to make suggestions. Point out that these phrases are followed by a verb (*go*, etc.).

11 `R8.14` `P` Play the recording (SB p124–p125). Students listen and practise the sentences in **10**. Point out that *shall* is pronounced /ʃəl/ in the questions.

You can ask students to turn to R8.14, SB p124–p125, where the stress and linking are marked. Play the recording again. Students listen, read and practise the stress and linking as shown in the Student's Book.

12 **a)** Students do the exercise on their own.

b) `R8.15` Play the recording (SB p125). Students listen and check their answers. Check answers with the class.

  3c) 4i) 5e) 6f) 7d) 8h) 9b)

c) Students practise the conversation in pairs. While students are working, help them with any pronunciation problems and make sure they sound polite and interested when asking and answering questions.

13 **a)** Students do the activity in new pairs.

b) Students practise their conversation until they can remember it.

c) Put two pairs together so that they are working in groups of four. Each pair takes turns to role-play their conversation. The other pair writes down what they decide to do.

d) Ask one pair in each group to role-play the conversation for the class. Students don't have to leave their seats. Finally, students can decide which conversation they liked best.

EXTRA PRACTICE AND HOMEWORK

8 Review Exercise 6 SB p69
CD-ROM Lesson 8C
Workbook Lesson 8C p41

8D Festivals

QUICK REVIEW ●●●
This activity reviews ways of making suggestions. Check students understand *tomorrow evening*. Students do the exercise in pairs. If students are having problems remembering what language to use, ask them to look at the flow chart in `RW8.2` SB p115.

Vocabulary big numbers
Review making suggestions; months and dates; *was and were*

1 **a)** Students do the exercise on their own before checking in pairs. Check answers with the class.

Point out that we don't use a plural *-s* with *hundred*, *thousand* or *million*: *three hundred* not ~~three hundreds~~, etc.

Also point out that we use *and* after *hundred*, but not after *thousand*: *a hundred **and** fifty*, but *sixteen thousand, two hundred* not ~~sixteen thousand **and** two hundred~~.

Highlight that we can say *a hundred* or *one hundred*, *a thousand* or *one thousand* and *a million* or *one million*. Point out that using *a* with these numbers is more common.

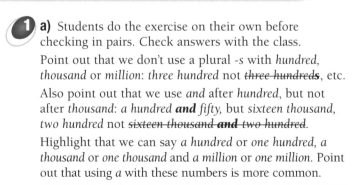

390 three hundred and ninety 1,000 a thousand
16,200 sixteen thousand, two hundred
750,000 seven hundred and fifty thousand
1,000,000 a million 50,000,000 fifty million

b) `R8.16` `P` Play the recording. Students listen and practise. Highlight the pronunciation of *hundred* /ˈhʌndrəd/ and *thousand* /ˈθaʊzənd/. Repeat the drill if necessary.

2 **a)** `R8.17` Play the recording (SB p125). Students listen and write the numbers. Play the recording again if necessary.

b) Students compare answers in pairs. ✍ Check answers with the class and write them on the board in numbers.

  a) 365 b) 999 c) 17,000
  d) 62,400 e) 250,000
  f) 1,200,000 g) 18,000,000

3 **a)** Students do the exercise on their own.

b) Students do the exercise in new pairs. While students are working, monitor and correct any pronunciation errors.

4 **a)** Pre-teach the vocabulary in the box. Drill the new words with the class.

b) Use the photo in the article to introduce the topic of festivals. Students read the article and try to fill in the gaps with the numbers in the box.

c) R8.18 Play the recording. Students listen and check their answers. Check answers with the class.

> a) 30,000 b) 125,000 c) 150,000
> d) 1,500 e) 177,500 f) 70,000,000

5 **a)** Students read the article again and answer the questions. Students compare answers in pairs. Check answers with the class.

> 1 It's on the last Wednesday in August in Buñol, Spain.
> 2 They throw tomatoes at each other. 3 It's in July.
> 4 They eat garlic bread, garlic chicken, garlic chocolate and garlic ice cream. 5 It was in June 1970.
> 6 It's in 2015.

b) Ask the class which two festivals from the article they would like to go to. Encourage students to give reasons for their choices if possible.

> ┌─ EXTRA PRACTICE AND HOMEWORK ─────┐
> **Ph** **Class Activity** 8D Numbers, years and dates p139 (Instructions p109)
> **CD-ROM** Lesson 8D
> **Workbook** Lesson 8D p42
> **Workbook** Reading and Writing Portfolio 8 p66
> **Progress Test 8** p172
> └──────────────────────────────────┘

> **Help with Sounds** /ɔ:/ **and** /ɜ:/

1 **a)** Focus students on the phonemes /ɔ:/ and /ɜ:/, the pictures and the words.
R8.19 Play the recording. Students listen to the sounds and the words.

Point out that *or* in *forty* is pronounced with a /ɔ:/ sound and *ur* in *burger* is pronounced with a /ɜ:/ sound. Note that in British English we don't usually pronounce the letter *r* after a vowel sound.

b) **P** Play the recording again. Students listen and practise. If students are having problems producing the sounds, help them with the mouth position for each sound.

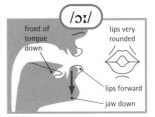 

Point out that when we make the /ɔ:/ sound, the lips are very rounded and pushed forward, the front of the tongue is down and the jaw is also down. Also point out that /ɔ:/ is a long sound.

Highlight that when we make the /ɜ:/ sound, the mouth is slightly open and the lips, tongue and jaw are in a relaxed position. Highlight that /ɜ:/ is also a long sound. Note that this is the same mouth position that we use for the schwa /ə/, which is a short sound.

2 **a)** R8.20 Focus students on the boxes. Play the recording. Students listen and notice how we say the pink and blue letters.

b) **P** Play the recording again. Students listen and practise.

3 **a)** R8.21 Play the recording. Students listen and read the sentences.
P Play the recording again. Students listen and practise the sentences. Check they pronounce the pink letters with an /ɔ:/ sound and the blue letters with an /ɜ:/ sound.

b) Students practise the sentences in pairs.
Finally, ask students to say the sentences for the class.

> ## 8 Review

See p29 for ideas on how to use this section.

> **1a)** → wrong, terrible, long, great, happy
> ↓ boring, full, easy
>
> **1b)** wrong → right, terrible → great/fantastic/amazing, long → short, great → awful/terrible, happy → unhappy, boring → interesting, full → empty, easy → difficult
>
> **2** 2 weren't, were 3 wasn't, was 4 were 5 wasn't
> 6 weren't, were
>
> **4a)** b) last c) yesterday d) last e) in f) ago
> **4b)** 1a) 2c) 3d) 4b) 5f) 6e)

> **5a)** 2 Were you in this country last year? 3 Where was your father born? 4 Were you in this class two months ago? 5 Where were you on your last birthday? 6 When was your first English class?
>
> **6a)** 2 Why 3 think 4 let's 5 good 6 Where 7 meet
> 8 shall 9 past

> **Progress Portfolio**
> ┄┄┄┄┄┄┄┄┄┄┄┄┄┄┄┄┄┄┄┄┄┄┄┄┄┄┄┄
> See p29 for ideas on how to use this section.
> ┄┄┄┄┄┄┄┄┄┄┄┄┄┄┄┄┄┄┄┄┄┄┄┄┄┄┄┄

9 Going away

Student's Book p70–p77

9A Amazing journeys

Vocabulary transport
Grammar Past Simple: positive (regular and irregular verbs)
Help with Listening Present Simple or Past Simple
Review years, months and dates

QUICK REVIEW ●●●

This activity reviews years, months and dates. Students do the first part of the activity on their own. Go through the example conversation with the class. Check students remember the question *Where was he/she born?* and how to say months, dates and years (*On June the second, nineteen ninety-four*, etc.). Students complete the activity in pairs.

Transport

1 a) Students work on their own and tick the words they know. Students then turn to Language Summary 9 **V9.1** SB p116 and check the meaning of the other words. Check answers with the class.

Highlight that we usually say *taxi* in British English and *cab* in American English. Note that *cab* is also used in the UK. Also remind students that *a bike = a bicycle*.

You can also teach *a scooter, a ferry* and *a tram* if they are relevant to your students.

b) **R9.1** **P** Play the recording. Students listen and practise.

c) Focus students on sentences 1–4. Students underline the verbs in the sentences. Check answers with the class (*go, come, travel, walk*).

Use the sentences to highlight the difference between *come* (travel from another place to where you are now) and *go* (travel to another place away from where you are now). Also check students understand the new verb *walk*.

Point out that we say *by car, by bus*, etc. Note that we say *on foot* not ~~by foot~~. However, this phrase is rarely used nowadays and we are more likely to use the verb *walk* (*I usually walk to school.*, etc.).

Also teach students that *go by plane = fly, go by car = drive* and *go by bike = cycle*.

Model and drill sentences 1–4 with the class. Highlight the difference in pronunciation between the vowel sounds in *walk* /wɔːk/ and *work* /wɜːk/ in sentence 4, which students studied in the Help with Sounds section in unit 8.

2 a) Students do the exercise on their own, as shown in the example.

b) Students work in pairs and take turns to say their sentences. Ask each pair to tell the class any sentences that are the same for both students.

Bangkok to Brighton

3 a) Pre-teach the vocabulary in the box. Note that *a tuk-tuk* is a small motorised taxi commonly used in Asian countries, as shown in the photo.

Drill the words chorally and individually, highlighting the pronunciation of *tuk-tuk* /ˈtʊk tʊk/, *Thailand* /ˈtaɪlænd/ and *journey* /ˈdʒɜːni/.

b) Focus students on the newspaper article and ask them to cover the text. Students look at the photo and discuss what they think the article is about. This can be done in pairs or with the whole class.

Ask students to share their ideas with the class.
 Write all students' ideas on the board, but don't say if they are right or wrong at this stage.

c) Students read the article to find out if their ideas in **3b)** are correct.
 Focus students on the ideas on the board and ask which are correct. Tick the correct ideas and cross out the wrong ideas.

Check students know that *Bangkok* is the capital of Thailand and that *Brighton* /ˈbraɪtən/ is a city in England.

Tell students not to worry about the pink and blue words in the text at this stage. If students ask about them, simply say that they are all verbs in the past.

4 Students do the exercise on their own. Point out that students should write dates, places and numbers in the table, not complete sentences.

Students compare their answers in pairs by saying the dates, places and numbers to each other. Check answers with the class. You can also ask students if they would like to do the same journey.

> b) May 28th 2006
> c) Bangkok, Thailand
> d) Brighton, England
> e) 12,500
> f) 12
> g) 98
> h) £50,000

Help with Grammar Past Simple: positive (regular and irregular verbs)

5 **a)–c)** Focus students on the Past Simple forms in blue and pink in the article. Point out that the words in blue are Past Simple forms of regular verbs and the words in pink are Past Simple forms of irregular verbs.

Students do the exercises on their own or in pairs, then check their answers in **G9.1** SB p117.

Check answers with the class, highlighting the following points.

- **a)** To make the Past Simple of regular verbs, we usually add -ed to the verb: want**ed**, start**ed**, etc.
- For regular verbs that end in -e (like, arrive, etc.), we add -d to the verb: lik**ed**, arriv**ed**, etc.
- Point out that the Past Simple of travel is trave**lled** and the Past Simple of study is stud**ied**. This is because travel ends in consonant + vowel + consonant and study ends in consonant + y. However, at this level we suggest that you don't overburden students with spelling rules as they are not asked to use any other Past Simple forms of this type in **face2face** Starter. Students study these spelling rules in **face2face** Elementary.
- Check students understand the meaning of the new verbs want, visit and arrive.

- **b)** 2 came 3 got 4 gave 5 went 6 had 7 left 8 met 9 told 10 wrote
- Check students understand the meaning of the new verbs give, leave, meet and tell.
- Point out that there are no spelling rules for irregular verbs.
- Also highlight that the Past Simple of both regular and irregular verbs is the same for all subjects (I, you, he, she, it, we, they).
- Remind students that the Past Simple of be is was or were.
- Highlight the lists of regular verbs and irregular verbs in **G9.1** SB p117. Encourage students to learn the irregular Past Simple forms at home.

--- EXTRA IDEA ---
- If your students are finding the lesson difficult, go through **5a)** and **5b)** with the whole class yourself, highlighting the points in **5a)–c)** above. You can then point out the verb lists in **G9.1** SB p117.

6 **a)** Point out that verbs 1–12 are all regular verbs. Students do the exercise on their own before checking in pairs.

Check answers with the class by writing them on the board so students can check their spelling. Include the answer to question 1 (visited).

1 visited 2 watched 3 played 4 hated 5 walked 6 worked 7 lived 8 wanted 9 loved 10 talked 11 started 12 finished

b) **R9.2** **P** Play the recording (SB p125). Students listen and practise. Note that students should repeat both the verb and its Past Simple form together (visit, visited, etc.), not separately.

Ask students which Past Simple forms end in /ɪd/ and underline them on the board (visited, hated, wanted, started). Point out that the -ed ending in these words is said as an extra syllable because the verbs end in t (visit, etc.). This is also true of verbs that end in d (needed /niːdɪd/, ended /endɪd/, etc.), but this has not been highlighted as students haven't met any of these verbs yet.

Also note that students often have difficulty pronouncing the 'consonant clusters' at the end of regular Past Simple forms (watched /wɒtʃt/, worked /wɜːkt/, finished /ˈfɪnɪʃt/, etc.), and often mistakenly say these -ed endings as extra syllables.

Play the recording again, pausing after each pair of words for students to repeat individually.

c) Focus students on the irregular Past Simple forms in **5b)**.

R9.3 **P** Play the recording. Students listen and practise. Note that only the Past Simple forms are included on the recording. Highlight the /ɔː/ sound in bought /bɔːt/, which students studied in the Help with Sounds section in unit 8. Repeat the drill if necessary.

--- EXTRA IDEA ---
- Students work in pairs and take turns to test each other on the regular and irregular Past Simple forms from the lesson. One student says a verb, for example buy, and his/her partner says the Past Simple form, for example bought.

Help with Listening
Present Simple or Past Simple

- This Help with Listening section helps students to hear the difference between Present Simple and Past Simple verb forms.

7 **a)** Focus students on sentences 1–3. Point out that the verbs in blue are in the Present Simple and the verbs in pink are in the Past Simple.

R9.4 Play the recording. Students listen and notice the different pronunciation of these verb forms. Play the recording again if necessary.

b) **R9.5** Play the recording (SB p125). Students listen and decide which they hear first, the Present Simple or the Past Simple, as shown in the example. Play the recording again if necessary. Check answers with the class.

2 Present Simple (live)
3 Past Simple (arrived)
4 Present Simple (talk)
5 Present Simple (want)
6 Past Simple (played)

Around the world by bike

8 **a)** Focus students on the photo of Mark Beaumont. Teach the phrase *travel around the world*. Ask how Mark travelled around the world (by bike).

Students do the exercise on their own.

b) Students compare answers in pairs. Check answers with the class. Also point out the regular verb *cycle* /'saɪkəl/ in the example.

> 2 had 3 left 4 started 5 travelled 6 visited
> 7 met 8 wrote 9 got 10 finished 11 went
> 12 told 13 was 14 raised

Get ready ... Get it right!

9 Put students into groups of three. Ask all students to turn to SB p99. Check they are all looking at the correct exercise.

a) Students do the exercise on their own. Remind students to put the verbs in brackets in the Past Simple. If necessary, go through the prompts with the class before they begin.

b) Students work on their own and practise saying their sentences until they can remember them.

c) Students work in their groups and take turns to tell each other about the last time they visited a different town or city, using the sentences they have memorised.

Students may start asking each other questions about the places they visited, but don't worry if these are inaccurate at this point. Note that Past Simple questions are taught in lesson 9B.

d) Finally, ask each student to tell the class two things about the place they visited.

— EXTRA IDEA —
* Introduce the activity by telling the class about the last time you visited a town or city.

— EXTRA PRACTICE AND HOMEWORK —
Ph **Class Activity** 9A My past p140 (Instructions p109)
9 Review Exercises 1 and 2 SB p77
CD-ROM Lesson 9A
Workbook Lesson 9A p43

 9B **My last holiday**

QUICK REVIEW ●●●
This activity reviews the Past Simple of regular and irregular verbs. Students do the first part of the activity on their own. Demonstrate the second part of the activity by asking students to say one or two of their verbs and then saying sentences with the correct Past Simple form, as in the example. Students complete the activity in pairs.

Holiday activities

1 **a)** Students work on their own and tick the phrases they know, then do the exercise in **V9.2** SB p116. They can then check answers in pairs. Check answers with the class.

Point out that we say *go on holiday* in British English and *go on vacation* in American English.

Check students understand *go sightseeing* (visit the famous buildings in a town, city or country) and *travel around* (travel from place to place in a town, city or country).

Highlight the different words and phrases that follow *go*: *go on holiday, go to the beach, go sightseeing, go swimming, go for a walk.*

Also tell students that we can say *rent a car* or *hire a car*.

> 2g) 3k) 4d) 5i) 6a) 7c) 8f) 9b) 10j) 11h)

Vocabulary holiday activities
Grammar Past Simple: negative, questions and short answers
Review Past Simple: positive; frequency adverbs

b) **R9.6** **P** Play the recording. Students listen and practise. Highlight the pronunciation of *beach* /biːtʃ/ and *sightseeing* /'saɪtsiːɪŋ/. Repeat the drill if necessary. Note that only the **main** stress is shown in the vocabulary boxes and Language Summaries.

c) Elicit the Past Simple forms of the verbs in **1a)** and write them on the board. Point out that *take* is irregular. Drill these words with the class, highlighting the extra syllable in *rented* /'rentɪd/.

> stay → stayed rent → rented travel → travelled
> have → had

2 **a)** Check students remember *always, usually* and *sometimes*. Students do the exercise on their own, as in the examples.

b) Students do the exercise in pairs. Ask students to tell the class which of their sentences are also true for their partner (*Nico and I always go to the beach.*, etc.).

Favourite places

 a) Pre-teach the vocabulary in the box. Drill the words with the class. Point out the silent *s* in *island* /'aɪlənd/ and the silent *c* in *scenery* /'siːnəri/.

b) Focus students on the photos of the people and the texts on SB p72, and the photos on SB p73.

R9.7 Play the recording. Students listen, match the people to the photos and decide which countries the places are in. Check answers with the class.

> **Nancy** Istanbul (in Turkey) **Jeff** Cartagena (in Colombia)
> **Bob and Liz** Guilin (in China)

c) Students do the exercise on their own before checking in pairs. Check answers with the class.

Ask students which of the three places they would like to visit.

> 1 Jeff 2 Nancy 3 Jeff 4 Bob, Liz 5 Nancy 6 Jeff, Bob, Liz

Help with Grammar Past Simple: negative

 a)–b) Students do the exercises on their own or in pairs.

While students are working, draw the table from **4a)** on the board. Check answers with the class.

- Focus students on the table on the board. Elicit which words in sentences 1 and 2 in **4b)** go in each column and complete the table (see the table in G9.2 SB p117).
- Highlight the word order in Past Simple negatives: subject + *didn't* + verb + ...
- Point out that *didn't* is the contracted form of *did not* and that we usually use this form when speaking and writing.
- Also point out that we use *didn't* with all subjects (*I, you, he, she, it, we, they*) and with all verbs except *be*.
- Highlight that we use the verb in negative sentences, not its Past Simple form: *I didn't* **stay** *in a hotel.* not ~~*I didn't stayed in a hotel.*~~, etc.
- Remind students that the Past Simple negative of *be* is *wasn't* or *weren't*, not ~~*didn't be*~~.

 R9.8 P Play the recording. Students listen and practise the sentences in **4**. Check that students copy the sentence stress correctly. Also point out that *didn't* is always stressed because it has a negative meaning.

 a) Focus students on the example. Point out that we use the verb *go* in the negative sentence (*didn't go*), but its Past Simple form in the positive sentence (*went*). Students do the exercise on their own.

b) Students compare answers in pairs. Check answers with the class.

1b) She didn't go sightseeing in the mornings. She went sightseeing in the afternoons.
2a) Jeff didn't travel around Colombia two years ago. He travelled around Colombia last year.
2b) He didn't stay with friends. He stayed in a hotel.
3a) Bob and Liz didn't stay in a big hotel. They stayed in a small hotel.
3b) They didn't rent bikes. They rented a car.

 Ask students to cover the texts on SB p72. Students answer the questions on their own before checking in pairs. Check answers with the class.

Highlight the position of *with* in question 2 and tell students that it is common in English to end a sentence with a preposition: *Who do you live with?, Where are you from?*, etc.

> 1 (She went to) Istanbul. 2 She stayed with friends (from university). 3 (He went to the beach) every afternoon. 4 No, he didn't. 5 No, they didn't. 6 (They took) 300 photos.

Help with Grammar Past Simple: questions and short answers

 a)–c) Students do the exercises on their own or in pairs. While they are working, draw the table from **8a)** on the board. Check answers with the class.

- **a)–b)** Focus students on the *Wh-* questions table on the board. Elicit which words in sentences 1 and 2 go in each column and complete the table (see the table in G9.3 SB p117).
- Highlight the word order in Past Simple *Wh-* questions: question word + *did* + subject + verb + ...
- Point out that the auxiliary *did* has no meaning, but is used to make the Past Simple questions.
- Use sentence 2 to highlight that we often use a noun after *How many*: **How many photos** *did they take?*.
- Point out that we use *did* with all subjects (*I, you, he, she, it, we, they*) and with all verbs except *be*.
- Highlight that we use the verb in questions, not its Past Simple form: *Where did Nancy* **go** *... ?* not ~~*Where did Nancy went ... ?*~~.
- Remind students that we don't use the auxiliary *did* in questions with *was* and *were*: *Where were you?* not ~~*Where did you be?*~~, etc.

- **c)** **Did** he go swimming? Yes, he did. No, he **didn't**. **Did** they visit China last year? Yes, they **did**. No, they didn't.
- Highlight the word order in Past Simple *yes/no* questions: *Did* + subject + verb + ...
- Point out that the form of *yes/no* questions and short answers is the same for all subjects: *Did* **you** *go swimming? Yes,* **I** *did./No,* **I** *didn't., Did* **she** *visit China last year? Yes,* **she** *did./No,* **she** *didn't.*, etc.

- Ask students to turn to **G9.3** SB p117. Focus students on the final **TIP!**. Use the table below the **TIP!** to highlight the difference between negative and question forms in the Present Simple and Past Simple. Point out that only the auxiliary in pink changes (*don't/doesn't* → *didn't*, *do/does* → *did*).

9 **R9.9** **P** Play the recording. Students listen and practise. Check that students copy the sentence stress correctly. If necessary, play the recording again, pausing after each sentence for students to repeat individually.

10 Put students into pairs, student A and student B. Student As turn to SB p91 and student Bs turn to SB p97. Check they are all looking at the correct exercise.

a) Focus students on the photos of Nancy and Jeff and ask students where they went on holiday last year (Istanbul and Cartagena). Check students understand the phrase *buy presents (for someone)*.

Students do the exercise on their own.

If necessary, check the questions with the whole class. Note that the questions are the same for student As and student Bs, apart from *he/she* and *his/her*.

> **Student A/Student B** **2** Did she/he visit any museums?
> **3** What did she/he do in the evenings?
> **4** How did she/he travel around?
> **5** Did she/he buy presents for her/his family?

b) Students work with their partners. Student A in each pair asks his/her questions from **a)** about Nancy. Tell student Bs that the answers are in column C of their table. Student As should write the answers in column B of their table.

c) Students swap roles so that student B in each pair asks his/her questions from **a)** about Jeff. Students can then compare tables and check their partner's answers.

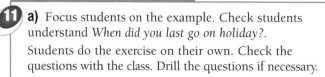

Get ready ... Get it right!

11 **a)** Focus students on the example. Check students understand *When did you last go on holiday?*. Students do the exercise on their own. Check the questions with the class. Drill the questions if necessary.

> Where did you go? What did you do there?
> Who did you go with? Where did you stay?
> How did you travel around? Did you have a good time?

b) Ask students to think about their last holiday and answer the questions in **11a)** for themselves. Students can make brief notes if necessary or just answer the questions in their heads.

12 **a)** Put students into pairs, student A and student B. If possible, ask students to work with someone they don't know very well. Student A in each pair asks his or her partner all the questions from **11a)**. Students then swap roles so that student B asks all his or her questions.

b) Finally, ask a few students to tell the class about their partner's holiday.

- Use **Class Activity** 9B What did you do on holiday? p141–p142 (Instructions p109) as an alternative way to finish the lesson.

─ EXTRA PRACTICE AND HOMEWORK ─

Ph **Class Activity** 9B What did you do on holiday? p141–p142 (Instructions p109)

9 Review Exercises 3 and 4 SB p77

CD-ROM Lesson 9B

Workbook Lesson 9B p44

9C Last weekend

QUICK REVIEW ●●●
This activity reviews holiday activities and the Past Simple. Students do the first part of the activity on their own before comparing lists in pairs. Students then talk about their favourite holiday with their partner. At the end of the activity, ask a few students to tell the class about their (or their partner's) favourite holiday.

Two days in Liverpool

1 **a)** Students do the exercise on their own. Remind them to use the Past Simple in their sentences.

> **Vocabulary** at the station
> **Real World** buying train tickets
> **Help with Listening** sentence stress (3)
> **Review** holiday activities; Past Simple

b) Put students into pairs. Students take turns to tell their partner about their weekend, using the sentences they prepared in **1a)**. Encourage students to ask questions in the Past Simple, as shown in the speech bubbles.

c) Ask students to tell the class two things their partner did last weekend.

a) Focus students on photos A and B. Ask students what they know about Liverpool.

We suggest you don't tell your students why the Cavern Club is famous at this stage, as this is featured in the listening activity.

> **Possible answers** Liverpool is a big city in the north of England. It has two famous football teams, Liverpool FC and Everton FC. The Beatles were all born in Liverpool and played their first concerts there. The airport is called Liverpool John Lennon Airport.

b) Focus students on photo C of James and Caroline. Ask students where they are (in a café). Tell the class that it's Monday morning.

Write these questions on the board: *When did Caroline go to Liverpool?*, *Did she have a good time?*.

R9.10 Play the recording (SB p125). Students listen and answer the questions. Check answers with the class. (Caroline went to Liverpool last weekend. She had a good time there.)

c) Give students time to read sentences 1–6. Play the recording again. Students listen and choose the correct answers.

d) Students compare answers in pairs. Check answers with the class.

Ask students why the Cavern Club is famous if this hasn't been mentioned earlier (it was the place where the Beatles first played).

> 2 Saturday 3 Chinese 4 sister 5 afternoon 6 train

Help with Listening Sentence stress (3)

- This Help with Listening activity reviews sentence stress in the context of an informal conversation.

 a) Focus students on the beginning of Caroline and James's conversation.

R9.10 Play the beginning of the recording again. Students listen and notice the sentence stress. Remind students that we stress the important words (the words that carry the meaning).

You can use the sentences to highlight what types of word are stressed (names, nouns, verbs, adjectives, negatives, etc.) and what types of word are not usually stressed (pronouns, auxiliaries, prepositions, *a, the, and, but*, etc.).

b) Ask students to turn to R9.10, SB p125, which has all the sentence stress marked. Play the complete recording again. Students listen, read and notice the sentence stress.

At the station

 a) Focus students on the photos on SB p75. Students do the exercise on their own or in pairs. Check answers with the class.

Point out that *a single* = a single ticket and *a return* = a return ticket. However, we rarely say *ticket* with these words.

> 2 a ticket office 3 a ticket machine
> 4 a platform 5 a single 6 a return

b) **P** Play the recording. Students listen and practise.

Real World Buying train tickets

 a) Focus students on the picture at the top of SB p75. Tell the class that it is now Saturday morning. Ask who the man is (James) and what the woman's job is (she's a ticket seller).

R9.12 Focus students on the flow chart. Play the recording. Students listen and fill in the gaps. Play the recording again if necessary.

b) Students compare answers in pairs. Check answers with the class.

Go through the sentences in the flow chart with the class and check students understand them. Point out the new phrases *come back*, *the next train* and *Which platform?*.

> b) £93.40 c) 9.17 d) six e) 12.29

 R9.13 **P** Play the recording (SB p125). Students listen and practise. Check that students copy the sentence stress correctly. Play the recording again if necessary.

 a) Students do the exercise in pairs, taking turns to be the customer. Ask students to practise a few times in each role and encourage them to memorise the conversation.

> ┌─ **EXTRA IDEA** ─
> - To help students with **7b)**, write the answers a)–e) in **5a)** on the board so that students don't have to remember the place, price, train times and platform number when they practise the conversation with their books closed.

b) Ask students to close their books. Students practise the conversation in pairs.

You can ask one or two pairs to role-play the conversation for the class.

 a) Ask students to cover the conversation in **5a)**. Students do the exercise on their own.

b) R9.14 Play the recording. Students listen and check their answers. Check answers with the class.

> 2 That's 3 your 4 next 5 at 6 Which 7 does 8 At 9 a lot

9 Put students into new pairs, student A and student B. Student As turn to SB p91 and student Bs turn to SB p97. Check they are all looking at the correct exercise.

a) Tell student As that they are customers and student Bs that they are ticket sellers. Give students a few moments to read the information in the table. Point out that student As must buy two different pairs of tickets. Tell the class that the time is now 9 a.m.

Students work with their partners. Student As buy two returns to Bath and fill in the gaps in the first row of the table.

Student As then buy two singles to Bristol and fill in the gaps in the second row of the table.

b) Students swap roles so that student Bs are customers and student As are ticket sellers. Give students time to read the information in the second table. Check the pronunciation of *Birmingham* /'bɜːmɪŋəm/ with the class before they begin.

Students work with their partners. Student Bs buy two returns to Birmingham and fill in the gaps in the first row of the table.

Student Bs then buy two singles to Manchester and fill in the gaps in the second row of the table.

At the end of the activity, ask students to compare tables and check the information is correct. Finally, ask one or two pairs to role-play a conversation for the class.

> **EXTRA PRACTICE AND HOMEWORK**
>
> **Ph** **Vocabulary Plus** 9 Irregular verbs p159 (Instructions p150)
> **9 Review** Exercise 5 SB p77
> **CD-ROM** Lesson 9C
> **Workbook** Lesson 9C p46

9D Who, what, when?

Vocabulary question words
Review questions in the present and the past; big numbers

QUICK REVIEW ●●●

This activity reviews Past Simple *yes/no* questions. Use the examples to remind students that we make Past Simple *yes/no* questions with *Did you ... ?* and that we answer these questions with *Yes, I did.* and *No, I didn't.* Students do the activity in pairs. At the end of the activity, ask each pair to tell the class things that they both did last weekend.

 a) Use the pictures in the quiz to pre-teach the vocabulary in the box. Point out that we say **the** *moon*. Note that *sink* is used as a verb in this lesson (a boat or ship sinks). Also point out *climb* is a verb and a noun. Drill the words with the class, highlighting the silent *b* in *climb* /klaɪm/.

b) Students do the quiz in pairs. You can set a time limit of five minutes.

c) Students check their answers on SB p126. Check answers with the class.
Ask each pair how many questions they got right.

> 1c) 2b) 3a) 4a) 5c) 6a) 7b) 8c)

Help with Vocabulary Question words

 Focus students on the words in **bold** in the quiz. Students do the exercise on their own, then compare answers in pairs. Check answers with the class.

> • **Answers** **What** a thing **When** a time **Where** a place **Why** a reason **How old** age **How many** a number **How much** an amount of money

• Point out that we also use *What time ... ?* to ask about a time:
  A **What time** do you go to bed?
  B *At half past eleven.*
• Highlight that we usually answer *Why ... ?* questions with *Because ...* :
  A *Why are you tired?*
  B *Because I got up at 5 a.m.*
• Use sentence 7 to highlight that we often use a noun after *How many*: **How many yellow cabs** are there in New York City?
• Note that the difference between *What* and *Which* is dealt with in **face2face** Elementary. We suggest you don't point out the difference here.

 Put students into pairs, student A and student B. Student As turn to SB p86 and student Bs turn to SB p92. Check they are all looking at the correct exercise.

a) Pre-teach *spend (money) on something* (food, clothes, CDs, etc.).

Students work on their own and choose the correct words.

Check the answers with the class. Only check the question words so that students don't hear the questions they are about to be asked. Note that the answers are the same for student As and student Bs.

> **Student A/Student B**
> 2 Who 3 How old 4 Why 5 Where 6 When
> 7 How many 8 How much

b) Students work in pairs and take turns to ask and answer the questions in **a)**. Encourage students to ask more follow-up questions if possible.

Ask a few students to tell the class one or two things they found out about their partner.

4 a) Students work on their own and write four questions, using the question words in **2**. These questions can be in the Present Simple or the Past Simple.

b) Put students into new pairs. If possible, ask students to work with someone they don't know very well. Students then take turns to ask their questions.

c) Finally, ask students to tell the class two things they found out about their partner.

— EXTRA IDEA —
- Students work in pairs and write four questions to ask you. Allow students to ask you the questions and try to give honest answers if possible!

— EXTRA PRACTICE AND HOMEWORK —
Ph Class Activity 9D Money, money, money!
p143–p144 (Instructions p110)
CD-ROM Lesson 9D
Workbook Lesson 9D p47
Workbook Reading and Writing Portfolio 9 p68
Progress Test 9 p173

Help with Sounds /l/ and /r/

1 a) Focus students on the phonemes /l/ and /r/, the pictures and the words.

R9.15 Play the recording. Students listen to the sounds and the words. Point out that *l* in *leave* is pronounced with a /l/ sound and *rr* in *arrive* is pronounced with a /r/ sound.

b) P Play the recording again. Students listen and practise. If students are having problems, help them with the mouth position for each sound.

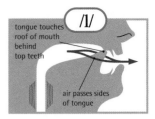
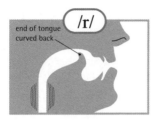

Point out that we make the /l/ sound by touching the roof of the mouth behind the top teeth with the tongue, so that the air passes either side of the tongue. Also highlight that /l/ is a voiced sound (there is vibration in the throat).

We make the /r/ sound by pointing the tip of the tongue upwards and backwards, but the tongue does not touch the roof of the mouth. There is some contact between the sides of the tongue and the teeth. /r/ is also a voiced sound (there is vibration in the throat).

2 a) R9.16 Focus students on the boxes. Play the recording. Students listen and notice how we say the pink and blue consonants.

b) P Play the recording again. Students listen and practise.

3 a) Tell the class that sometimes we don't say the letter *r* in standard British English, particularly after certain vowel sounds like /ə/ and /ɔː/, or at the end of a word. Highlight that we always pronounce *rr* (*double r*). Also point out that in standard American English the letter *r* is always pronounced.

Focus students on the examples in the box. Point out that we say the *r* in *friend*, but not the *r* in *first*. Students do the exercise on their own or in pairs.

b) R9.17 P Play the recording. Students listen and check their answers.

Play the recording again. Students listen and practise.

✗	✓	✗	✓	✗	✗	✓
doctor	green	morning	radio	sport	park	right
✗	✓	✗	✓	✓	✓
theatre	fruit	start	tomorrow	great	terrible

9 Review

See p29 for ideas on how to use this section.

1a) train, taxi, boat, bike, plane, bus, motorbike

2a) left, watched, had, started, bought, played, went
regular watched, started, played

2b) 2 left 3 started 4 had 5 bought 6 went 7 watched
8 played

3a) rent a car, stay in a hotel, take photos, go swimming
go for a walk, go to the beach, stay with friends, go sightseeing

4a) 1 Did you get up early today? 2 What did you do last Sunday? 3 Did you go shopping last weekend? 4 What did you have for breakfast today?

5a) 2 tickets 3 next 4 There's 5 platform 6 Platform 7 arrive

Progress Portfolio

See p29 for ideas on how to use this section.

10 My future

Student's Book p78–p85

10A Life changes

Vocabulary future plans; future time phrases
Grammar *be going to*: positive and negative
Review question words

QUICK REVIEW ●●●

This activity reviews questions words and question forms. Write these question words on the board: *Who, What, When, Where, Why, How old, How many, How much*. Students do the first part of the activity on their own. Put students into pairs. Students take turns to ask their questions. Encourage them to ask follow-up questions if possible. At the end of the activity, ask a few students to tell the class one thing they found out about their partner.

Future plans

1 a) Focus students on the diagram and highlight the example *start*. Point out that we can say *start school, start university* or *start a new job*.

Students do the exercise on their own or in pairs before checking in Language Summary 10 **V10.1** SB p118. Check answers with the class.

Point out that in this lesson, *start/leave school or university* are used to mean 'start or finish our education at that place', rather than the time that people begin classes or leave the building as part of their daily routine. Also highlight that we say *start school*, etc. not ~~*start the school*~~, etc.

Point out the difference between *start a new job* and *look for a new job*.

Also highlight that we say **do** *a (computer) course/an exam*, not ~~**make** *a (computer) course/an exam*~~. Elicit other types of course people do, for example, *do an English course, do a film course*, etc. Note that we can also say *take an exam*.

Check that students understand the difference between *get engaged* and *get married*.

Establish that *move house* means 'go and live in a different house or flat', and that we say *move house* not ~~*move a house*~~ or ~~*move flat*~~.

Point out that we also say *look for **a** house/**a** flat* not ~~*look for house/flat*~~.

Highlight that we can also say *move to* + city or country: *move to London, move to the USA*, etc.

> **leave** school or university/your job
> **do** a (computer) course/an exam
> **move** house/to another city or country
> **get** engaged/married
> **look for** a house or a flat/a (new) job

b) **R10.1** **P** Play the recording. Students listen and practise. Note that each phrase is said separately on the recording (*start school, start university*, etc.). Highlight the pronunciation of *university* /ˌjuːnɪˈvɜːsəti/, *course* /kɔːs/ and *engaged* /ɪnˈɡeɪdʒd/. Repeat the drill if necessary, pausing after each phrase for students to repeat individually.

c) Students do the activity in pairs, as shown in the speech bubbles. Remind students that we can sometimes use more than one verb with some nouns (*start school, leave school*, etc.).

A world language

2 a) Focus students on the photos of the four people and the texts. Tell the class that these people all study English in different parts of the world.

R10.2 Play the recording. Students listen, read and decide where each person studies English. Students compare answers in pairs. Check answers with the class.

If students ask you the meaning of *'m/'re/is going to* in the texts, you can simply say that these sentences are about the future and that students are going to study *be going to* later in the lesson.

> **Sabrina** studies English at school. **Carmen** studies English online. **Luca** studies English at university. **Wing Yu** studies English at a language school in London.

b) Students do the exercise on their own.

c) Students compare answers in pairs. Check answers with the class.

> 2 Sabrina 3 Wing Yu 4 Carmen
> 5 Sabrina 6 Wing Yu 7 Luca

> ─ EXTRA IDEA ─
> ● Put students into pairs, student A and student B. Student As read the texts about Sabrina and Carmen and underline all the phrases from **1a)** they can find. Student Bs do the same for the texts about Luca and Wing Yu. Students compare answers with their partners.

Help with Grammar *be going to:*
positive and negative

 3 a)–b) Focus students on the bullet point. Point out that we use *be going to* + verb to talk about future plans. You can use the sentences in **2b)** to help students understand what we mean by 'a future plan'.

Note that while there are various different ways to express the future in English, we feel that *be going to* is the most useful for Starter students and is most likely to be correct in the majority of situations, particularly when talking about plans for the future.

Students do the exercises on their own or in pairs. Early finishers can check in **G10.1** SB p119. While students are working, draw the table from **3a)** on the board. Check answers with the class.

- Focus students on the table on the board. Elicit which words in sentences 1 and 2 in **3b)** go in each column and complete the table (see the table in **G10.1** SB p119).
- Ask students when the people decided to do these things, 'now' or 'before now' (before now).
- Ask students which sentences are negative (*We **aren't** going to stay here.* and *I'm **not** going to start university this year.*).
- Highlight the word order: subject + *be* (+ *not*) + *going to* + verb + ...
- Point out that *be* changes according to the subject and whether the sentence is positive or negative:
  (+) *I'm, you're, he's, she's, it's, we're, they're*
  (−) *I'm not, you aren't, he/she/it isn't, we/they aren't.*
  Note that we can also use the alternative negative forms *you're not, he's not,* etc.
- Also highlight that with the verb *go* we usually say *I'm going to the cinema.* not *I'm going to go to the cinema.*, but that both sentences are correct.

 4 Focus students on the example. Highlight the sentence stress and the weak form of *to* /tə/.

R10.3 **P** Play the recording. Students listen and practise the sentences in **3**. Check students copy the sentence stress and the weak form of *to* correctly. Play the recording again, pausing after each sentence for students to practise individually.

5 a) Students do the exercise on their own.

b) Students compare answers in pairs, then match the sentences to the people in the photos. Check answers with the class.

Point out that we write *Our sons are ...* in question **1b)**, not *Our sons're ...* , as *are* comes after a noun (*sons*).

1b) are going to look for (Carmen) **2a)** aren't / 're not going to have **2b)** isn't / 's not going to leave (Luca) **3a)** 's going to stay **3b)** 're going to visit (Wing Yu) **4a)** 'm going to do **4b)** 'm not going to look for (Sabrina)

Future time phrases

 6 a) Students do the exercise on their own before checking in pairs. Check answers with the class.

Point out that we say *tonight* not ~~this night~~, and that we can say *tomorrow morning, tomorrow afternoon, tomorrow evening* and *tomorrow night*.

Highlight that we use *next* in these phrases: *next weekend, next week, next month, next year.*

Point out that we also use *in* with months (*in December,* etc.) and years (*in 2025,* etc.) to refer to the future. We can also use *next* with months (*next June,* etc.) and days (*next Monday,* etc.).

Highlight that we also use *on* with days (*on Monday,* etc.) to refer to the future.

Tell students that it is very common to use a future time phrase in sentences or questions with *be going to.*

2e)
3f)
4d)
5c)
6a)

b) Students do the activity on their own, as shown in the example. While students are working, monitor and check their sentences for accuracy.

c) Students work in pairs and take turns to tell each other their sentences. Encourage students to give more information if possible.

Ask each student to tell the class one of their sentences.

Get ready ... Get it right!

 7 Students do the exercise on their own. Tell students to write phrases, as in the example, not complete sentences. Students should write six things in total, one for each time phrase (*after class, tomorrow evening,* etc.).

 8 a) Put students into groups of three or four. Students tell each other their plans, using their phrases from **7**. Students make a note of any plans that are the same for more than one student in the group.

b) Finally, ask students to tell the class about their group's plans, as shown in the speech bubble.

EXTRA IDEA

- Students write about their future plans, and those of their family and friends, for homework.

EXTRA PRACTICE AND HOMEWORK

10 Review Exercises 1 and 2 SB p84
CD-ROM Lesson 10A
Workbook Lesson 10A p48

10B What are you going to do?

Vocabulary phrases with *have, watch, go, go to*
Grammar *be going to*: questions and short answers
Review future plans; *be going to*: positive and negative

Phrases with *have, watch, go, go to*

 a) Focus students on the four ovals and highlight the verbs *have, watch, go* and *go to* in each oval.

Students do the exercise on their own or in pairs, then check their answers in **V10.3** SB p118.

Check answers with the class. Point out the difference between *have a party* (it's your party) and *go to a party* (it's another person's party). Also point out that we don't say ~~make a party~~.

Highlight *the* in these phrases: *watch **the** news, go to **the** cinema* and *go to **the** gym*.

You can also tell the class that we say *the news* to refer to what is happening in the world and a type of TV or radio programme. Also point out that *the news* takes a singular verb: *The news **is** on at ten o'clock.*

Establish that we usually use *go* with verb+*ing* forms: *go shop**ping**, go swim**ming**, go run**ning**,* etc.

You can also point out the double letters in the verb+*ing* forms: *sho**pp**ing, swi**mm**ing, ru**nn**ing.* Note that this is because the verbs *shop, swim* and *run* end in consonant + vowel + consonant (see **V7.2** SB p112).

> **have** coffee with friends, a party
> **watch** TV, the news, sport on TV
> **go** shopping, swimming, running
> **go to** the cinema, the gym, a party

b) **R10.4** **P** Play the recording. Students listen and practise. Repeat the drill if necessary, pausing after each phrase for students to repeat individually.

c) Students do the exercise in pairs.

While students are working, draw a table with four columns on the board. Write *have, watch, go* and *go to* at the top of each column.

Elicit students' ideas and write correct phrases in the appropriate column on the board for other students to copy. Encourage students to record collocations such as these as fixed phrases in their notebooks.

> **Possible answers**
> **have** breakfast, lunch, children, a brother, a sister, a car, a computer
> **watch** a DVD, a video, a TV programme, a soap opera, a horror film, football, tennis
> **go** sightseeing, home, on holiday, for a walk, skiing, out with friends
> **go to** a concert, the theatre, a museum, the beach, work, school, university, bed

--- **EXTRA IDEA** ---

- Write the phrases (but not the verbs) from the **Possible answers** box above in random order on a handout. Give each student a copy of the handout. Students work in pairs and decide which verb goes with each word or phrase. Check answers on the board as in **1c)**.

 a) Students do the exercise on their own. Students can use phrases from **1a)** or those in the table on the board.

b) Students do the exercise in pairs. Ask each student to tell the class one of their true sentences.

A new start

 a) Focus students on the photo on SB p81. Ask students where Darla, Liam and Wesley are (in a café or bar). **R10.5** Play the recording (SB p125). Students listen and decide what Darla, Liam and Wesley are going to do on Saturday.

Check the answer with the class. (They're going to have dinner together in a restaurant.)

b) Give students time to read questions 1–6. Play the recording again. Students listen and answer the questions. Students compare answers in pairs.

Check answers with the class.

> 1 She's going to move to Australia next month.
> 2 He's going to work for a travel company.
> 3 Yes, she is.
> 4 They're going to live in Darla and her husband's flat in London.
> 5 No, they aren't.
> 6 He's going to (go to) the cinema.

Help with Grammar *be going to:* questions and short answers

 a)–c) Students do the exercises on their own or in pairs. Early finishers can check their answers in G10.2 SB p119. ✍ While students are working, draw the table from **4a)** on the board.

Check answers with the class.

- **a)–b)** Focus students on the table on the board. Elicit which words in questions 1 and 2 in **4b)** go in each column and complete the table (see the table in G10.2 SB p119).
- Highlight the word order in *Wh-* questions with *be going to:* question word + *be* + subject + *going to* + verb + ...
- Check students understand that *When's* = *When is* and *What's* = *What is*.

- **c) yes/no questions** Is, Are, Are
  short answers am, isn't, are, aren't
- Use the questions in the first column to highlight that the word order in *yes/no* questions with *be going to* is the same as for *Wh-* questions, but without the question word.
- Highlight that we only use a form of the verb *be* in the short answers, not *going to.*
- Also point out that the short answers are the same as for *yes/no* questions with the verb *be* (*Are you British?*, *Is she a doctor?*, etc.).
- Remind students that we can also say *No, you're not.*, *No, he's not.*, etc.

--- EXTRA IDEA ---
- Ask students to look at R10.5, SB p125. Play the recording again. Students listen, read and underline all the questions with *be going to.* Students can then compare answers in pairs.

 a) Students do the exercise on their own.

b) R10.6 Play the recording (SB p125). Students listen and check their answers. Check answers with the class.

P Focus students on the example. Highlight the sentence stress and the weak form of *to* /tə/. Play the recording again. Students listen and practise.

Alternatively, ask students to turn to R10.6, SB p125, where the stress in the questions is marked. Play the recording again. Students listen, read and copy the sentence stress as shown in the Student's Book.

2 What are you going to do after class?
3 When are you going to do your homework?
4 What time are you going to get up tomorrow?
5 Where are you going to have dinner tomorrow evening?
6 Where are you going to go on holiday next year?

c) Students do the activity in pairs. Remind students to make notes on their partner's answers before they begin.

d) Put students into new pairs. Students take turns to talk about their partner in **5c)**.

Ask students to tell the class two things they found out about their partner in **5c)**.

Get ready ... Get it right!

 Focus students on the prompts and go through the example with the class.

Students do the exercise on their own.

If necessary, check and drill the questions with the class. Also remind students that for questions with *go*, we can say *Are you going to go shopping on Saturday?* or *Are you going shopping on Saturday?* and that both questions are correct. Also point out the alternative questions *Are you going to have a party next weekend?* and *Are you going to go to a party next weekend?*.

Are you going to watch TV tonight?
Are you going to (go to) the cinema this week?
Are you going to have coffee with friends after class?
Are you going (to go) swimming or running next weekend?
Are you going to (go to) the gym next week?
Are you going to have/go to a party next weekend?
Are you going to have dinner with friends on Saturday evening?

7 a) Students move around the room and ask their questions from **6**, or ask as many people as they can sitting near them. When they find a student who answers *yes*, they write the person's name next to the question. Students then ask one follow-up question, as shown in the speech bubbles. Students should try and find a different person who answers *yes* for each question.

b) Finally, ask students to tell the class about one student's plans.

--- EXTRA IDEA ---
- When students have finished **7a)**, put them into pairs. Students take turns to tell each other what they have found out about other students' plans.

--- EXTRA PRACTICE AND HOMEWORK ---

Ph **Class Activity** 10B Guess your partner's future p145 (Instructions p111)

Ph **Vocabulary Plus** 10 The weather p160 (Instructions p150)

10 Review Exercises 3 and 4 SB p84

CD-ROM Lesson 10B

Workbook Lesson 10B p49

10C Good luck!

How do you feel?

1 **a)** Focus students on pictures 1–8. Students do the exercise on their own or in pairs, then check their answers in **V10.4** SB p118. Check answers with the class.

Point out that the opposite of *happy* is *sad* or *unhappy*.

Use the **TIP!** to highlight that we use the verbs *be* or *feel* with these adjectives: *I'm excited.* = *I **feel** excited.*, etc.

Depending on your students' first language, you may want to point out that *excited* is a positive adjective, and that we feel excited before something good or interesting happens (a holiday, a party, a concert, etc.). We feel *nervous* /ˈnɜːvəs/ before something we are worried about or don't want to do (an exam, speaking in public, a driving test, etc.).

You can also point out that the woman in picture 5 is *bored* because the man is *boring* (which students learned in lesson 8A). However, we suggest that you don't focus on the difference between -*ed* and -*ing* adjectives too much at this level.

With a strong class you can also teach *thirsty* /ˈθɜːsti/ and *frightened* /ˈfraɪtənd/. Note that *frightened* is a synonym of *scared*.

> 1 happy 2 sad 3 excited 4 angry
> 5 bored 6 hungry 7 tired 8 scared

b) **R10.7** **P** Play the recording. Students listen and practise. Alternatively, model and drill the words yourself. Highlight the difference in pronunciation between *hungry* /ˈhʌŋgri/ and *angry* /ˈæŋgri/. Also point out that *scared* /skeəd/ is one syllable, not two. Repeat the drill if necessary.

c) Focus students on the speech bubbles and highlight the use of *Who's ... ?* in the question. Students do the activity in pairs.

2 **a)** Check students remember *always, usually, sometimes* and *never*. Drill these words with the class if necessary.
Students do the exercise on their own.

b) Students work in pairs and take turns to say their sentences to each other. You can also ask students to tick any sentences that are the same.

Ask students to tell the class one or two things about their partner.

See you soon!

3 **a)** Focus students on photos A–C. Students do the exercise on their own.
Check answers with the class.

> 1B 2C 3A

b) **R10.8** Play the recording. Students listen and choose the correct words. Play the recording again if necessary.

c) Students compare answers in pairs. Check answers with the class.

> 2 holiday
> 3 two
> 4 course
> 5 September
> 6 job
> 7 exam
> 8 day

Real World Saying goodbye and good luck

4 **a)** Students do the exercise on their own, then check answers in pairs.
Check answers with the class.

- **Answers** Have a good (**holiday**)! Thanks a **lot**. See you (in **September**). Yes, **see** you. Good luck with your (**exam**). Thanks very **much**.
- Highlight the preposition in *Good luck **with** your exam.* and tell students we can also say *Good luck **in** your exam*.
- Check students understand that *Thanks a lot.* and *Thanks very much.* mean the same.

b) Students do the exercise on their own or in pairs. Early finishers can check answers in **RW10.1** SB p119. Check answers with the class.

- **Answers** Have a good **journey/day/weekend/ birthday/time**! See you **in two weeks/next month/on Monday**. Good luck with your **new job/English test/new school**.
- Check students remember *journey* and remind them that *a journey* is in one direction only. You can compare this to *a trip*, which is when you travel to a place and come back again. You can also teach the phrase *Have a good trip!*.
- You can also teach the phrase *Good luck with your driving test.*

5 R10.9 P Play the recording (SB p125). Students listen and practise the sentences in **4**. Highlight the /ɜː/ sounds in *journey* /ˈdʒɜːni/ and *birthday* /ˈbɜːθdeɪ/, which students studied in the Help with Sounds section in unit 8. Also encourage students to copy the interested intonation on the recording. Repeat the drill if necessary.

You can ask students to turn to R10.9, SB p125, where the stress is marked on all phrases. Play the recording again. Students listen, read and copy the stress as shown in the Student's Book.

6 a) Students do the exercise on their own, then compare answers in pairs.

b) R10.10 Play the recording (SB p125). Students listen and check their answers. Check answers with the class.

See R10.10 SB p125.

c) Students practise the conversations in pairs. While students are working, monitor and check they are saying the phrases with correct stress and that they sound cheerful and interested.

— EXTRA IDEA —
- R10.10 Before doing **6c)**, play the recording again, pausing after each sentence for students to repeat chorally and individually. Students can then practise the conversations in pairs.

7 a) Students do the exercise on their own. Ask students not to write anything at this stage.

b) Ask students to move around the room and talk about their plans with other students. Remind students to use *I'm going to ...* to talk about their plans, and to respond to other people's plans with phrases from **4** (*Have a good time!*, etc.). Encourage students to have natural conversations and ask questions or give more information as necessary. Alternatively, students can do the activity in groups.

Finally, ask students to tell the class about any interesting or exciting plans they talked about.

— EXTRA IDEAS —
- Introduce or finish the activity in **7** by talking about your own future plans.
- As a non-personalised alternative to the activity in **7**, use **Class Activity** 10C After the course p146 (Instructions p111).

— EXTRA PRACTICE AND HOMEWORK —
Ph **Class Activity** 10C After the course p146 (Instructions p111)
10 Review Exercise 5 SB p84
CD-ROM Lesson 10C
Workbook Lesson 10C p51
Workbook Reading and Writing Portfolio 10 p70
Progress Test 10 p174–p175 (note that this is a two-page test with a listening section)

10 Review

See p29 for ideas on how to use this section.

1 2 ~~married~~ 3 ~~a flat~~ 4 ~~a job~~ 5 ~~school~~ 6 ~~engaged~~

2 2 's going to play 3 'm going to stay 4 aren't/'re not going to eat 5 're going to study 6 isn't/'s not going to get up

3 go to a party, watch sport on TV, go swimming, have dinner with friends, watch the news, go running, go to the gym, watch TV, have coffee with friends, go shopping, go to the cinema

4a) 2 Where **are** you going to be next Sunday?
3 Are you going to **have** coffee with friends next weekend?
4 Are you going to study English **next** month?
5 What are you going **to** do after this class?
6 Are **you** going to have a party on your next birthday?

5a) → happy, angry, excited, hungry, scared
↓ bored, tired, sad

Progress Portfolio

See p29 for ideas on how to use this section.

End of Course Review

- The aim of this activity is to review language that students have learned throughout the course in a fun, student-centred way. The activity takes about 25–40 minutes.

  Pre-teach *a counter, throw a dice, land on a square, move forward/back* and *have a rest.*

  Give students time to read the rules on SB p84 and answer any questions they may have. Alternatively, go through the instructions section by section with the class. If possible, demonstrate how to play the game to the whole class while you go through the instructions. If you have a monolingual class, you can give the instructions in the students' own language.

  To check students have understood, ask what happens when a student lands on a Grammar or Vocabulary square for the first time (he/she answers question 1 only). Ask what happens when a second student lands on the same square (he/she answers question 2). Also check what happens when a third student lands on the square (he/she can stay there without answering a question).

  Put students into groups of four and give a dice and counters to each group (or students can make their own counters).

  Ask a student with a watch in each group to be the time-keeper for the group. He/She should time students when they land on a Talk About square and have to talk about a topic for 15 seconds.

  Students take turns to throw the dice and move around the board.

  If a student thinks another student's answer to a question on a Grammar or Vocabulary square is wrong, he/she can check in the Language Summaries in the Student's Book, or ask you to adjudicate.

  While students are working, monitor and help with any problems.

  The first student to get to FINISH is the winner. Students can continue playing until three students have finished.

  If one group finishes early, ask them to look at all the squares they didn't land on and answer the questions.

1 1 'm, 's 2 's, 're

3 1 men, chairs, sandwiches, people
2 women, watches, parents, children

5 1 See V1.2 SB p100. 2 See V2.1 SB p102.

6 1 What does he do in the evenings?
2 What did you do on Sunday?

8 1 Are there any shops near your flat?
2 What are you going to do tomorrow?

10 1 was, wasn't 2 did, were

12 1 She doesn't like watching TV.
2 We didn't go out last night.

13 1 See V2.2 SB p102. 2 See V6.1 and V6.2 SB p110.

15 1 some 2 shopping

17 1 cold, expensive, beautiful, unfriendly
2 short, interesting, empty, difficult

18 1 Yes, they are. No, they aren't./No, they're not.
2 Yes, she does. No, she doesn't.

20 1 I didn't **go** out, I stayed at home.
2 Karen always **gets** up early.

23 1 **at** the weekend, **at** night, **in** the evening
2 **on** Friday, **at** midday, **in** the morning

25 1 half past seven/seven thirty, five to four/three fifty-five, eight o'clock/eight, (a) quarter past two/two fifteen
2 (a) quarter to seven/six forty-five, twenty past eleven/eleven twenty, twenty-five to five/four thirty-five, half past twelve/twelve thirty

27 1 See V7.5 SB p113.
2 See V4.2 SB p106 and V10.3 SB p118.

29 1 have a party, do a course, get married
2 get engaged, do an exam, have coffee with friends

30 1 bought, travelled, got, met
2 told, came, visited, left

32 1 See V3.4 SB p104, V3.5 SB p104 and V5.3 SB p108.
2 See V9.2 SB p116.

34 1 Where **did you** go last Saturday?
2 What food **does** your sister like?

35 1 go to the cinema, go shopping, play football
2 play tennis, go to concerts, go on holiday

36 1 my, She 2 He, them

38 1 Yes, there is. No, there isn't.
2 Yes, I did./Yes, we did. No, I didn't./No, we didn't.

Photocopiable Materials

Class Activities

Instructions

There are 29 Class Activities worksheets (p112–p146). These worksheets give extra communicative speaking practice of the key language taught in the Student's Book. Each activity matches a lesson in the Student's Book, for example, *1B Where's he from?* matches lesson 1B, etc. There are three activities for units 1–9 and two activities for unit 10.

The Class Activities can be used as extra practice when you have finished the relevant lesson, or as review activities in the next class or later in the course.

Many of the activities involve students working in pairs or groups. When you have an odd number of students, you can:
- ask two students to share a role card or worksheet
- give extra cards to stronger students
- vary the size of the groups.

At this level it is usually advisable to demonstrate the activity to the class before students begin working in pairs or groups.

1B Where's he from? p112

Language

countries; *What's his / her name?*; *Where's he / she from?*

Activity type, when to use and time

Memory game. Use any time after lesson 1B. 10–20 minutes.

Preparation

Photocopy one worksheet for each pair of students. Cut into separate worksheets.

Procedure

- ✍ Write *What's his name?*, *Where's he from?*, *What's her name?*, *Where's she from?* and *I don't know.* on the board. Check students remember the questions by asking the names and countries of students in the class. Teach and drill *I don't know.*

- Put students into pairs. Give a copy of worksheet A to each pair. Tell students that they have two minutes to remember the names and countries of all the people in the picture. Students are not allowed to make notes.

- Collect the worksheets from each pair (or ask students to turn over their worksheets). Give a copy of worksheet B to each pair.

- Students work in the same pairs. They take turns to point at a person on the worksheet and ask their partner the person's name and country, using the questions on the board. Demonstrate this activity before they begin by holding up a copy of worksheet B, pointing to a person on the worksheet and asking the class to tell you the person's name and country.

- Students continue working in pairs until they have asked about all the people on the worksheet. If they are finding it hard to remember the information, collect in worksheet B and give out worksheet A again. Allow the class one minute to look at worksheet A again, then collect the worksheets and redistribute worksheet B.

- Finally, check the name and country of each person on worksheet B with the whole class.

1C Real names p113

Language

first names and surnames; the alphabet; *How do you spell that?*

Activity type, when to use and time

Information gap. Use any time after lesson 1C. 15–20 minutes.

Preparation

Photocopy one worksheet for each pair of students. Cut into separate worksheets.

Procedure

- Pre-teach *real name*, for example by showing the class a photo of the singer Sting or writing his name on the board, and asking the class if they think this is his real name. (His real name is Gordon Sumner.)

- Put students into pairs, A and B. Give each student a copy of the appropriate worksheet. Students are not allowed to look at their partner's worksheet.

- If you have a monolingual class, you can discuss where the people are from and what they do (see answer key).

- ✍ Write *Number 1. What's his real name?*, *Number 2. What's her real name?*, *His/Her first name's ...* , *His/Her surname's ...* , *How do you spell that?* and *Can you repeat that, please?* on the board. Drill these sentences with the class if necessary.

- Students take turns to ask their partner the real names of four people on their worksheets, using the questions on the board. Student A asks about people 1, 3, 5 and 7. Student B asks about people 2, 4, 6 and 8. Students must spell difficult names to each other. They are not allowed to copy them from their partner's worksheet.

- Students compare worksheets and check spelling.

Bono is the singer of the Irish rock band U2 and a well-known anti-poverty campaigner. **Elle Macpherson** is an Australian model, actress and businesswoman. **Nicolas Cage** is an American actor and the nephew of film director Francis Ford Coppola. **Winona Ryder** is an American actress. **Stevie Wonder** is an American singer and songwriter. **Elton John** is a British singer and songwriter. **Demi Moore** is an American actress. **Fatboy Slim** is a British DJ and record producer.

1D Pictures and words p114

Language

people; things; plurals

Activity type, when to use and time

Pelmanism. Use any time after lesson 1D. 10–20 minutes.

Preparation

Photocopy one worksheet for each group of three students. Cut into sets. Shuffle each set.

Procedure

- Put students into groups of three. Give each group a set of cards. Ask them to spread the cards out **face-down** on the table in front of them, with the small cards on the left and the big cards on the right.
- Students take turns to turn over one small card and one big card. If a student thinks that the two cards match, he/she must say and spell the plural form of the word. If the two cards match and plural form is correct, the student keeps the pair of cards and has another turn. If the student thinks that the two cards don't match, he/she puts both cards back on the table face-down **in exactly the same place**.
- If a student thinks that another student's cards don't match or that the plural is not correct, he/she can challenge him/her. If students can't agree, they can ask you to adjudicate. If the cards don't match or the plural form is incorrect, the student puts the cards back and the turn passes to the next student.
- Demonstrate the activity to the whole class before students begin working in groups.
- The activity continues until all the cards are matched up. The student who collects the most cards is the winner.
- If a group finishes early, students can take turns to test each other on the words by holding up a small card and asking the other students to say the word and its plural form.

2B New identities p115

Language

be (singular): *Wh-* questions; jobs; countries

Activity type, when to use and time

Mingle role play. Use any time after lesson 2B. 15–25 minutes.

Preparation

Photocopy one worksheet for every ten students in the class. Cut into separate role cards.

Procedure

- Give each student a role card. If you have more than ten students in the class, give out duplicate role cards. If you are using more than one set of cards, try to give the first role card to a female student and the duplicate role card to a male student. Students are not allowed to look at each other's cards.
- Tell students that the information on their role card is their new identity. Point out that the names with a ♂ sign are for male students and those with a ♀ sign are for female students.
- Students look at the pictures on their cards and complete the words for the country and the job. Monitor and check that students have written the correct words. Give students time to memorise their new name, country and job.
- Students move around the room and introduce themselves to each other. Before they begin, tell students that they must try to remember other people's names, countries and jobs, but they are not allowed to write anything down. If students are not able to leave their seats, they should talk to as many students sitting near them as they can.
- Encourage students to use the following language during this stage of the activity: *Hello / Hi, my name's (Bob).*, *What's your name?*, *Nice to meet you.*, *You too.*, *Where are you from?*, *I'm from (the UK).*, *What's your job?*, *I'm a (taxi driver).* 🖊 If necessary, write this language on the board before students begin the activity.
- When students have finished, put them into pairs. Students take turns to ask their partner about the other students in the room. Encourage students to use these questions and answers when working in pairs: *What's his / her name?*, *Where's he / she from?*, *What's his / her job?*, *He's / She's a (teacher).*, *I don't know.* 🖊 If necessary, write this language on the board during the mingle stage of the activity.
- Finally, ask each student to tell the class about another student's new identity.

2C The nine2five Employment Agency p116

Language

personal information questions

Activity type, when to use and time

Information gap.
Procedure A: use in place of exercise 9a) in lesson 2C.
Procedure B: use any time after lesson 2C. 10–20 minutes.

Preparation

Procedures A and B: photocopy one worksheet for each pair of students. Cut into separate worksheets.

Procedure A

This procedure is suitable for classes where the students know each other well, or classes where you feel it is inappropriate for students to reveal their personal details to each other.

- After the class has done exercise 8 in lesson 2C (SB p19), put students into pairs, A and B. Give each student a copy of the appropriate worksheet. Students are not allowed to look at each other's worksheets.
- Tell students that they now live in London and that their new personal information is on form 1 on their worksheets. Note that Sam and Alex are names for men and women in English, so both worksheets can be used by male and female students.

- Students take turns to interview each other, using the personal information questions with *you* from exercise 7 in lesson 2C. Students answer the questions using the information on their form, not their real personal details. The interviewers can either fill in form 2 on the worksheet or the form in the Student's Book. Before students begin, remind them of the questions *How do you spell that?* and *Can you repeat that, please?*.

- When students have finished, they compare forms and check their spelling.

Procedure B

This procedure provides practice of personal information questions with *his* and *her*.

- ✄ Draw a blank nine2five Employment Agency form on the board and elicit the following questions with *he, she, his* and *her*: *What's his / her first name?, What's his / her surname?, Is he / she married?, What's his / her nationality?, What's his / her address?, What's his / her mobile number?, What's his / her email address?*. Drill these questions with the class.

- Put students into pairs, A and B. Give each student a copy of the appropriate worksheet. Students are not allowed to look at each other's worksheets.

- Tell the class that Sam (form 1 on worksheet A) is a man and Alex (form 1 on worksheet B) is a woman. Student A in each pair asks his/her partner about Alex and writes the personal information in form 2 on his/her worksheet, using the questions on the board. Before students begin, remind them of the questions *How do you spell that?* and *Can you repeat that, please?*.

- When student A has completed his/her form, student B asks his/her partner about Sam and writes the personal information in form 2 in his/her worksheet.

- When students have finished, they compare forms and check their spelling.

2D Hear a number, say a number p117

Language

numbers 0–100

Activity type, when to use and time

Hear/Say activity. Use any time after lesson 2D. 10–15 minutes.

Preparation

Photocopy one worksheet for every three students. Cut into separate worksheets.

Procedure

- Put students into groups of three, A, B and C. Give each student a copy of the appropriate worksheet. If you have extra students, have one or two groups of four and ask two students to share one worksheet.

- Explain that students must listen to the numbers that the other two students in the group say. If the number is in the HEAR column on their worksheet, they must say the number next to it in the SAY column.

- Students do the activity in their groups. Student A in each group starts by saying *forty-one*. Student B hears *forty-one* and says *fifteen*. Student C hears *fifteen* and says *fifty*, etc. The activity continues until the students reach FINISH. Students should cross out numbers on their worksheets when they hear or say them.

- Demonstrate this activity by doing the first five numbers with the whole class before asking students to work in their groups.

3A Where are they? p118

Language

be (plural): questions and short answers; adjectives (1)

Activity type, when to use and time

Information gap. Use any time after lesson 3A. 15–25 minutes.

Preparation

Photocopy one worksheet for each pair of students. Cut into separate worksheets.

Procedure

- Put students into pairs, A and B. Give each student a copy of the appropriate worksheet. Students are not allowed to look at their partner's worksheet.

- Focus students on the prompts in the first column on their worksheets. ✄ Elicit the following questions about Tom and Alice and write them on the board: *Where are Tom and Alice from?, How old are they?, What are their jobs?, Are they married?, Where are they now?, Are they in a new hotel?, Are the rooms very big?, Are the restaurants cheap?*. Drill the questions with the class.

- Students work with their partners and take turns to ask questions about the four couples. Student A starts by asking all the questions about Tom and Alice, then Student B asks all the questions about Paco and Ana. Remind students to use correct short answers (*Yes, they are.* and *No, they aren't.*) when answering *yes / no* questions. Students write the answers on their worksheets. Before students begin, remind them of the questions *How do you spell that?* and *Can you repeat that, please?*.

- When students have finished, they compare answers with their partner and check their spelling.

3B Barry and Wendy's family p119–p120

Language

family; possessive *'s*; jobs; *How old … ?*

Activity type, when to use and time

Information gap. Use any time after lesson 3B. 15–25 minutes.

Preparation

Photocopy one student A worksheet and one student B worksheet for each pair of students.

Procedure

- Pre-teach *a writer* and *a footballer*.

- Put students into pairs, A and B. Give each student a copy of the appropriate worksheet. Students are not allowed to look at each other's worksheets.

- Tell students that their worksheet has some names, jobs and ages of ten people in the same family. Students must ask their partner questions to complete the information about each person in the family.

- ✍ Elicit the questions for 1–7 from the whole class and write them on the board: 1 *What's Barry's job?* 2 *How old is he?* 3 *What's his wife's name?* 4 *What's Wendy's / her job?* 5 *How old is she?* 6 *What's their daughter's name?* 7 *What's her husband's name?*. Drill these questions with the class.

- Students work with their partners and take turns to ask questions about the people on their worksheet **in number order**. Students write the information on their worksheets.

- When students have finished, they compare answers and check their spelling.

3D From start to finish p121

Language

Review of lessons 1A–3D

Activity type, when to use and time

Board game. Use any time after lesson 3D. 20–30 minutes.

Preparation

Photocopy one board for each group of three or four students. You also need a dice for each group and a counter for each student (or students can make their own counters).

Procedure

- Put the class into groups of three or four. Give each group a copy of the board, a dice and counters.

- Check students understand these squares on the board: START, FINISH, THROW AGAIN, MOVE FORWARD TWO / THREE SQUARES, MOVE BACK TWO / THREE SQUARES.

- Students take turns to throw the dice and move around the board. When a student lands on a square, he/she must answer the question correctly in order to stay on the square. If a student can't answer the question correctly, he/she must move back to his/her previous square.

- If a student thinks another student's answer is wrong, they can check in the Language Summaries in the Student's Book or ask you to adjudicate. If the answer is wrong, the student must move back to his/her previous square.

- If a student lands on a square where the question has already been answered, he/she must answer the question again to show that he/she has been listening!

- The game ends when one student reaches the FINISH square. If some groups finish early, they can go through the squares in number order and take turns to answer the questions again.

---

1 five, fourteen, forty, sixty-three, ninety-nine 2 Brazilian, Spanish, American 4 I**'m not** from the UK. He **isn't** Russian. / He**'s not** Russian. They **aren't** students. / They**'re not** students. 5 **What's** your name? **Where's** he from? **How** old are they? 6 See V2.2 SB p102. 8 women, girls, babies, children 9 Yes, I am., Yes, he is., Yes, they are. 10 **an** apple, **a** book, **a** pencil, **an** iPod 11 A Ben, **this** is Carol. B Hello, Carol. Nice to **meet** you. C You **too**. 12 See SB p26. 13 See V3.3 SB p104. 15 three pounds seventy-five, fifty p/pence, sixty-four dollars, eight euros fifty, ninety-nine cents 16 China, Germany, Russia 17 It's an old car. Their dog is very nice. 18 cold, big, expensive 20 Where **are** you from? What's your job? **Are** you married? 21 See V1.3 SB p100. 22 No, she isn't. / No, she's not., No, I'm not., No, they aren't. / No, they're not. 24 unfriendly, old, beautiful 25 See V3.4 and V3.5 SB p104. 26 eleven, twenty-seven, fifty-four, seventy-six, a/one hundred 27 Is she **your** sister? This is **our** cat. Are **they** actors? 29 things, people, watches, men 30 Italian, Turkish, Mexican 31 She **isn't** German. / She**'s not** German. We **aren't** from Egypt. / We**'re not** from Egypt. You **aren't** a teacher. / You**'re not** a teacher. 32 oh two oh, seven six double nine, three oh double seven; oh one six double seven, three double two oh nine eight; c dot page at webmail dot com 33 **How** do you spell that? **Can** you repeat that, please? What does 'bag' **mean**?

4B Find two people p122

Language

free time activities; Present Simple (*I, you, we, they*): *yes* / *no* questions and short answers

Activity type, when to use and time

'Find someone who' activity. Use any time after lesson 4B. 15–25 minutes.

Preparation

Photocopy one worksheet for each student.

Procedure

- Give a copy of the worksheet to each student. Students work on their own and choose the correct verb for each phrase in the first column. Check answers with the whole class (see answer key).

- Elicit questions with *Do you ... ?* for prompts 1–12. Drill these questions if necessary.

- Tell students that they must find two people in the class who answer *yes* to each question and write their names in the second and third columns on their worksheets. Demonstrate this stage of the activity by asking individual students question 1 and writing the names of two students who answer *yes* on your copy of the worksheet.

- Students move around the room and ask each other questions 1–12. When they find a student who answers *yes* to a question, they should write his/her name in the second or third column on the worksheet. They must try to find two students who answer *yes* to each question.

- When they have finished, ask students to tick all the questions for which two students have answered *yes*.
- Put students into pairs. Students take turns to make sentences about each pair of students on their worksheets, for example, *Marco and Carolina watch TV a lot.*, *Yi Ling and Henri go to rock concerts.*, etc. Students should not make sentences about any prompt for which only one student has answered *yes*, as these would require the *he/she* form of the Present Simple.
- Finally, ask students to tell the class two things they have found out about their class.

> 1 watch 2 go to 3 play 4 go 5 eat 6 go 7 play 8 go to 9 work 10 live 11 have 12 like

4C Shopping bingo p123

Language
things to buy; food and drink (2)

Activity type, when to use and time
Bingo game. Use any time after lesson 4C. 10–15 minutes.

Preparation
Photocopy one worksheet for every four students. Cut into separate bingo cards.

Procedure
- Give one bingo card to each student in random order. Try to avoid giving the same bingo card to two students sitting next to each other.
- Give students a few minutes to check they know the words for all the pictures on their cards. Students can check in **V3.5** SB p104 and **V4.3** SB p106. Students are not allowed to write the words on their cards. While they are working, monitor and help students with any words they don't know.
- Read out these things to the whole class **in this order**: *a magazine, cheese, a map, orange juice, coffee, fruit, a birthday card, milk, batteries, tissues, tea, chewing gum, eggs, a box of chocolates, vegetables, sweets, sugar, a postcard, bread, a newspaper, fish, meat* (student C card is completed), *rice* (student B card is completed), *pasta* (student A and student D cards are completed).
- When students hear the word for a picture on their card, they put a cross through it.
- When a student has crossed out all the pictures on his/her card, he/she shouts *Bingo!*. The first student to shout *Bingo!* wins the game.
- If necessary, check students understand how to play the game before you begin. Note that students must cross out **all** the pictures on the card, not just one line or one column.
- If you want to play the game again, distribute new cards and read out the words in random order.

4D Time dominoes p124

Language
telling the time

Activity type, when to use and time
Dominoes. Use any time after lesson 4D. 15–20 minutes.

Preparation
Photocopy one set of dominoes for each pair of students. Cut into sets and shuffle each set.

Procedure
- Put students into pairs. Give one set of dominoes to each pair. Students share out the dominoes equally. Students are not allowed to look at their partner's dominoes. If you have an extra student, have one group of three and ask them to share one set of dominoes equally between them.
- One student puts a domino on the table. His/Her partner puts another domino at either end of the first domino so that the time in words on one domino matches the digital clock on the other domino. Students must say the time aloud when they match the dominoes. Students then continue taking turns to put dominoes at either end of the domino chain.
- If a student thinks that a pair of dominoes doesn't match, he/she can challenge his/her partner. If the match is incorrect, the student must take back his/her domino and the turn passes to his/her partner. If students can't agree, they should ask you to adjudicate.
- If a student can't put down a domino, the turn passes to his/her partner. The game continues until one student has put down all his/her dominoes, or until neither student can make a correct match. The student who finishes first, or who has fewer dominoes remaining, is the winner.

5A My partner's life p125

Language
Present Simple (*he, she, it*): positive and negative; daily routines; free time activities

Activity type, when to use and time
Personalised information gap. Use any time after lesson 5A. 15–25 minutes.

Preparation
Photocopy one worksheet for each pair of students. Cut into separate worksheets.

Procedure
- Pre-teach **in** *the week* and **at** *the weekend*. Highlight the prepositions in these phrases.
- Put students into pairs, A and B. If possible, put students with someone they don't know very well. Give each student a copy of the appropriate worksheet. Students write their partner's name at the top of their worksheet. Students are not allowed to look at their partner's worksheet.

- ✍ Write sentence 1 from student A's worksheet on the board and elicit the two possible ways to complete the sentence by using the positive or negative Present Simple form of the verb in brackets (*gets up* or *doesn't get up*).

- Students work on their own and make sentences they think are true about their partner by putting the verb in brackets into the correct positive or negative form of the Present Simple. Students are not allowed to speak to their partner at this stage of the activity.

- ✍ Focus students on the sentence on the board and elicit the *yes / no* question: *Do you get up before 7.00 in the week?*. Remind students of the short answers *Yes, I do.* and *No, I don't.*

- Students work on their own and prepare *yes / no* questions with *Do you ... ?* for each sentence on their worksheet.

- Students work with their partner and take turns to ask and answer questions. Students put a tick in the second column of their worksheet if their sentence is correct and a cross if their sentence is incorrect. The student with more ticks is the winner.

- Finally, students can work in new pairs and tell their new partner about the person they have just talked to.

5B A writer's week p126–p127

Language

time phrases with *on, in, at*; Present Simple (*he, she, it*): Wh- questions

Activity type, when to use and time

Information gap. Use any time after lesson 5B.
15–25 minutes.

Preparation

Photocopy one student A worksheet and one student B worksheet for each pair of students.

Procedure

- Pre-teach *a writer, at home, a bookshop* and *quiet*.

- Put students into two groups, A and B. Give each student a copy of the appropriate worksheet.

- Focus students on the article on their worksheets. Ask them to look at the heading and the photo and say what the man's name and job is. (Oliver Richardson. He's a writer.)

- Students read the article on their own and choose *on, in* or *at* in time phrases 1–8. Tell the class not to worry about the gaps in the article at this stage. Check the answers with the class (see answer key).

- Students work in pairs with another student **from the same group**. They read the article about Oliver again and complete questions b)–f) at the bottom of their worksheets, as in the example in question a). Check answers if necessary.

- Put students into pairs, with one student from group A and one student from group B in each pair. Students are not allowed to look at each other's worksheets. Students take turns to ask their questions and fill in the gaps in the article. Tell student A to ask the first question.

- When students have finished, they look at their partner's worksheet and check their answers.

> **Prepositions** 2 in 3 at 4 In 5 at 6 at 7 On 8 in
>
> **Student A b)** What time **does** he **get** up in the **week**? **c)** When **does** Ingrid **go** to **work**? **d)** What time **does** Oliver **start work**? **e)** Where **does** he **have lunch**? **f)** What **does** he **do** on Saturday **morning**?
>
> **Student B b)** When **does** he **have breakfast**? **c)** Where **does** Ingrid **work**? **d)** What time **does** Oliver **have lunch**? **e)** What **does** he **do** in the **evening**? **f)** What **does** he **do** on Saturday **afternoon**?

5D Always, sometimes, never p128

Language

frequency adverbs and phrases with *every*; Present Simple

Activity type, when to use and time

Personalised guessing game. Use any time after lesson 5D.
15–25 minutes.

Preparation

Photocopy one worksheet for each student.

Procedure

- Pre-teach *something* and *a TV programme*.

- Give a copy of the worksheet to each student. Tell students to read the prompts in box A and then write eight people, things, places and times in the empty boxes. Point out that students only need to write words or phrases for eight of the twelve prompts. Students should write single words or short phrases, for example, *play tennis, my sister Juliana, cheese*, etc., not complete sentences. They can write their words or phrases in any box they want, but **not** in the same order as the prompts. ✍ Demonstrate this before students begin by drawing eight boxes on the board and writing in your own ideas in random order.

- When students have finished, put them into pairs and ask them to swap worksheets.

- Students work on their own and write eight sentences beginning with *You ...* about their partner at the bottom of their partner's worksheet, based on the people, things, places and times that he/she has written in the boxes. For example, if a student has written *play tennis*, his/her partner could write: *You never play tennis at the weekend.* or *You sometimes play tennis at the weekend.* Students are not allowed to talk to their partners during this stage of the activity. ✍ You can demonstrate this stage of the activity before students begin by eliciting sentences about you for the ideas in the boxes on the board.

- Students work in their pairs and take turns to say their sentences about their partner. Their partner says if the sentences are true or false. Students tick their true sentences. The student with more true sentences is the winner.

- Finally, ask each student to tell the class one or two true things they have found out about their partner.

6B London Road p129–p130

Language

there is / there are; places in a town or city (1) and (2); *a, some, a lot of, any*

Activity type, when to use and time

Spot the difference. Use any time after lesson 6B. 15–25 minutes.

Preparation

Photocopy one student A worksheet and one student B worksheet for each pair of students.

Procedure

- Put students into pairs, A and B. Give each student a copy of the appropriate worksheet.
- Tell the class that there are ten differences between the pictures. Students must work together to find the ten differences by asking questions or saying sentences with *there is / there are*. Students are not allowed to look at each other's worksheets.
- ✏ If necessary, write these prompts on the board before giving out the worksheets: *There's a (café) in my picture.*, *There are two (people) at the bus stop.*, *There are some (cars).*, *Is there a (bank) in your picture?*, *Yes, there is.*, *No, there isn't.*, *Are there any (children)?*, *Yes, there are.*, *No, there aren't.* Model and drill the sentences with the class.
- Students work with their partners and take turns to ask questions or say sentences about their picture. When students find a difference, they should mark it on their picture.
- When students have finished, they compare worksheets and check their differences.
- Finally, ask students to tell the class one difference they have found.

> 1 **A** There's a chemist's. **B** There's a post office. 2 **A** There isn't a cashpoint / an ATM. **B** There's a cashpoint / an ATM. 3 **A** There are a lot of / some people in the café. **B** There aren't any people in the café. 4 **A** There's a theatre. **B** There's a museum. 5 **A** There's a cat. **B** There isn't a cat. 6 **A** There are two women at the bus stop. **B** There are two men at the bus stop. 7 **A** There aren't any children. **B** There are some / four children (near the bank). 8 **A** There's a dog. **B** There are two dogs. 9 **A** There are two cars. **B** There are three cars. 10 **A** There's a bus. **B** There isn't a bus.

6C What's in your bag? p131

Language

things in your bag (1) and (2)

Activity type, when to use and time

Bingo game. Use any time after lesson 6C. 10–15 minutes.

Preparation

Photocopy one worksheet for every four students. Cut into separate bingo cards.

Procedure

- Give one bingo card to each student in random order. Try to avoid giving the same bingo card to two students sitting next to each other. Tell students that each card shows what they have in their bags.
- Give students a few minutes to check they know the words for all the things in the bag on their cards. Students can check in V1.4 SB p100, V1.7 SB p100 and V6.3 SB p110. Students are not allowed to write the words on their cards.
- Read out these things to the whole class **in this order**: *purse, pen, keys, credit card, passport, dictionary, iPod, money, pencil, camera, guide book, wallet, mobile phone, notebook, laptop, map, ID card, umbrella* (student D card is completed), *apple* (student A card is completed), *sandwich* (student C card is completed), *watch* (student B card is completed).
- When students hear the word for something in the bag on their bingo card, they put a cross through it on their card.
- When a student has crossed out all the things in the bag on his/her bingo card, he/she shouts *Bingo!*. The first student to shout *Bingo!* wins the game.
- If you want to play the game again, distribute new cards and read out the words in random order.

6D Review snakes and ladders p132

Language

Review of lessons 4A–6D

Activity type, when to use and time

Board game. Use any time after lesson 6D. 20–30 minutes.

Preparation

Photocopy one board for each group of three students. You also need a dice for each group and a counter for each student (or students can make their own counters).

Procedure

- Put the students into groups of three. If you have extra students, have one or two groups of four. Give each group a copy of the snakes and ladders board, a dice and counters.
- Students take turns to throw the dice and move around the board. When a student lands on a square, he/she must answer the question correctly in order to stay on the square. If a student can't answer the question correctly, he/she must move back to his/her previous square.
- If a student lands on the bottom of a ladder, he/she must answer the question correctly before he/she is allowed to go up it. He/She does not have to answer the question at the top of the ladder. If he/she lands on the head of a snake, he/she must always go down the snake to its tail. He/She does not have to answer the question at the snake's tail.

- If a student thinks another student's answer is wrong, they can check in the Language Summaries in the Student's Book, or ask you to adjudicate. If the answer is wrong, the student must move back to his/her previous square.

- The first student to reach the FINISH square is the winner. If some groups finish early, they can go through the squares in number order and answer the questions in their groups.

1 See **V6.5** SB p110. **2 in** the week, **at** night, **on** Monday
3 See **V4.2** SB p106. 4 half past six / six thirty, quarter to eight / seven forty-five, quarter past three / three fifteen, nine o'clock / nine 5 always, usually, sometimes, not usually, never 6 Monday, Tuesday, Wednesday, Thursday, Friday, Saturday, Sunday 7 Does he like coffee? What music do you like? 8 I don't like football. He doesn't have a car. 9 I never have lunch. He works every day. 10 have breakfast, leave home, go to bed 11 1 minute = 60 **seconds**, 1 day = 24 **hours**, 1 year = 12 **months** 14 studies, watches, leaves, goes 15 See **V6.1** and **V6.2** SB p110.
16 Yes, there are. / No, there aren't. Yes, there is. / No, there isn't. 18 Can you show me on this map? 20 Yes, I (we) do. / No, I (we) don't. Yes, she does. / No, she doesn't. 22 I live here. She likes it. 23 See **V6.4** SB p110. 24 Are there **any** cafés? There are **some** shops. 26 study languages, have a car, live in a flat 27 See SB p42. **28 in** the morning, **at** midnight, **on** Sunday morning 29 does, finishes, likes, has 30 Where does your son live? Do you have a car? 31 ten past four, five to one, twenty to three, twenty past eleven 33 There isn't a market. There aren't any restaurants.

7A I like dominoes p133

Language

things you like and don't like; *like, love, hate*; object pronouns

Activity type, when to use and time

Dominoes. Use any time after lesson 7A. 15–20 minutes.

Preparation

Photocopy one set of dominoes for each pair of students. Cut into sets and shuffle each set.

Procedure

- Put students into pairs. Give one set of dominoes to each pair. Students share out the dominoes equally. Students are not allowed to look at their partner's dominoes. If you have an extra student, have one group of three and ask them to share one set of dominoes between them.

- Students work with their partners. One student puts a domino on the table. His/Her partner puts another domino at either end of the first domino so that the question and the short answer on the two dominoes match. Students must say the question and answer aloud when they match the dominoes. Students then continue taking turns to put dominoes at either end of the domino chain.

- If a student thinks that a pair of dominoes doesn't match, he/she can challenge his/her partner. If the match is incorrect, the student must take back his/her domino and the turn passes to his/her partner.

- If a student can't put down a domino, the turn passes to his/her partner. The game continues until one student has put down all his/her dominoes, or until neither student can make a correct match. The student who finishes first, or who has fewer dominoes remaining, is the winner.

- If a pair finishes early, students can take turns to ask each other the questions with *you* on the dominoes and answer for themselves.

7B What can the class do? p134

Language

can for ability; abilities

Activity type, when to use and time

Class survey. Use any time after lesson 7B. 10–15 minutes.

Preparation

Procedure A: photocopy one worksheet for every twelve students in the class. Cut into separate cards.

Procedure B: photocopy one worksheet for every four students in the class. Cut into separate cards. Keep each set of cards separate.

Procedure A

This procedure is suitable for smaller classes and for classes where students can move around the room.

- Pre-teach *a musical instrument, a motorbike, metres, backgammon, chess, golf, a horse* and *run* by using photos, board illustrations, mime, examples or translation.

- Give one card to each student. If you have more than twelve students in the class, give out duplicate cards. Tell the class that they must find out the number of students who can do the activity on the card by talking to every person in the class.

- Students work on their own and make a question with *you* to ask other students. Tell students that they make this question with *Can you ...* + the phrase in **bold** on their card. For example, a student with card A should ask *Can you play a musical instrument?*, etc.

- Students move around the room and ask their questions. Students should talk to all the students in the class if possible. Before they begin, tell students to keep a record of how many people say *yes* and *no* to their question on the back of their cards or in their notebooks.

- When they have finished, students complete the sentence on their card by writing a number in the gap. Finally, ask each student to tell the class the result of their survey by reading the sentence from their card. For example, a student with card A might say: *Four students in the class can play a musical instrument.*

Procedure B

This procedure is suitable for larger classes and for classes where students can't move around the room.

- Pre-teach the new vocabulary as in procedure A.

- Put students into groups of four. If you have extra students, have one or two groups of five.

107

- Give each group a set of 12 cards. Ask students to share the cards equally between them.

- Give students time to prepare their questions with *Can you ... ?* as in procedure A.

- Students take turns to ask the other people in the group their questions. Before they begin, tell students to keep a record of how many people say *yes* and *no* to each question on the back of their cards or in their notebooks.

- When they have finished, ask each student to tell the class one or two things they have found out about their group. For example, a student with card A might say: *Four students in our group can play a musical instrument.*

7C It's on the left p135–p136

Language

asking for and giving directions; prepositions of place

Activity type, when to use and time

Information gap. Use any time after lesson 7C. 15–25 minutes.

Preparation

Photocopy one student A worksheet and one student B worksheet for each pair of students.

Procedure

- Put students into pairs, A and B. Give each student a copy of the appropriate worksheet. Students are not allowed to look at each other's worksheets.

- Tell the students that they are at ✳ on the map. Students must ask their partner for directions to places 1–5 in the box at the top of their worksheets. Also explain that the places shaded in grey (the park, the shopping centre, the station and the supermarket) are on both maps.

- ✍ Before they begin, elicit the questions they need to ask for the first place on each worksheet and write them on the board, underlining *the* and *a*: *Excuse me. Where's the cinema?* and *Excuse me. Is there a bank near here?*. Point out that students should use *Where's the ... ?* for places with *the* on their worksheets, and *Is there a ... near here?* for places with *a* on their worksheets.

- ✍ If necessary, write the following prompts on the board to help students during the activity: *Go along this road and turn left / right.*, *That's (New Street).*, *The ... is on the left / right, next to ...* , *The ... is on the left / right, opposite ...* , *It's over there, near the ... .*

- Students work with their partner and take turns to ask directions to the places at the top of their worksheets. Student A asks the first question. Encourage students to refer to the places shaded in grey on both maps if possible. Also remind them to thank their partner each time he/she gives directions. Students are not allowed to look at each other's worksheets at this stage of the activity.

- When a student thinks he/she has identified the correct location, he/she should write the place on the map.

- When students have finished, they compare worksheets and see if they have identified the places correctly.

8A Opposite adjectives p137

Language

adjectives (1) and (2)

Activity type, when to use and time

Pelmanism. Use any time after lesson 8A. 10–20 minutes.

Preparation

Photocopy one worksheet for each group of three students. Cut into sets. Shuffle each set.

Procedure

- Put students into groups of three. Give each group a set of cards. Ask them to spread the cards out **face-down** on the table in front of them, with the small cards on the left and the big cards on the right.

- Students take turns to turn over one small card and one big card. If a student thinks that the adjectives on the two cards are opposites, he/she says a sentence for each adjective. If the student is correct, he/she keeps the pair of cards and has another turn. If the student thinks that the two words are not opposites, he/she puts both cards back on the table face-down **in exactly the same place**.

- If a student thinks that another student's cards aren't a pair of opposite adjectives or one of his/her sentences is incorrect, he/she can challenge him/her. If students can't agree, they can ask you to adjudicate. If the cards aren't a pair of opposite adjectives or one of the sentences is incorrect, the student puts the cards back and the turn passes to the next student.

- The activity continues until all the opposite adjectives are matched up. The student who collects the most cards wins.

- If a group finishes early, students can test each other on the adjectives by taking turns to hold up a card and asking the other students to say the opposite adjective.

8B Were you or weren't you? p138

Language

past time phrases; Past Simple of *be*; *was born / were born*

Activity type, when to use and time

'Find someone who' activity. Use any time after lesson 8B. 15–25 minutes.

Preparation

Photocopy one worksheet for each student.

Procedure

- Teach students how we say *the 1980s* (*the nineteen eighties*). Also check students remember *a bus*, *a train* and *different*.

- Give a copy of the worksheet to each student. Students work on their own and choose the correct word for each time phrase in the first column. Students can compare answers in pairs before you check answers with the whole class (see answer key).

- Elicit questions with *Were you ... ?* for prompts 1–12. Drill these questions if necessary.

- Tell students that they must find one person in the class who answers *yes* to each question and write his/her name in the second column on their worksheets. Demonstrate this stage of the activity by asking individual students question 1 and writing the name of a student who answers *yes* on your copy of the worksheet.

- Students move around the room and ask questions 1–12. When they find a student who answers *yes* to a question, they should write his/her name in the second column on the worksheet. Encourage students to talk to as many people as possible. If students are not able to leave their seats, they should ask as many students sitting near them as they can.

- When they have finished, put students into pairs. Students take turns to tell their partners what they have found out about the class.

- Finally, ask students to tell the class two things they have found out about their class.

1 yesterday 2 last 3 in 4 ago 5 last 6 yesterday 7 ago
8 in 9 last 10 ago 11 yesterday 12 ago

8D Numbers, years and dates p139

Language

big numbers; years; months and dates

Activity type, when to use and time

Hear/Say activity. Use any time after lesson 8D. 10–15 minutes.

Preparation

Photocopy one worksheet for every three students. Cut into separate worksheets.

Procedure

- Put the students into groups of three, A, B and C. Give each student a copy of the appropriate worksheet. If you have extra students, have one or two groups of four and ask two students to share one worksheet.

- Explain that students must listen to the big numbers, years and dates that the other two students in the group say. If the number, year or date is in the HEAR column on their worksheet, they must say the number, year or date next to it in the SAY column.

- Students do the activity in their groups. Student A in each group starts by saying *three hundred and sixty-five*. Student C hears *three hundred and sixty-five* and says *April the first*. Student B hears *April the first* and says *nineteen eighty*, etc. The activity continues until the students reach FINISH. Students should cross out the numbers, years or dates on their worksheets when they hear or say them.

- Demonstrate this activity by doing the first five numbers, years or dates together with the whole class before asking students to work in their groups.

9A My past p140

Language

Past Simple: positive (regular and irregular verbs)

Activity type, when to use and time

Personalised guessing game. Use any time after lesson 9A. 15–25 minutes.

Preparation

Photocopy one worksheet for each student.

Procedure

- Give a copy of the worksheet to each student. Tell students to read the prompts in the box and then write eight people, things, places and times in the circles. Point out that students only need to write words or phrases for eight of the twelve prompts. Students should write single words or short phrases, for example, *Madrid, my friend Antonio, a new suit*, etc., not complete sentences. They can write their words or phrases in any circle they want, but **not** in the same order as the prompts. Demonstrate this before students begin by drawing eight circles on the board and writing in your own ideas in random order.

- When students have finished, put them into pairs and ask them to swap worksheets.

- Students work on their own and write eight sentences beginning with *I think you ...* about their partner at the bottom of their partner's worksheet, based on the people, things, places and times that he/she has written in the circles. For example, if a student has written *Madrid*, his/her partner could write: *I think you lived in Madrid when you were ten.*, *I think you went to Madrid last year.* or *I think you visited Madrid last month.* Students are not allowed to talk to their partners during this stage of the activity. You can demonstrate this stage of the activity before students begin by eliciting sentences about you for the ideas in the circles on the board.

- Students work in their pairs and take turns to say their sentences about their partner. Their partner says if the sentences are true or false. Students tick their true sentences. The student with more true sentences is the winner.

- Finally, ask each student to tell the class one or two true things they have found out about their partner.

9B What did you do on holiday? p141–p142

Language

Past Simple: questions and short answers; holiday activities

Activity type, when to use and time

'Find someone who' activity with role cards. Use any time after lesson 9B. 20–30 minutes.

Preparation

Photocopy one worksheet for each student and one set of role cards for every ten students in the class. Cut the role cards into separate cards. Shuffle the cards.

Procedure

- Pre-teach *the American President, a dolphin, an elephant, kilometres, a footballer, a football team* and *Africa*. Check students remember *a tuk-tuk* and *cycle* (verb). Also check students know where *Dubai, Cairo, Cape Town* and *New Zealand* are. Drill the new vocabulary with the class.

- Give each student a copy of the worksheet. Tell the class that they all went on holiday last year and that sentences 1–10 on the worksheet give information about the students' holidays. Focus students on sentences 1 and 2. ✍ Elicit the correct *yes / no* questions for each sentence and write them on the board (see answer key).

- Students work on their own or in pairs and write questions for sentences 3–10. ✍ While students are working, write these prompts on the board:
  A *Where did you go on holiday last year?*
  B *I went to ... .*
  A *Did you ... ?*
  B *Yes, I did. / No, I didn't.*

- Check questions 3–10 with the class (see answer key). Drill the questions with the class if necessary.

- Give each student a role card. If you have more than ten students in the class, distribute extra role cards. If you have fewer than ten students in the class, do not give out the extra role cards. Give students a few minutes to read their role cards and ask you any questions. Students are not allowed to look at each other's role cards.

- Tell the class they must find out which student in the class did the things on the worksheet. ✍ Focus students on the prompts on the board and drill the question *Where did you go on holiday last year?* with the class. Point out that students must ask where each person went on holiday before they ask any *Did you ... ?* questions on their worksheet.

- Students then move around the room and ask each other questions about where they went and what they did on their last holiday. When students find someone who did one of the things on the worksheet, they write his/her name in the second column. Encourage students to continue talking about their holidays for as long as possible, using the information on the cards and their own ideas. The aim of the activity is to find one person who did each of the things on the worksheet.

- When students have finished, they can compare answers and discuss what else they have found out about each person's holiday.

- Finally, ask each student to tell the class about one person's holiday.

1 Did you meet the American President? 2 Did you buy a tuk-tuk? 3 Did you stay in a seven-star hotel? 4 Did you go swimming with dolphins? 5 Did you cycle 13,000 kilometres? 6 Did you play football with some famous footballers? 7 Did you travel around on an elephant? 8 Did you take 15,000 photos? 9 Did you stay with Daniel Craig? 10 Did you walk 4,000 miles?

9D Money, money, money! p143–p144

Language
Review of lessons 7A–9D

Activity type, when to use and time
Board game. Use any time after lesson 9D. 20–30 minutes.

Preparation
Photocopy one board, one set of Vocabulary cards and one set of Grammar cards for each group of four students. Cut the Vocabulary cards and Grammar cards into sets. Shuffle each set. Each group also needs a dice and counters (or students can make their own counters).

Procedure

- Put students into groups of four. Give each group a copy of the board, a set of Vocabulary cards and a set of Grammar cards, dice and counters. Students place the cards face-down in two separate piles in the middle of the board.

- Tell students that they collect £1,000 every time they pass the START square. Students will need a pen and paper to keep a record of how much money they have during the game. Tell students that they all start with £2,000. Check students understand what to do if they land on the *Throw again!, Miss a turn!* or *Double your money!* squares.

- Students take turns to throw the dice and move around the board. When a student lands on a Vocabulary card or Grammar card square, he/she turns over the top card of the appropriate pile and reads out the question to the group. He/She must then answer the question himself/herself. If he/she answers it correctly, he/she wins the amount of money on the square. He/She then puts the card at the bottom of the appropriate pile.

- Students always stay on the square they landed on, whether they win money or not. Students don't have to leave the game if they have a negative amount of money. They should keep playing to try and win more money.

- The game can continue as long as you wish. Alternatively, students can continue playing until they've answered all the Grammar and Vocabulary cards. The student with the most money when the game finishes is the winner.

Vocabulary cards 1 visiting new places, shopping for clothes, watching sport on TV 2 nineteen eighty-seven, nineteen ninety-eight, two thousand and nine, twenty twelve (two thousand and twelve) 3 short, right, easy, interesting 4 What, Who, Where, When / What time 5 **How much** was your car? **How many** people were there? 6 **take** photos, **rent** a car, **stay** in a hotel 7 See V8.3 SB p114. 8 ride a bike, play the guitar, speak German 9 unhappy, terrible / awful, empty, old 10 **go to** the beach, **go** sightseeing, **go for** a walk 11 eight hundred and fifty thousand, seven million, fifteen thousand, four hundred and fifty 12 Students' answers 13 April the first, May the second, June the third, July the fourth 14 chat to friends, book a holiday, download music 15 See V9.1 SB p116. 16 It's **in** New Road. It's **on** the right. It's **near** the café.

Grammar cards 1 had, travelled, went, left 2 Yes, I (we) can. / No, I (we) can't. Yes, he was. / No, he wasn't. 3 Where did you go on holiday last year? 4 Where **were** you? Where **did** you go? 5 We **weren't** late for class. I **didn't watch** TV last night. 6 **They** know **us**. **She** loves **him**. 7 came, got, wrote, told 8 Yes, he did. / No, he didn't. Yes, she can. / No, she can't. 9 What did your children do yesterday afternoon? 10 What **did** he say? What **was** his name? 11 Students' answers 12 I **was born** in 1987. Where **was** Jo born? 13 Yes, I (we) did. / No, I (we) didn't. Yes, they were. / No, they weren't. 14 bought, met, gave, took 15 I **wasn't** at home at 2 p.m. He **didn't go** to the beach. 16 I bought a new computer four months ago.

10B Guess your partner's future p145

Language

be going to: *yes / no* questions and short answers; phrases with *have, watch, go, go to*

Activity type, when to use and time

Personalised information gap. Use any time after lesson 10B. 15–25 minutes.

Preparation

Photocopy one worksheet for each pair of students. Cut into separate worksheets.

Procedure

- Put students into pairs, A and B. If possible, put students with someone they don't know very well. Give each student a copy of the appropriate worksheet. Students are not allowed to look at their partner's worksheet.

- ✏️ Write sentence 1 from student A's worksheet on the board and elicit the correct verb (*have*). Highlight the collocation *have a party*.

- Students work on their own and choose the correct verb in each sentence on their worksheets. Tell students to look at the word or phrase in **bold** after the verbs when making their choice. Check answers with the class (see answer key). Note that the answers are the same for both the student A and student B worksheets.

- Students work on their own and make sentences they think are true about their partner by filling in the gaps with *'s going to* or *isn't going to*. Students are not allowed to speak to their partner at this stage of the activity.

- ✏️ Focus students on the sentence on the board and elicit the *yes / no* question with *you*: *Are you going to have a party on your next birthday?*. Remind students of the short answers *Yes, I am.* and *No, I'm not.*

- Students work on their own and prepare *yes / no* questions with *Are you ... ?* for each sentence on their worksheet.

- Students work with their partner and take turns to ask and answer questions. Students put a tick in the second column of their worksheet if their sentence is correct and a cross if their sentence is incorrect. The student with more ticks is the winner.

- Finally, students can work in new pairs and tell their new partner about the person they have just talked to.

1 have 2 go to 3 watch 4 go 5 move 6 stay 7 get 8 go to

10C After the course p146

Language

saying goodbye and good luck; *be going to*; question words

Activity type, when to use and time

Mingle. Use instead of exercise 7 in lesson 10C, or any time after lesson 10C. 15–20 minutes.

Preparation

Photocopy one worksheet for every twelve students in the class. Cut into separate role cards.

Procedure

- Pre-teach *a club* (a place where you go to listen to music and dance), *sail* (v), *a journalist* /ˈdʒɜːnəlɪst/, *dive* (go into the sea with scuba equipment to look at fish) and *Nepal* /nəˈpɔːl/. Drill the new vocabulary with the class.

- Give each student a role card. If you have more than twelve students, give out duplicate role cards. Students are not allowed to look at each other's cards.

- Tell students that the role cards say what they are going to do at the end of their English course. Ask students to read the information and write their own answers for the question words in **bold** on their cards in the gaps. Be prepared to help any students with ideas during this stage of the activity. Give students time to read their role cards and ask them to remember the information.

- ✏️ Write these prompts on the board: *What are you going to do after the course?*, *I'm going to ... , Have a good ... , See you ... , Good luck with your ...* . Drill the question with the class and elicit some phrases for saying goodbye and good luck (*Have a good holiday!, See you in December., Good luck with your exam.*, etc.).

- Students move around the room asking each other about their plans after the course. Encourage students to continue each conversation by asking more questions and telling each other the information on their cards. Also tell students to finish each conversation with a phrase beginning with *Have a good ... , See you ...* or *Good luck with your ...* . If students are not able to leave their seats, they should ask as many students sitting near them as they can.

- Before they begin, tell the class that they must remember other students' plans. Students are not allowed to make notes at any time during the activity.

- When students have finished, put them into pairs or small groups. Students work in their pairs/groups and see how much they can remember about the plans of the other students in the class.

- Finally, ask each student to tell the class about another student's plans for after the course.

1B Where's he from? countries; *What's his / her name?*; *Where's he / she from?*

Worksheet A

Shane, Australia

Alberto, Mexico

Layla, Egypt

Tanya, Russia

Isabel, Spain

Helga, Germany

Silvia, Brazil

Ping, China

Scott, the USA

Enzo, Italy

Diana, the UK

Osman, Turkey

Worksheet B

Instructions p100

1C Real names first names and surnames; the alphabet; *How do you spell that?*

Student A

1 *Bono* real name	**2** *Elle Macpherson* real name **Eleanor Gow**	**3** *Nicolas Cage* real name	**4** *Winona Ryder* real name **Winona Horowitz**
5 *Stevie Wonder* real name	**6** *Elton John* real name **Reginald Dwight**	**7** *Demi Moore* real name	**8** *Fatboy Slim* real name **Norman Cook**

Student B

1 *Bono* real name **Paul Hewson**	**2** *Elle Macpherson* real name	**3** *Nicolas Cage* real name **Nicolas Coppola**	**4** *Winona Ryder* real name ....
5 *Stevie Wonder* real name **Steveland Judkins**	**6** *Elton John* real name	**7** *Demi Moore* real name **Demetria Guynes**	**8** *Fatboy Slim* real name ....

Instructions p100   © Cambridge University Press 2009   face2face Starter Photocopiable

CLASS ACTIVITIES: PHOTOCOPIABLE

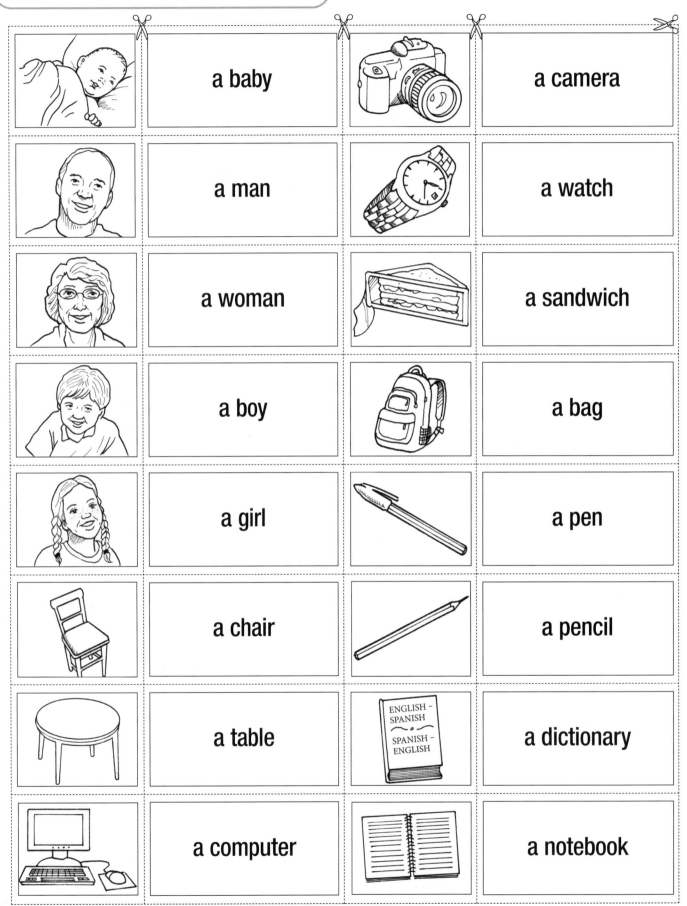

a baby

a camera

a man

a watch

a woman

a sandwich

a boy

a bag

a girl

a pen

a chair

a pencil

a table

a dictionary

ENGLISH – SPANISH
SPANISH – ENGLISH

a computer

a notebook

 Instructions p101

2B New identities *be* (singular): *Wh-* questions; jobs; countries

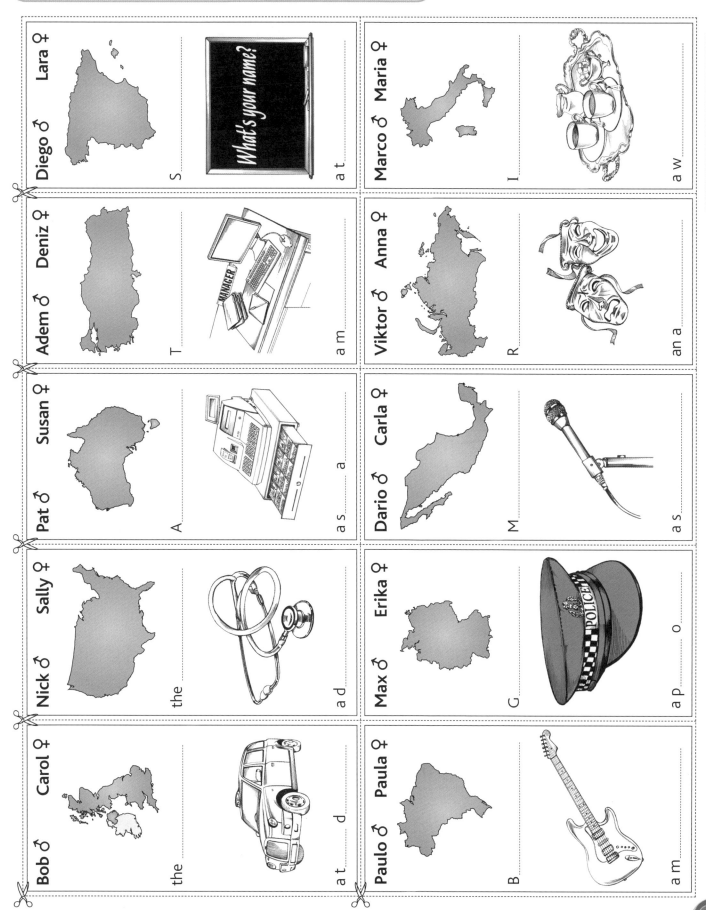

Diego ♂ Lara ♀	Marco ♂ Maria ♀
S	I
What's your name?	
a t	a w
Adem ♂ Deniz ♀	Viktor ♂ Anna ♀
T	R
a m	an a
Pat ♂ Susan ♀	Dario ♂ Carla ♀
A	M
a s a	a s
Nick ♂ Sally ♀	Max ♂ Erika ♀
the	G
a d	a p o
Bob ♂ Carol ♀	Paulo ♂ Paula ♀
the	B
a t d	a m

Student A

✂

Student B

2D Hear a number, say a number numbers 0–100

Student A

HEAR	SAY
43 ⇨	86
96 ⇨	8
START ⇨	41
35 ⇨	16
29 ⇨	18
0 ⇨	11
17 ⇨	30
71 ⇨	7
50 ⇨	82
12 ⇨	90

Student B

HEAR	SAY
90 ⇨	19
16 ⇨	100
86 ⇨	12
77 ⇨	60
41 ⇨	15
64 ⇨	17
18 ⇨	80
68 ⇨	0
8 ⇨	23
30 ⇨	70

Student C

HEAR	SAY
11 ⇨	29
15 ⇨	50
7 ⇨	64
100 ⇨	68
82 ⇨	77
70 ⇨	96
60 ⇨	35
23 ⇨	FINISH
80 ⇨	43
19 ⇨	71

Student A

	Tom and Alice	Paco and Ana	Ian and Sonia	Kang and Li
PERSONAL DETAILS				
country?	....	Spanish	....	Chinese
age?	Tom: .... Alice:	Paco: 57 Ana: 54	Ian: .... Sonia:	Kang: 35 Li: 32
job?	Tom: .... Alice:	Paco: taxi driver Ana: manager	Ian: .... Sonia:	Kang: doctor Li: actress
married?		✓		✓
NOW				
where?	....	Buenos Aires	....	Athens
in a new hotel?		✗		✗
rooms very big?		✓		✗
restaurants cheap?		✓		✓

Student B

	Tom and Alice	Paco and Ana	Ian and Sonia	Kang and Li
PERSONAL DETAILS				
country?	Australian	....	British	....
age?	Tom: 34 Alice: 31	Paco: .... Ana:	Ian: 24 Sonia: 26	Kang: .... Li: ....
job?	Tom: waiter Alice: teacher	Paco: .... Ana:	Ian: musician Sonia: waitress	Kang: .... Li: ....
married?	✓		✓	
NOW				
where?	Tokyo	....	Melbourne	....
in a new hotel?	✓		✗	
rooms very big?	✗		✓	
restaurants cheap?	✗		✓	

Instructions p102

3B Barry and Wendy's family family; possessive 's; jobs; How old ... ?

Student A

Instructions p102

3D From start to finish Review of lessons 1A–3D

30 Say the nationalities.
Italy, Turkey, Mexico

31 Make these sentences negative (–).
She's German.
We're from Egypt.
You're a teacher.

32 Say the phone numbers and the email address.
020 7699 3077
01677 322098
c.page@webmail.com

33 Say the missing words.
.... do you spell that?
.... you repeat that, please?
What does 'bag' .... ?

FINISH

29 Say and spell the plurals.
thing, person, watch, man

28 MOVE BACK THREE SQUARES

27 Choose the correct words.
Is she *you* / *your* sister?
This is *we* / *our* cat.
Are *they* / *their* actors?

26 Say these numbers.
11, 27, 54, 76, 100

25 Say ten words for food and drink.

20 Say the missing words.
Where .... you from?
What .... your job?
.... you married?

21 Say the alphabet.

22 Say the negative (–) short answers.
Is she British?
Are you a student?
Are they from Cairo?

23 THROW AGAIN!

24 Say the opposites.
friendly, new, ugly

19 MOVE FORWARD TWO SQUARES

18 Say the opposites.
hot, small, cheap

17 Make sentences with these words.
an / It's / car / old .
dog / is / nice / very / Their .

16 Say the countries.
Chinese, German, Russian

15 Say the prices.
£3.75, 50p, $64.00, €8.50, 99c

10 Choose *a* or *an*.
.... apple, ... book,
.... pencil, ... iPod

11 Say the missing words.
A Ben, ... is Carol.
B Hello, Carol. Nice to .... you.
C You ....

12 Say five things on the Café Pronto price list.

13 Say eight family words. Are they male (♂), female (♀) or both (♀♂)?

14 MOVE BACK TWO SQUARES

9 Say the positive (+) short answers.
Are you a student?
Is he from Mexico?
Are they friendly?

8 Say and spell the plurals.
woman, girl, baby, child

7 THROW AGAIN!

6 Say six jobs.

5 Say the missing words.
.... your name?
.... he from?
.... old are they?

START

1 Say these numbers.
5, 14, 40, 63, 99

2 Say the nationalities.
Brazil, Spain, the USA

3 MOVE FORWARD THREE SQUARES

4 Make these sentences negative (–).
I'm from the UK.
He's Russian.
They're students.

© Cambridge University Press 2009   face2face Starter Photocopiable

4B Find two people free time activities; Present Simple (*I*, *you*, *we*, *they*): *yes / no* questions and short answers

Do you ...	Name	Name
1 *live / play / watch* TV a lot?		
2 *go / go to / work* rock concerts?		
3 *play / go / live* tennis?		
4 *like / go / have* out with friends after class?		
5 *watch / eat / like* out a lot?		
6 *go / go to / have* shopping with friends?		
7 *work / live / play* computer games?		
8 *go / go to / watch* the cinema a lot?		
9 *like / work / have* in an office?		
10 *watch / like / live* in a flat?		
11 *have / go / play* a car?		
12 *go / work / like* football?		

4C Shopping bingo things to buy, food and drink (2)

Student A

Student B

Student C

Student D

© Cambridge University Press 2009 face2face Starter Photocopiable

twenty past twelve	2.30	half past two	6.50
ten to seven	7.40	twenty to eight	5.20
twenty past five	1.45	one forty-five	4.00
four o'clock	3.40	twenty to four	9.55
five to ten	2.25	twenty-five past two	1.05
five past one	4.15	four fifteen	10.00
ten o'clock	12.50	ten to one	4.45
quarter to five	9.35	twenty-five to ten	6.30
six thirty	3.15	quarter past three	2.35
twenty-five to three	9.10	ten past nine	6.25
twenty-five past six	0.00	midnight	10.55
five to eleven	8.10	ten past eight	12.20

Instructions p104

5A My partner's life Present Simple (*he*, *she*, *it*): positive and negative; daily routines; free time activities

Student A

My partner's name	✓ or ✗
1 He / She .... before 7.00 in the week. (**get up**)	
2 He / She .... breakfast after 10.30 at the weekend. (**have**)	
3 He / She .... home before 9.00 in the week. (**leave**)	
4 He / She .... dinner after 9.00 at the weekend. (**have**)	
5 He / She .... to bed before 11.30 in the week. (**go**)	
6 He / She .... computer games. (**play**)	
7 He / She .... out in the week. (**eat**)	
8 He / She .... to the cinema a lot. (**go**)	

Student B

My partner's name	✓ or ✗
a) He / She .... after 10.30 at the weekend. (**get up**)	
b) He / She .... breakfast before 8.00 in the week. (**have**)	
c) He / She .... home after 6.30 in the week. (**get**)	
d) He / She .... dinner with his / her family in the week. (**have**)	
e) He / She .... to bed after 11.00 at the weekend. (**go**)	
f) He / She .... tennis. (**play**)	
g) He / She .... TV in the morning. (**watch**)	
h) He / She .... to concerts. (**go**)	

Student A

A week in the life of...

Oliver Richardson, writer

Oliver Richardson writes a)_____
_____ . He lives in London with
his wife, Ingrid, and their seven-year-old
son, Charlie.

Oliver works at home and ¹*on* / *in* / *at*
the week he gets up at b)_____ . He
has breakfast at 7.30 with his family. After
breakfast Charlie goes to school and then
Ingrid goes to work at c)_____ .
She works in a bookshop.

Oliver starts work at d)_____ .
"I like writing ²*on* / *in* / *at* the morning
because it's very quiet at home," he says. He has lunch at 1.30 in e)_____
and he finishes work ³*on* / *in* / *at* 6.30. ⁴*On* / *In* / *At* the evening Oliver watches TV and he goes to
bed ⁵*on* / *in* / *at* midnight.

Oliver doesn't work ⁶*on* / *in* / *at* the weekend. "Saturday and Sunday are family days," he says.
⁷*On* / *In* / *At* Saturday morning he f)_____ with Ingrid, and he goes to the
cinema with his son ⁸*on* / *in* / *at* the afternoon. "I have a very good life," says Oliver.

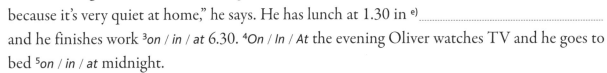

a) What d <u>o e s</u> Oliver w <u>r i t e</u> ?

b) What time d __ __ __ he g __ __ up in the w __ __ __ __ ?

c) When d __ __ __ Ingrid g __ to w __ __ __ __ ?

d) What time d __ __ __ Oliver s __ __ __ __ __ w __ __ __ ?

e) Where d __ __ __ he h __ __ __ __ l __ __ __ __ __ ?

f) What d __ __ __ he d __ on Saturday m __ __ __ __ __ __ ?

Student B

A week in the life of ...

Oliver Richardson, writer

Oliver Richardson writes children's books. He lives in ᵃ⁾_____ with his wife, Ingrid, and their seven-year-old son, Charlie.

Oliver works at home and ¹*on /in/ at* the week he gets up at 7.00. He has breakfast at ᵇ⁾_____ with his family. After breakfast Charlie goes to school and then Ingrid goes to work at 8.30. She works in ᶜ⁾_____ .

Oliver starts work at 8.45. "I like writing ²*on / in / at* the morning because it's very quiet at home," he says. He has lunch at ᵈ⁾_____ in a small café and he finishes work ³*on / in / at* 6.30. ⁴*On / In / At* the evening Oliver ᵉ⁾_____ and he goes to bed ⁵*on / in / at* midnight.

Oliver doesn't work ⁶*on / in / at* the weekend. "Saturday and Sunday are family days," he says. ⁷*On / In / At* Saturday morning he goes shopping with Ingrid, and he ᶠ⁾_____ with his son ⁸*on / in / at* the afternoon. "I have a very good life," says Oliver.

---

a) Where d _o_ _e_ _s_ Oliver l _i_ _v_ _e_ ?

b) When d __ __ __ he h __ __ __ b __ __ __ __ __ __ __ __ ?

c) Where d __ __ __ Ingrid w __ __ __ ?

d) What time d __ __ __ Oliver h __ __ __ l __ __ __ __ __ ?

e) What d __ __ __ he d __ in the e __ __ __ __ __ __ g ?

f) What d __ __ __ he d __ on Saturday a __ __ __ __ __ __ __ __ ?

© Cambridge University Press 2009   **face2face** Starter Photocopiable

5D Always, sometimes, never frequency adverbs and phrases with *every*; Present Simple

A

Write **eight** of these people, things, places and times in the boxes. **Don't** write them in this order.

- a person you email **every week**
- something you **don't usually** eat or drink
- a free time activity you **never** do at the weekend
- a place you go to **every month**
- the time you **usually** get up in the week
- something you eat or drink **every day**
- a person you **sometimes** see at the weekend
- a TV programme you **always** watch
- a place you go to **every week**
- the time you **usually** get up at the weekend
- a TV programme you **never** watch
- a free time activity you **sometimes** do at the weekend

Look at your partner's answers in the boxes. Write eight sentences about your partner. Use ideas from box A.

1 You ....

2 You ....

3 You ....

4 You ....

5 You ....

6 You ....

7 You ....

8 You ....

Instructions p105

Student A

Student B

6C What's in your bag? things in your bag (1) and (2)

Student A

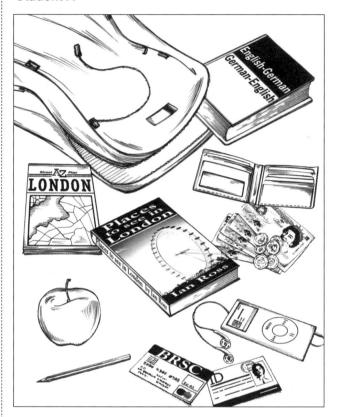

Student B

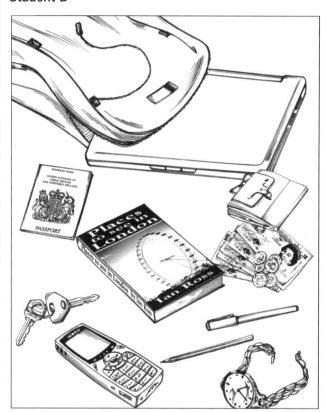

Student C

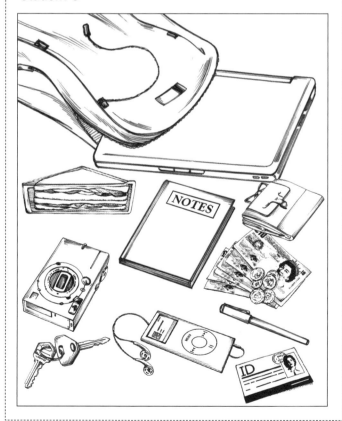

Student D

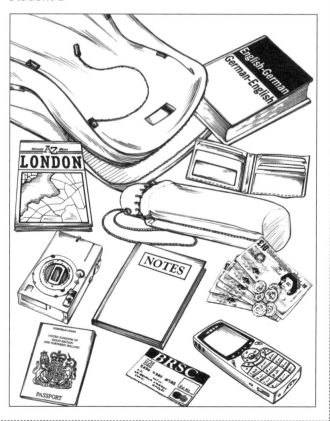

CLASS ACTIVITIES: PHOTOCOPIABLE

30 Make questions.

your / Where / does / son / live ?
Do / a / car / you / have ?

31 Say these times with *past* or *to*.

4.10, 12.55, 2.40, 11.20

32

33 Make these sentences negative (–).

There's a market.
There are some restaurants.

FINISH

29 Spell the *he, she, it* form of these verbs.

do, finish, like, have

28 *On, in* or *at*?

the morning
midnight
Sunday morning

27 Say five things on the menu at the New Moon restaurant.

26 Match the words and phrases.

study   a car
have   in a flat
live   languages

25

20 Say the (+) and (–) short answers.

Do you live here?
Does she have a cat?

21

22 Make these sentences positive (+).

I don't live here.
She doesn't like it.

23 Say eight words for clothes.

24 *Some* or *any*?

Are there ____ cafés?
There are ____ shops.

19 Say three sentences with *favourite* about you.

18 Make a question.

on / map / you / Can / me / this / show ?

17 Say four sentences about your daily routine.

16 Say the (+) and (–) short answers.

Are there any shops?
Is there a bank?

15 Say eight places in a town or city.

10 Match the words and phrases.

have   bed
leave   breakfast
go to   home

11 Fill in the gaps.

1 minute = 60 ____
1 day = 24 ____
1 year = 12 ____

12

13 Say four sentences with *there is / there are* about your town or city.

14 Spell the *he, she, it* form of these verbs.

study, watch, leave, go

9 Make sentences.

have / I / lunch / never .
every / He / works / day .

8 Make these sentences negative (–).

I like football.
He has a car.

7 Make questions.

he / Does / coffee / like ?
What / do / like / you / music ?

6 Say the days of the week.

5 Put these adverbs in order.

usually, never, not usually, sometimes, always

START

1 Say six colours.

2 *On, in* or *at*?

the week
night
Monday

3 Say five free time activities.

4 Say these times in two ways.

6.30, 7.45, 3.15, 9.00

Yes, they love it.	Do you like flying?	No, I hate it.	Does your sister like Kylie Minogue?
Yes, she likes her a lot.	Does your husband like soap operas?	No, he hates them.	Do your parents like visiting new places?
Yes, they do.	Do you like Johnny Depp?	Yes, I love him.	Does your mother like shopping for clothes?
No, she doesn't.	Do your children like vegetables?	No, they hate them.	Do you like animals?
Yes, I love them.	Does your daughter like Madonna?	Yes, she loves her.	Do you like Will Smith?
Yes, I like him a lot.	Do your brothers like playing tennis?	No, they hate it.	Do you like going to the cinema?
Yes, I do.	Does your brother like dancing?	Yes, he loves it.	Do you like Cameron Diaz?
Yes, I like her a lot.	Do your grandchildren like Italian food?	No, they don't.	Do you like horror films?
No, I hate them.	Do you like playing computer games?	No, I don't.	Do your daughters like Daniel Craig?
Yes, they love him.	Does your wife like Chinese food?	Yes, she does.	Do your grandparents like classical music?

CLASS ACTIVITIES: PHOTOCOPIABLE

A _____ students can **play a musical instrument**.

B _____ students can **ride a motorbike**.

C _____ students can **say 'hello' in four languages**.

Hello!

D _____ students can **cook a lasagne**.

E _____ students can **swim a hundred metres**.

F _____ students can **play backgammon**.

G _____ students can **drive**.

H _____ students can **play golf**.

I _____ students can **ride a horse**.

J _____ students can **say 'goodbye' in four languages**.

Goodbye!

K _____ students can **run for twenty minutes**.

L _____ students can **play chess**.

Instructions p107

7C It's on the left asking for and giving directions; prepositions of place

Student A

You are at ✳ on the map. Ask your partner for directions to these places.

1 the cinema   2 a post office   3 the market   4 a restaurant   5 a chemist's

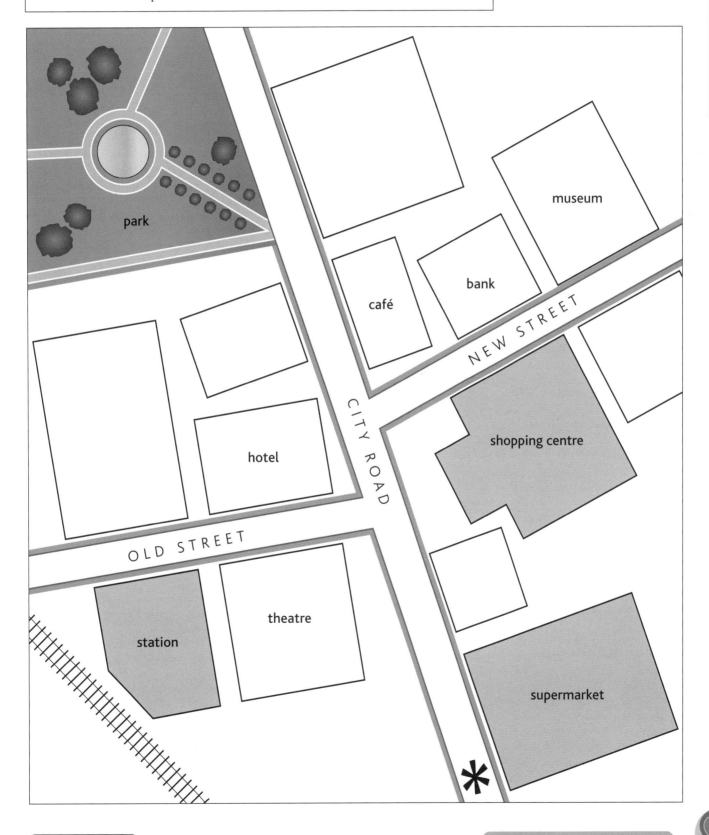

© Cambridge University Press 2009   **face2face** Starter Photocopiable   135

Student B

You are at ✳ on the map. Ask your partner for directions to these places.

1 a bank   2 the theatre   3 the museum   4 a hotel   5 a café

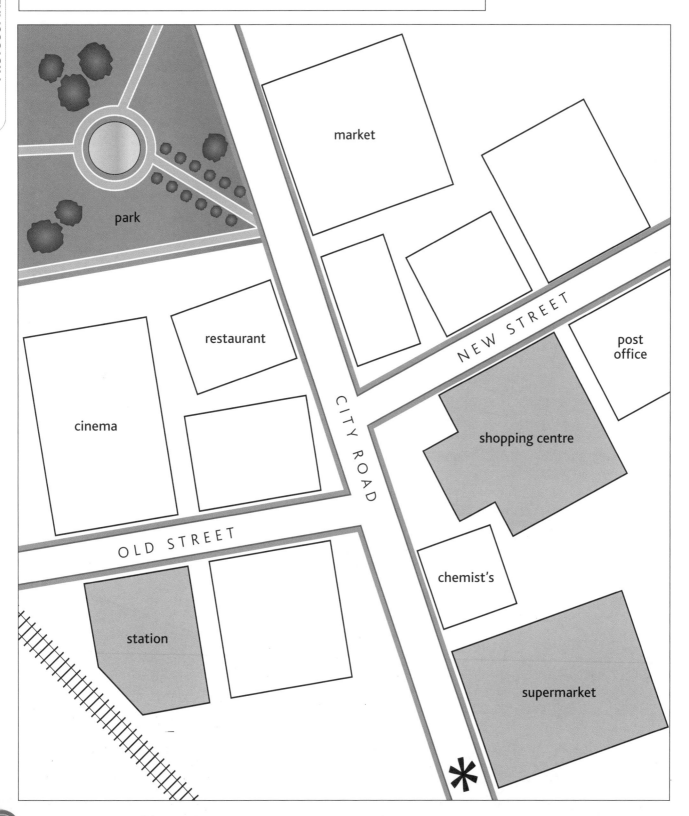

CLASS ACTIVITIES: PHOTOCOPIABLE

boring

  small

easy

 young

   unfriendly

Were you …	NAME
1 … at home *yesterday / last / ago* evening?	
2 … on holiday *yesterday / last / ago* month?	
3 … born *on / in / at* December?	
4 … in this town or city five years *yesterday / last / ago* ?	
5 … with some friends *yesterday / last / ago* Sunday?	
6 … in a restaurant *yesterday / last / ago* evening?	
7 … in this class two months *yesterday / last / ago* ?	
8 … born *on / in / at* the 1980s?	
9 … at work *yesterday / last / ago* Friday?	
10 … on a bus or a train two hours *yesterday / last / ago* ?	
11 … in a café at 10.30 *yesterday / last / ago* morning?	
12 … in a different town or city two weeks *yesterday / last / ago* ?	

Student A

HEAR	SAY
May 17th ⇨	**2009**
December 25th ⇨	6,000,000
2010 ⇨	February 14th
August 19th ⇨	October 8th
750,000 ⇨	**1965**
45,400 ⇨	60,000
February 4th ⇨	**2018**
START ⇨	365
July 2nd ⇨	January 30th
60,000,000 ⇨	November 6th

Student B

HEAR	SAY
1965 ⇨	July 2nd
November 6th ⇨	**1956**
June 20th ⇨	**FINISH**
January 30th ⇨	54,500
16,000 ⇨	February 4th
April 1st ⇨	**1980**
60,000 ⇨	May 17th
March 3rd ⇨	45,400
6,000,000 ⇨	January 13th
September 7th ⇨	570,000

Student C

HEAR	SAY
February 14th ⇨	16,000
2018 ⇨	September 7th
1956 ⇨	March 3rd
October 8th ⇨	60,000,000
365 ⇨	April 1st
January 13th ⇨	750,000
1980 ⇨	December 25th
54,500 ⇨	**2010**
2009 ⇨	June 20th
570,000 ⇨	August 19th

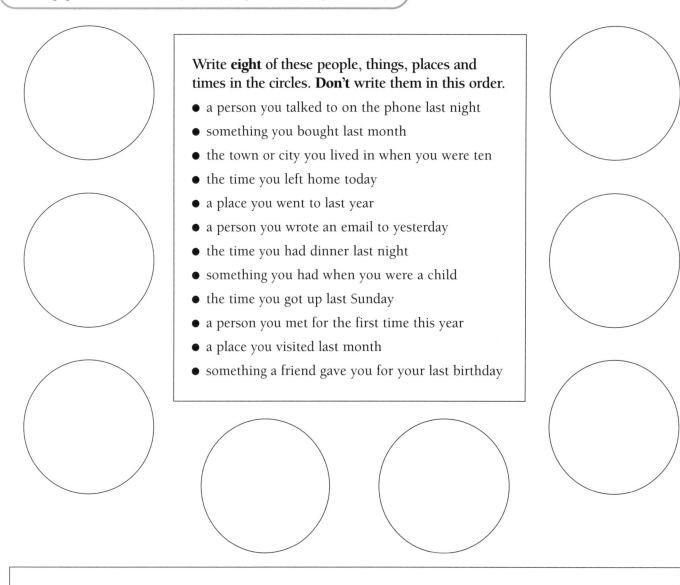

Write **eight** of these people, things, places and times in the circles. **Don't** write them in this order.

- a person you talked to on the phone last night
- something you bought last month
- the town or city you lived in when you were ten
- the time you left home today
- a place you went to last year
- a person you wrote an email to yesterday
- the time you had dinner last night
- something you had when you were a child
- the time you got up last Sunday
- a person you met for the first time this year
- a place you visited last month
- something a friend gave you for your last birthday

Look at your partner's answers in the circles. Write eight sentences about your partner. Use ideas from the box.

1 I think you ....

2 I think you ....

3 I think you ....

4 I think you ....

5 I think you ....

6 I think you ....

7 I think you ....

8 I think you ....

On holiday last year	NAME
1 This person met the American President. **Question:** *Did you* _____ ?	
2 This person bought a tuk-tuk. **Question:** *Did you* _____ ?	
3 This person stayed in a seven-star hotel. **Question:** _____ ?	
4 This person went swimming with dolphins. **Question:** _____ ?	
5 This person cycled 13,000 kilometres. **Question:** _____ ?	
6 This person played football with some famous footballers. **Question:** _____ ?	
7 This person travelled around on an elephant. **Question:** _____ ?	
8 This person took 15,000 photos. **Question:** _____ ?	
9 This person stayed with Daniel Craig. **Question:** _____ ?	
10 This person walked 4,000 miles. **Question:** _____ ?	

   face2face Starter Photocopiable

Role cards

CLASS ACTIVITIES: PHOTOCOPIABLE

STUDENT A

You went on holiday to the USA last year. You stayed with some friends in Washington. On the last day of your holiday you met the American President at a party. You talked to him for ten minutes and he was very friendly.

STUDENT B

You went on holiday to Thailand last year. On the second day of your holiday you bought a yellow tuk-tuk. You travelled around the country in your tuk-tuk for six months and you had a fantastic time!

STUDENT C

You went on holiday to Dubai last year. You stayed in a seven-star hotel called the Burj Al Arab. It was very expensive and the rooms were very big. There were eight restaurants and cafés in the hotel, and the food was amazing!

STUDENT D

You went on holiday to New Zealand last year. You travelled around the country by bus. The scenery was beautiful and you went for a lot of walks. On the last day you went swimming with dolphins. They were very friendly!

STUDENT E

You went on holiday to Africa last year. You cycled from South Africa to Egypt. You travelled 13,000 kilometres and visited 10 countries. You arrived in Cairo 165 days after you left Cape Town and you raised £10,000 for charity.

STUDENT F

You went on holiday to Brazil last year. You stayed in a hotel near the beach in Rio de Janeiro. You went sightseeing every day and you also went swimming a lot. On the last day of your holiday you played football on the beach with the Brazilian football team!

STUDENT G

You went on holiday to India last year. First you went to a friend's wedding in Mumbai. Then you travelled around the country on an elephant called Raja. You went to some fantastic festivals – at one festival there were 2,000 elephants!

STUDENT H

You went on holiday to Australia last year. You stayed with your brother in Sydney and then you rented a motorbike and travelled around the country. You stayed in Australia for eight months and you took 15,000 photos!

STUDENT I

You went on holiday to England last year. You stayed with the actor, Daniel Craig. You and Daniel are friends because your brother was in a James Bond film with him. You also went sightseeing in London and you had a great time.

STUDENT J

You went on holiday to China last year. You were there for nine months. You walked 4,000 miles along the Great Wall of China. It was an amazing journey and you met a lot of friendly people. You also raised £20,000 for charity.

Instructions p109

9D Money, money, money! Review of lessons 7A–9D

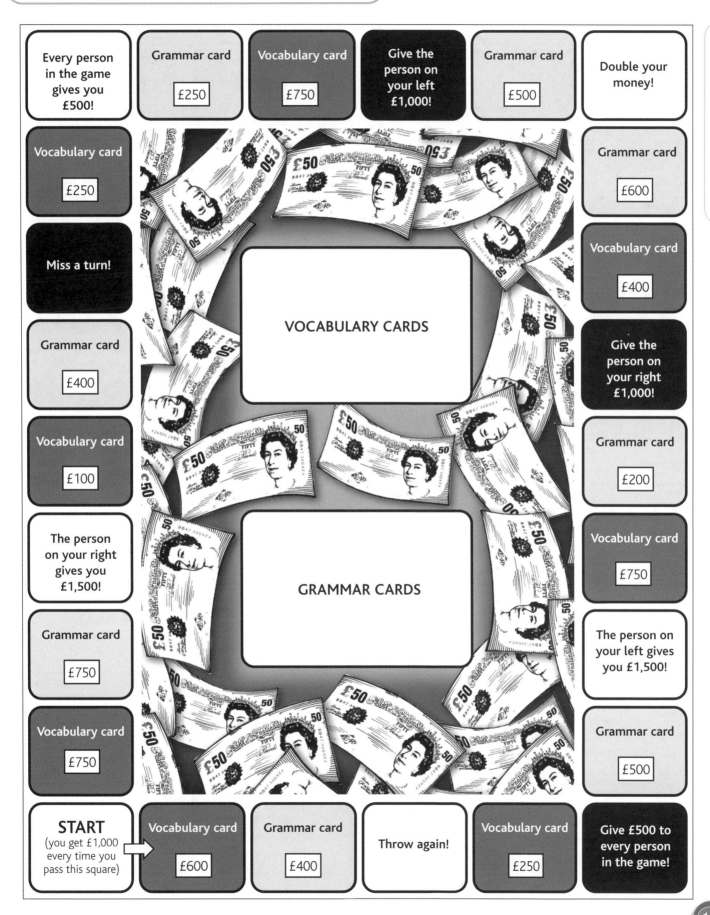

Every person in the game gives you £500!

Grammar card £250

Vocabulary card £750

Give the person on your left £1,000!

Grammar card £500

Double your money!

Vocabulary card £250

Grammar card £600

Miss a turn!

Vocabulary card £400

VOCABULARY CARDS

Grammar card £400

Give the person on your right £1,000!

Vocabulary card £100

Grammar card £200

The person on your right gives you £1,500!

GRAMMAR CARDS

Vocabulary card £750

Grammar card £750

The person on your left gives you £1,500!

Vocabulary card £750

Grammar card £500

START (you get £1,000 every time you pass this square)

Vocabulary card £600

Grammar card £400

Throw again!

Vocabulary card £250

Give £500 to every person in the game!

CLASS ACTIVITIES: PHOTOCOPIABLE

Vocabulary cards

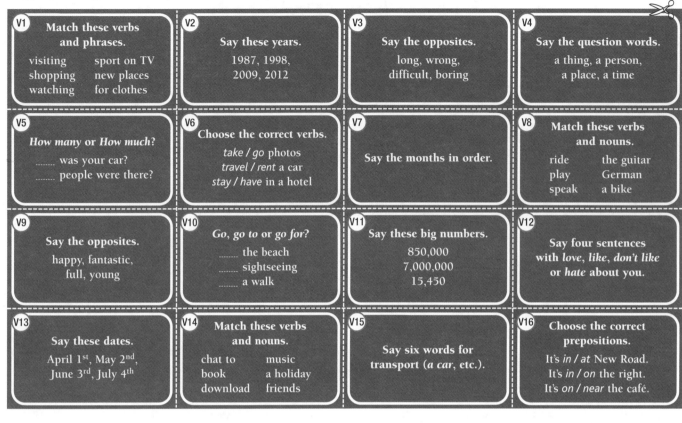

V1 Match these verbs and phrases.
visiting   sport on TV
shopping   new places
watching   for clothes

V2 Say these years.
1987, 1998,
2009, 2012

V3 Say the opposites.
long, wrong,
difficult, boring

V4 Say the question words.
a thing, a person,
a place, a time

V5 *How many* or *How much*?
.... was your car?
.... people were there?

V6 Choose the correct verbs.
take / go photos
travel / rent a car
stay / have in a hotel

V7 Say the months in order.

V8 Match these verbs and nouns.
ride   the guitar
play   German
speak   a bike

V9 Say the opposites.
happy, fantastic,
full, young

V10 *Go, go to* or *go for*?
.... the beach
.... sightseeing
.... a walk

V11 Say these big numbers.
850,000
7,000,000
15,450

V12 Say four sentences with *love, like, don't like* or *hate* about you.

V13 Say these dates.
April 1st, May 2nd,
June 3rd, July 4th

V14 Match these verbs and nouns.
chat to   music
book   a holiday
download   friends

V15 Say six words for transport (*a car*, etc.).

V16 Choose the correct prepositions.
It's *in / at* New Road.
It's *in / on* the right.
It's *on / near* the café.

Grammar cards

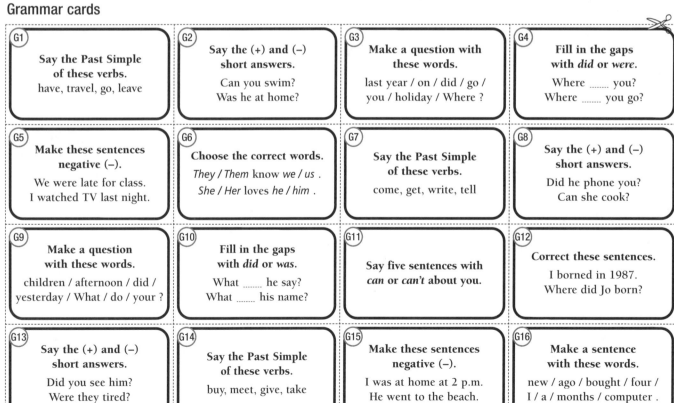

G1 Say the Past Simple of these verbs.
have, travel, go, leave

G2 Say the (+) and (–) short answers.
Can you swim?
Was he at home?

G3 Make a question with these words.
last year / on / did / go /
you / holiday / Where ?

G4 Fill in the gaps with *did* or *were*.
Where .... you?
Where .... you go?

G5 Make these sentences negative (–).
We were late for class.
I watched TV last night.

G6 Choose the correct words.
They / Them know *we / us* .
She / Her loves *he / him* .

G7 Say the Past Simple of these verbs.
come, get, write, tell

G8 Say the (+) and (–) short answers.
Did he phone you?
Can she cook?

G9 Make a question with these words.
children / afternoon / did /
yesterday / What / do / your ?

G10 Fill in the gaps with *did* or *was*.
What .... he say?
What .... his name?

G11 Say five sentences with *can* or *can't* about you.

G12 Correct these sentences.
I borned in 1987.
Where did Jo born?

G13 Say the (+) and (–) short answers.
Did you see him?
Were they tired?

G14 Say the Past Simple of these verbs.
buy, meet, give, take

G15 Make these sentences negative (–).
I was at home at 2 p.m.
He went to the beach.

G16 Make a sentence with these words.
new / ago / bought / four /
I / a / months / computer .

Instructions p110

10B Guess your partner's future

be going to: yes / no questions and short answers; phrases with *have, watch, go, go to*

Student A

		✓ or ✗
1 My partner	*go / have / watch* **a party** on his or her next birthday.	
2 My partner	*go to / go / play* **the gym** next weekend.	
3 My partner	*go / look / watch* **the news** this evening.	
4 My partner	*go to / go / get* **shopping** for clothes this month.	
5 My partner	*move / stay / have* **house** next year.	
6 My partner	*visit / go / stay* **in a hotel** next month.	
7 My partner	*get / do / have* **home** before 7 p.m. tomorrow.	
8 My partner	*stay / go to / get* **bed** before midnight this evening.	

✂

Student B

		✓ or ✗
1 My partner	*watch / have / go* **dinner** with friends next Friday.	
2 My partner	*go to / go / play* **a party** next weekend.	
3 My partner	*go / look / watch* **a DVD** this evening.	
4 My partner	*go to / go / get* **on holiday** next month.	
5 My partner	*move / stay / have* **to another city or country** next year.	
6 My partner	*visit / go / stay* **at home** next Saturday evening.	
7 My partner	*get / do / have* **married** this year.	
8 My partner	*stay / go to / get* **a wedding** next month.	

10C After the course saying goodbye and good luck; *be going to*; question words

STUDENT A

It's your birthday on Sunday. You're going to have a party at a famous club in your town or city. _____ (**how many?**) people are going to be there. And _____ (**who?**) is / are going to play at midnight!

STUDENT B

You're going to fly to Nepal tomorrow. Then next week you're going to climb Mount Everest with _____ (**who?**). You're going to come back to this country _____ (**when?**). Then you're going to write a book about the climb.

STUDENT C

You're going to move to Los Angeles next week. You bought Leonardo diCaprio's house last month for _____ (**how much?**). And in August you're going to be in a big Hollywood film with _____ (**who?**).

STUDENT D

You're going to sail around the world next month with _____ (**who?**). You're also going to make a film about your journey. You're going to be away for about _____ (**how long?**).

STUDENT E

You're going to start a new job next Monday. You're going to be a journalist for a famous newspaper called _____ (**what?**). And on Tuesday you're going to interview _____ (**who?**).

STUDENT F

You're going to go on holiday to _____ (**where?**) next week. You're going to stay in a beautiful hotel near the beach. You're also going to learn how to dive. You're going to be on holiday for _____ (**how long?**).

STUDENT G

You're going to fly to _____ (**where?**) for the weekend. You're going to go with _____ (**who?**) and you're going to stay in a five-star hotel. You're going to come back on Monday.

STUDENT H

You're the singer in a rock band called No Future. You're going to play a concert for _____ (**how many?**) people in _____ (**where?**) next week. There were only 200 people at your last concert!

STUDENT I

It's your wedding anniversary next Tuesday. You are going to buy your husband or wife _____ (**what?**). And on Tuesday evening you're going to have a very expensive dinner at _____ (**where?**).

STUDENT J

You're going to start university next September. You're very excited because you're going to study music at _____ (**where?**). You're going to come back to your country in December _____ (**why?**).

STUDENT K

You're going to do an English exam next Monday. Then you're going to fly to _____ (**where?**) on Friday. You're going to study English there, and then you're going to travel around the country with _____ (**who?**).

STUDENT L

You're going to open a restaurant in the city centre next Friday. _____ (**who?**) is / are going to be there! Then you're going to open a second restaurant in _____ (**where?**) next month.

Vocabulary Plus

Instructions

There are ten Vocabulary Plus worksheets (p151–p160). These worksheets introduce additional vocabulary that is **not** presented in the Student's Book. The topic of each Vocabulary Plus worksheet is linked to the topic of the corresponding unit in the Student's Book. There is an answer key at the bottom of each worksheet, which can be cut off if necessary.

- Use these worksheets for extra vocabulary input in class. The instructions give additional communicative stages you can include in each lesson. We suggest you cut off the answer keys from the bottom of the worksheets and check the answers yourself after each exercise.

- Give the worksheets for homework. You can leave the answer keys on the worksheets so students can check the answers themselves. Alternatively, cut off the answer keys before handing out the worksheets and check the answers yourself at the beginning of the next class.

- Give the worksheets to fast finishers in class. This is often useful when you have a mixed-level class and some students finish speaking activities early. Students can begin the worksheets in class and finish them for homework if necessary. You can then give copies of the worksheet to the other students for homework at the end of the class.

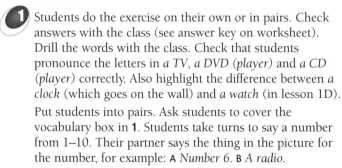

1 Things in a room p151

Language

a clock, a radio, a phone / a telephone, a TV / a television, a DVD, a DVD player, a CD, a CD player, a door, a window

When to use and time

Use any time after lesson 1D. 15–20 minutes.

Procedure

1 Students do the exercise on their own or in pairs. Check answers with the class (see answer key on worksheet). Drill the words with the class. Check that students pronounce the letters in *a TV*, *a DVD* (*player*) and *a CD* (*player*) correctly. Also highlight the difference between *a clock* (which goes on the wall) and *a watch* (in lesson 1D).

Put students into pairs. Ask students to cover the vocabulary box in **1**. Students take turns to say a number from 1–10. Their partner says the thing in the picture for the number, for example: A *Number 6.* B *A radio.*

2 Students do the crossword on their own or in pairs. Check answers with the class.

3 Students do the exercise on their own before checking in pairs. Check answers with the class. Point out that all these words have regular plural forms with an *-s* added to the singular word. Drill the plural forms with the class.

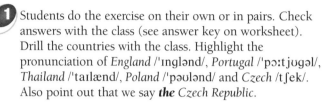

2 Countries and nationalities p152

Language

England / English, India / Indian, Switzerland / Swiss, Portugal / Portuguese, Ireland / Irish, Peru / Peruvian, Thailand / Thai, Poland / Polish, the Czech Republic / Czech, South Africa / South African

When to use and time

Use any time after lesson 2A. 15–25 minutes.

Procedure

1 Students do the exercise on their own or in pairs. Check answers with the class (see answer key on worksheet). Drill the countries with the class. Highlight the pronunciation of *England* /ˈɪŋɡlənd/, *Portugal* /ˈpɔːtjʊɡəl/, *Thailand* /ˈtaɪlænd/, *Poland* /ˈpəʊlənd/ and *Czech* /tʃek/. Also point out that we say **the** *Czech Republic.*

Put students into pairs. Ask students to cover the sentences in **1**. Students take turns to point to a person on the worksheet and ask where he/she is from. For example, student A points to person 3 and asks *Where's he from?*. Student B replies *He's from India.*

2 Students do the exercise on their own or in pairs. Check answers with the class. Drill the nationalities with the class. Highlight the pronunciation of *Czech* /tʃek/ and *Thai* /taɪ/, and the different stress patterns in *Portugal* and *Portuguese* /pɔːtjʊˈɡiːz/. Also highlight the extra *v* in *Peruvian*.

✍ Write the questions *What's his nationality?* and *What's her nationality?* on the board. Drill the questions with the class. Put students into new pairs. Ask students to cover the sentences in **2**. Students take turns to point to a person on the worksheet and ask what his/her nationality is. For example, A *What's his nationality?* B *He's Indian.*

3 a) Focus students on the table. Point out the endings for nationality words in the first column and the examples in the second column. Students do the exercise on their own before checking in pairs. Check answers with the class.

b) Students do the exercise on their own before checking in pairs. Check answers with the class.

Put students into pairs. Ask the class to cover the vocabulary box in **2**. Students test each other on the nationalities by taking turns to say a country from **1**, for example: A *Portugal.* B *Portuguese.*

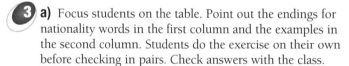

3 Food and drink p153

Language

tomatoes, potatoes, oranges, beer, lemons, red wine, chicken, onions, sausages, bananas, white wine, steak

When to use and time

Use any time after lesson 3D. 15–25 minutes.

Procedure

1 Students do the exercise on their own or in pairs. Check answers with the class (see answer key on worksheet). Drill the words with the class. Highlight the pronunciation of oranges /'ɒrɪndʒɪz/, chicken /'tʃɪkɪn/, onions /'ʌnjənz/, sausages /'sɒsɪdʒɪz/ and steak /steɪk/. Note that *tomatoes* is pronounced /tə'mɑːtəʊz/ in British English and /tə'meɪtəʊz/ in American English. Also point out that the singular of *tomatoes* is *a tomato*, not ~~a tomatoe~~, and the singular of *potatoes* is *a potato*, not ~~a potatoe~~.

Put students into pairs. Ask the class to cover the vocabulary box in **1**. Students take turns to say a number. Their partner says what the food and drink is, for example: A *Number 11.* B *Tomatoes.*

2 Students do the exercise on their own before checking in pairs. Check answers with the class.

3 Students do the exercise on their own before checking in pairs. While they are working, draw the table on the board. Check answers with the class by saying a word from **1** and asking the class which category it goes in. Note that although *tomatoes* are botanically classed as a fruit, from a culinary point of view (and in supermarkets, on menus, etc.) they are usually classed as a vegetable.

4 Students do the exercise on their own. Remind students that they can use words from **1** and their own ideas.

Put students into groups of three or four. Students compare sentences in their groups. Finally, ask students to tell the class one or two of their sentences.

4 Free time activities p154

Language

listen to music, go to the theatre, go clubbing, play golf, go to museums, play cards, read books or magazines, go cycling

When to use and time

Use any time after lesson 4B. 20–30 minutes.

Procedure

1 Students do the exercise on their own or in pairs. Check answers with the class (see answer key on worksheet). Drill the phrases with the class. Highlight the pronunciation of *listen* /'lɪsən/, *theatre* /'θɪətə/ and *cycling* /'saɪklɪŋ/. Point out that we usually say *go to **the** theatre* but *go to museums*. Check students understand that when people *go clubbing*, they go to a club to listen to music and dance. You can also highlight that we often use *go + verb+ing* (*go shopping*, etc.).

2 Students do the exercise on their own before checking in pairs. Check answers with the class.

Put students into pairs. Students take turns to say a word or phrase in column B. Their partner says the complete phrase, for example, A *the theatre.* B *go to the theatre.*

3 Students do the exercise on their own. Put students into pairs. Students take turns to say their sentences. Ask students to tell the class one or two of their sentences.

4 a) Students do the exercise on their own before checking answers in pairs. Check answers with the class.

b) Students answer the questions on their own. Remind them of the short answers *Yes, I do.* and *No, I don't.* before they begin. Put students into new pairs. Students take turns to ask each other the questions in **4a)**. Ask students to tick any of the free time activities they both do. Finally, ask students to tell the class about things they and their partner both do in their free time.

5 Jobs p155

Language

a nurse, an artist, a journalist, a mechanic, a secretary, a chef, a farmer, a DJ

When to use and time

Use any time after lesson 5B. 15–25 minutes.

Procedure

1 Students do the exercise on their own or in pairs. Check answers with the class (see answer key on worksheet). Drill the words chorally and individually, focusing on word stress. Pay particular attention to the pronunciation of *nurse* /nɜːs/, *journalist* /'dʒɜːnəlɪst/, *mechanic* /mɪ'kænɪk/ and *chef* /ʃef/. Also highlight that the stress on *a DJ* is on D, not J. Note that *a DJ* stands for *a disc jockey*, although this term is rarely used nowadays. Also note that there are two different ways to pronounce *secretary* /'sekrətri/ and /'sekrəteri/. You can also teach students that we sometimes say *a PA* /piː'eɪ/ (= *a personal assistant*) instead of *a secretary*.

Put students into pairs. Ask the class to cover the vocabulary box in **1**. Students take turns to point to a picture and ask their partner what the person's job is, for example: A *What's her job?* B *She's a nurse.*

2 Focus students on the example and picture 7. Students do the rest of the exercise in pairs. While students are working, be prepared to help them with any of the new vocabulary in **bold**, or encourage them to check the words in their bilingual dictionaries. Check answers with the class and check any vocabulary in **bold** that students are still unsure about. Drill the sentences with the class.

3 Focus students on the pictures and the example. Point out that students must write their sentences in picture order 1–8. Students do the exercise on their own before checking in pairs. Before they begin, remind students that they must use the *he, she, it* form of the verbs in **2** and tell the class that all these verbs are regular. Check answers with the class.

Ask students to cover **2** and **3**. Put students into pairs. Students take turns to ask their partner what people do in the jobs in **1**, for example: A *What does a mechanic do?* B *He repairs cars.*

4 Students do the crossword on their own or in pairs. Check answers with the class.

6 Rooms and furniture p156

Language

the kitchen, the living room, the bedroom, the bathroom, the toilet, the balcony, a sofa, a bed, a cooker, a fridge, a shower, a bath, a carpet, a table, a chair, a desk

When to use and time

Use any time after lesson 6B. 15–25 minutes.

Procedure

1 Focus students on the picture of the flat. Ask the class who lives there (Danny). Students do the exercise on their own or in pairs. Check answers with the class (see answer key on worksheet). Drill the words with the class. Highlight the pronunciation of *kitchen* /ˈkɪtʃɪn/, *toilet* /ˈtɔɪlət/ and *balcony* /ˈbælkənɪ/. Point out that we say **the** *kitchen*, **the** *living room*, etc. because there is only one kitchen, one living room, etc. in Danny's flat. Also tell students that we say **in** *the kitchen*, **in** *the living room*, etc. but **on** *the balcony*.

2 Students do the exercise on their own. Check answers with the class. Drill the words and highlight the pronunciation of *sofa* /ˈsəʊfə/ and *fridge* /frɪdʒ/.

Put students into pairs. Ask the class to cover the vocabulary boxes in **1** and **2**. Students take turns to test each other on the rooms and things in the picture, for example, A *What's number 8?* B *It's a sofa.*

3 Focus students on the examples. Students do the exercise on their own before checking in pairs. Check answers with the class.

4 Students do the exercise on their own before checking in pairs. Check answers with the class.

Students work on their own and write four more questions with *Is there ... ?* or *Are there ... ?* about Danny's flat. Put students into pairs. Ask students to cover the picture of Danny's flat on their worksheets. Students then take turns to ask their questions and say if their partner's answers are right or wrong.

5 Students do the exercise on their own. You can tell students to look at **3** if they need more guidance about what type of sentences to write.

Put students into pairs or small groups. Students take turns to tell their partner about their flat or house. Finally, ask students to tell the class one or two things about their flat or house.

7 Parts of the body p157

Language

head, face, arm, leg, hand, foot, back, hair, mouth, eye, nose, ear, teeth

When to use and time

Use any time after lesson 7B. 10–20 minutes.

Procedure

1 Students do the exercise on their own or in pairs. Check answers with the class (see answer key on worksheet). Drill the words with the class. Highlight the pronunciation of *mouth* /maʊθ/, *eye* /aɪ/ and *teeth* /tiːθ/. Point out that the singular of *teeth* is *tooth* and the plural of *foot* is *feet*. Tell the class that all the other words have regular plural forms.

Put students into pairs. Ask the class to cover the vocabulary box in **1**. Students take turns to test each other on the parts of the body of the man in the picture, for example, A *What's number 4?* B *It's his nose.* Alternatively, students can point to parts of their own body and their partner says the word.

2 Students do the exercise on their own before checking in pairs. Check answers with the class.

3 a) Draw four people on the board, one with long hair, one with short hair, one with a round face and one who is very thin. Use these drawings to teach *long, short, round* and *thin*.

b) Focus students on the picture and check they understand what *an alien* /ˈeɪlɪən/ is. Students do the exercise on their own before checking in pairs. Check answers with the class.

4 Students work on their own and draw a picture of a different alien on the back of their worksheets or in their notebooks. Encourage them to use their imagination during this stage of the activity. Students then write a description of their aliens, similar to the description in **3b)**. Remind them to use words from **1** and **3a)** in their descriptions.

Put students into pairs. Students are not allowed to see their partner's picture. Students take turns to read out their description of their alien to their partner. He/She draws his/her partner's alien. When students have finished, they compare pictures and see if they are the same.

If you have a weaker class, ask students to do **4** in pairs, and do the communicative stage of the activity in groups of four.

8 Places with *at, in, on* p158

Language

at home, at work, at school, at a party, in bed, in the garden, in the kitchen, in town, in the shower, on holiday, on the train, on the bus

When to use and time

Use any time after lesson 8B. 15–25 minutes.

Procedure

1 Students do the exercise on their own or in pairs. Check answers with the class (see answer key on worksheet). Drill the phrases. Point out that each phrase begins with a preposition (*at, in* or *on*).

Note that although it is sometimes possible to use other prepositions with these nouns, the phrases taught on the worksheet are the most common, and the most likely to be used when answering a question with *Where ... ?* (*Where are you?*, etc.). If you have done Vocabulary Plus worksheet 6 (Rooms and furniture), point out that we also use *in* with other rooms (*in the bedroom*, *in the bathroom*, etc.) and in the phrase *in the bath*. You can also point out that we use *in* with towns, cities and countries: *He's **in** New York.*, *They're **in** Germany.* and that we can say ***at** a restaurant / café* or ***in** a restaurant / café*.

2 Ask students to cover the vocabulary box in **1**. Students do the exercise on their own before checking in pairs. Check answers with the class.

Ask students to cover the sentences in **2**. Put students into pairs. Students take turns to ask and answer questions about the people in the pictures, for example: A *Where are the people in picture 1?* B *They're at a party.*

3 Focus students on the nouns in **bold** in **2**. Students do the exercise on their own before checking in pairs. While students are working, draw the table on the board. Check answers with the class by saying a noun in **bold** from **2** and asking students where it goes in the table.

4 Students do the exercise on their own. Put students into groups. Students take turns to say their sentences to the other people in the group. Students can ask follow-up questions if they wish. Finally, ask students to tell the class one or two of their sentences.

9 Irregular verbs p159

Language
drive (drove), think (thought), sleep (slept), wake up (woke up), see (saw), break (broke), lose (lost), find (found), send (sent), read (read /red/)

When to use and time
Use any time after lesson 9C. 15–25 minutes.

Procedure

1 Students do the exercise on their own or in pairs. Check answers with the class (see answer key on worksheet). Drill the words with the class. Highlight the pronunciation of *break* /breɪk/ and *lose* /luːz/. Check students understand the difference between *wake up* and *get up*.

2 Students do the exercise on their own before checking in pairs. Check answers with the class. Drill the Past Simple forms with the class. Highlight the pronunciation of *thought* /θɔːt/ and *saw* /sɔː/. Point out that the Past Simple of *read* is pronounced /red/, but the spelling is the same.

Put students into pairs. Ask students to cover the table in **2**. Students test each other on the verbs in **1** and their Past Simple forms, for example, A *think.* B *thought.*

3 a) Focus students on the email. Students read the email and find out if Vicky had a good weekend. (She didn't.)

b) Students do the exercise on their own before checking in pairs. Check answers with the class.

4 a) Pre-teach *an arm*. Students do the exercise on their own. Check answers with the class.

b) Students work on their own and tick the sentences in **4a)** that are true for them.

Put students into groups. Students take turns to tell each other which sentences are true for them. Encourage students to continue the conversation if possible. Finally, ask students to tell the class one or two sentences that are true for them.

10 The weather p160

Language
dry, wet, hot, warm, cold, sunny, cloudy, windy, foggy, (26)° / (26) degrees.

When to use and time
Use any time after lesson 10B. 15–20 minutes.

Procedure

1 Focus students on the pictures. You can ask students which countries the cities are in. Tell the class that this is the weather in these cities today. Students do the exercise on their own or in pairs. Check answers with the class (see answer key on worksheet). Drill the sentences chorally and individually. Pay particular attention to the pronunciation of *cloudy* /'klaʊdi/ and *degrees* /dɪ'griːz/. With a strong class you can also teach *It's raining.* and *It's snowing.* However, as students have not studied the Present Continuous yet, we suggest you teach these as fixed phrases at this level.

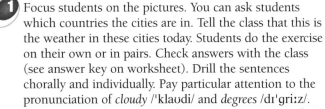 Write the question *What's the weather like in Sydney?* on the board. Drill the question with the class. Elicit the answer (*It's warm.*) and write it on the board. Point out that we use *like* in the question, but not in the answer (*It's like warm.*).

Put students into pairs. Tell students to cover the sentences in **1**. Students take turns to ask what the weather is like in the places in the pictures, for example, A *What's the weather like in Barcelona?* B *It's sunny.*

2 Focus students on the table. Check students understand that this is the weather forecast for tomorrow. Then focus students on sentence 1 and point out that we use *be going to* because we're talking about the future. Students do the exercise on their own before checking in pairs. Check answers with the class.

3 a) Students do the exercise on their own. Check answers with the class.

b) Students do the exercise on their own before checking in pairs. Check answers with the class.

1 Look at the picture of a room. Match these things to 1–10.

a clock [1] a radio [ ] a phone / a telephone [ ] a TV / a television [ ] a DVD [ ]
a DVD player [ ] a CD [ ] a CD player [ ] a door [ ] a window [ ]

2 Write words from **1** in the crossword.

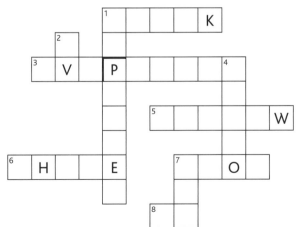

3 Look again at the picture. Write the plurals of words 1–10.

1 c _l_ _o_ _c_ _k_ _s_
2 d _ _ _ _ _
3 w _ _ _ _ _ _ _
4 T _ _ _ / t _ _ _ _ _ _ _ _ _ _
5 p _ _ _ _ _ _ / t _ _ _ _ _ _ _ _ _ _
6 r _ _ _ _ _ _
7 D _ _ _ p _ _ _ _ _ _ _
8 D _ _ _ _
9 C _ _ _
10 C _ p _ _ _ _ _ _ _

---

1 a radio 6, a telephone 5, a TV / a television 4, a DVD 8, a DVD player 7, a CD 9, a CD player 10, a door 2, a window 3
2 1 → clock 1 ↑ CD player 2 TV 3 DVD player 4 radio 5 window 6 phone 7 door 7 → door 7 ↑ DVD 8 CD **3** 2 doors 3 windows
4 TVs / televisions 5 phones / telephones 6 radios 7 DVD players 8 DVDs 9 CDs 10 CD players

© Cambridge University Press 2009   face2face Starter Photocopiable   151

2 Countries and nationalities

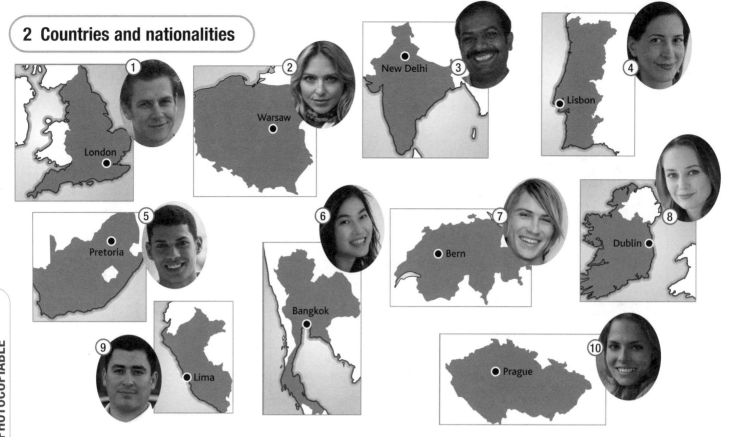

1 Look at the photos and the countries. Fill in the gaps in sentences 1–10 with these countries.

> ~~England~~ India Switzerland Portugal Ireland Peru
> Thailand Poland the Czech Republic South Africa

1 He's from _England_ .
2 She's from ....
3 He's from ....
4 She's from ....
5 He's from ....
6 She's from ....
7 He's from ....
8 She's from ....
9 He's from ....
10 She's from ....

2 Look again at the photos and the countries. Fill in the gaps with these nationalities.

> ~~English~~ Indian Portuguese Swiss Polish
> Czech South African Thai Irish Peruvian

1 He's _English_ .
2 She's ....
3 He's ....
4 She's ....
5 He's ....
6 She's ....
7 He's ....
8 She's ....
9 He's ....
10 She's ....

3 a) Write the nationalities in **2** in the table.

-ish	English
-n -an -ian	Indian
-ese	Portuguese
other	Swiss

b) Write the nationalities for these countries in the table in **3a)**.

> Brazil Spain China the USA
> Turkey France the UK
> Colombia Japan Italy

---

1 2 Poland 3 India 4 Portugal 5 South Africa 6 Thailand 7 Switzerland 8 Ireland 9 Peru 10 the Czech Republic **2** 2 Polish
3 Indian 4 Portuguese 5 South African 6 Thai 7 Swiss 8 Irish 9 Peruvian 10 Czech **3 a) and b)** **-ish:** Polish, Irish, Spanish,
Turkish, British; **-n, -an, -ian:** South African, Peruvian, Brazilian, American, Colombian, Italian; **-ese:** Chinese, Japanese; **other:** Czech,
Thai, French.

3 Food and drink

1 Look at the picture. Match these words to 1–12.

tomatoes [11] potatoes [ ] oranges [ ] beer [ ] lemons [ ] red wine [ ]
chicken [ ] onions [ ] sausages [ ] bananas [ ] white wine [ ] steak [ ]

TIP! • The singular of *tomatoes* is a tomato. The singular of potatoes is a potato.

VOCABULARY PLUS: PHOTOCOPIABLE

2 Find the words in **1** in the puzzle (→↓).

L	E	M	O	N	S	A	W	F	S	C	O
H	W	E	U	F	D	E	H	R	T	H	D
O	R	A	N	G	E	S	I	E	E	I	Y
N	P	S	A	V	C	X	T	Z	A	C	T
I	S	A	U	S	A	G	E	S	K	K	O
O	I	J	S	R	E	D	W	I	N	E	M
N	E	A	T	R	K	O	I	N	E	N	A
S	T	V	E	D	U	I	N	S	B	I	T
D	P	O	T	A	T	O	E	S	E	P	O
W	E	Q	K	J	P	L	E	G	E	Q	E
B	A	N	A	N	A	S	D	O	R	J	S

3 Write the words in **1** in the table.

vegetables	*tomatoes*
fruit	
meat	
drinks	

4 Complete the sentences. Use words from **1** or your own ideas.

1 I like .... and ....

2 I love .... and ....

3 I eat a lot of .... and ....

4 I drink .... with my food.

5 In my country people eat a lot of ....

6 In my country people drink a lot of ....

---

4 Free time activities

1 Match these phrases to pictures 1–8.

listen to music 8   go to the theatre ☐   go clubbing ☐   play golf ☐
go to museums ☐   play cards ☐   read books or magazines ☐   go cycling ☐

2 Match the verbs in A to the words / phrases in B.

A	B
listen to	the theatre
go	music
go to	cycling
go	books
read	cards
play	clubbing
go to	golf
play	magazines
read	museums

3 Complete these sentences about your free time. Use phrases from **1** or your own ideas.

1 I ....

2 I don't ....

3 I .... a lot.

4 My friends ....

5 My friends don't ....

6 My friends .... a lot.

4 **a)** Make questions with these words.

1 cycling / you / go / in your free time / Do ?
   Do you go cycling in your free time?

2 the theatre / you / Do / go to / a lot ?
   .... ?

3 in the car / you / music / listen to / Do ?
   .... ?

4 clubbing / Do / you / with your friends / go ?
   .... ?

5 play / in your free time / you / golf / Do ?
   .... ?

6 you / museums / a lot / go to / Do ?
   .... ?

7 cards / with your family / you / Do / play ?
   .... ?

8 you / books or magazines / in English / read / Do ?
   .... ?

b) Answer the questions for you.

----

1 go to the theatre 1, go clubbing 6, play golf 4, go to museums 2, play cards 3, read books or magazines 7, go cycling 5 **2** go cycling, go to the theatre, go clubbing, read books, play golf, read magazines **4 a)** 2 Do you go to the theatre a lot? 3 Do you listen to music in the car? 4 Do you go clubbing with your friends? 5 Do you play golf in your free time? 6 Do you go to museums a lot? 7 Do you play cards with your family? 8 Do you read books or magazines in English?

5 Jobs

1 Match these jobs to pictures 1–8.

a nurse 5   an artist ☐   a journalist ☐   a mechanic ☐   a secretary ☐   a chef ☐   a farmer ☐   a DJ ☐

VOCABULARY PLUS: PHOTOCOPIABLE

2 Match these sentences to the people in pictures 1–8. Check new words in **bold** with your teacher or in a dictionary.

a) I work for a TV company.   7

b) I **cook** food in a restaurant. ☐

c) I **paint** pictures. ☐

d) I play music in **clubs** or on the radio. ☐

e) I write **letters** and answer the phone. ☐

f) I **repair** cars. ☐

g) I work in a **hospital**. ☐

h) I **produce** food. ☐

3 Look again at pictures 1–8. Write sentences about the people. Use the phrases in **2**.

1 She _paints pictures_ .

2 He ....

3 She ....

4 He ....

5 She ....

6 He ....

7 She ....

8 He ....

4 Write the jobs from **1** in the crossword.

---

6 Rooms and furniture

1 Look at the picture of Danny's flat. Match these words to A–F.

the kitchen [B] the living room ☐ the bedroom ☐ the bathroom ☐ the toilet ☐ the balcony ☐

Danny

VOCABULARY PLUS: PHOTOCOPIABLE

2 Look at the picture again. Match these things to 1–10.

a sofa [8] a bed ☐ a cooker ☐ a fridge ☐
a shower ☐ a bath ☐ a carpet ☐ a table ☐
a chair ☐ a desk ☐

3 Tick (✓) the true sentences. Correct the wrong sentences.

five

1 There are ~~four~~ *five* rooms in Danny's flat.

2 There's a bed and a chair in the bedroom. ✓

3 There's a sofa in the living room.

4 There aren't any chairs on the balcony.

5 There's a carpet in the kitchen.

6 There's a bath and a shower in the bathroom.

7 There's a table in the kitchen.

8 There's a cooker and a fridge in the living room.

4 Answer these questions about Danny's flat.

1 Is there a table on the balcony?
   Yes, there is.

2 Are there any chairs in the kitchen?
   ....

3 Is there a table in the bathroom?
   ....

4 Is there a desk in the bedroom?
   ....

5 Are there any chairs in the bathroom?
   ....

5 Write five sentences about your flat or house. Use *there is / there are* and words from **1** and **2**.
There are four rooms in my flat.

---

❶ the living room E, the bedroom A, the bathroom C, the toilet D, the balcony F ❷ a bed 1, a cooker 5, a fridge 3, a shower 6, a bath 7, a carpet 9, a table 10, a chair 4, a desk 2 ❸ 3 ✓ 4 **There are two** chairs on the balcony. 5 **There isn't** a carpet in the kitchen. 6 ✓ 7 ✓ 8 There's a cooker and a fridge in the **kitchen.** ❹ 2 Yes, there are. 3 No, there isn't. 4 Yes, there is. 5 No, there aren't.

7 Parts of the body

1 Match these words to parts of the body 1–13.

head ☐7	face ☐3	arm ☐	leg ☐	hand ☐
foot ☐	back ☐	hair ☐	mouth ☐	
eye ☐	nose ☐	ear ☐	teeth ☐	

TIPS! • The singular of teeth is tooth.
• The plural of foot is feet.

2 Find the words from **1** in the puzzle (→ ↓).

E	Y	E	M	G	H	P	N	S	O	B	J
T	R	I	O	H	A	H	O	Z	Q	A	K
E	L	E	U	I	I	A	S	F	A	C	E
E	A	R	T	L	R	N	E	O	R	K	T
T	U	D	H	E	A	D	K	O	Y	P	W
H	Y	A	R	M	I	D	F	T	L	E	G

3 **a)** Check these adjectives with your teacher or in a dictionary.

> long   short   round   thin

b) Look at the picture of an alien. Fill in the gaps with the singular or plural form of words from **1**.

He has a big ¹*head* , a round ²................................
and six ³................................ . He has short
⁴................................ and four small ⁵................................ .
He also has a long ⁶................................ and a very
big ⁷................................ , but he only has five
⁸................................ .
He has two very thin ⁹................................ and small
¹⁰................................ . He also has very short
¹¹................................ and big ¹²................................ !

4 Draw a picture of a different alien. Then write about your alien. Use words from **1** and **3a)**.

---

1 arm 11, leg 6, hand 5, foot 13, back 12, hair 12, mouth 2, eye 9, nose 7, ear 8, teeth 10 ➜ face, ear, head, arm, leg ↓ teeth, mouth, hair, hand, nose, foot, back **3 b)** 2 face 3 eyes 4 hair 5 ears 6 nose 7 mouth 8 teeth 9 arms 10 hands 11 legs 12 feet

8 Places with *at*, *in*, *on*

1 Match these phrases to pictures 1–12.

at home [6]   at work [ ]   at school [ ]   at a party [ ]   in bed [ ]   in the garden [ ]   in the kitchen [ ]
in town [ ]   in the shower [ ]   on holiday [ ]   on the train [ ]   on the bus [ ]

TIPS! • We use *in* with towns, cities and countries: He's *in* New York. They're *in* Germany.
• We can say *at* a restaurant / café or *in* a restaurant / café.

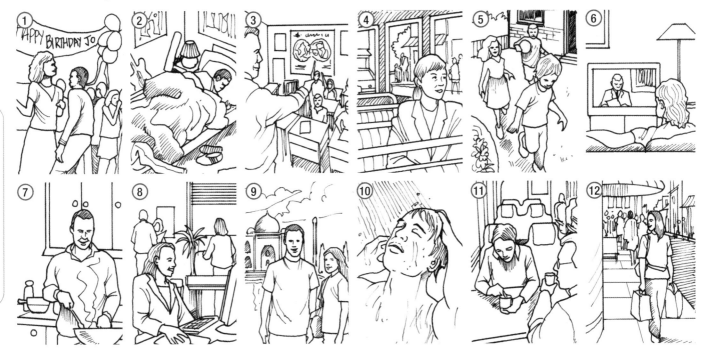

2 Look again at pictures 1–12. Fill in the gaps with *at*, *in* or *on*.

1 They're .at. **a party**.
2 He's .... **bed**.
3 They're .... **school**.
4 She's .... **the bus**.
5 They're .... **the garden**.
6 She's .... **home**.
7 He's .... **the kitchen**.
8 She's .... **work**.
9 They're .... **holiday**.
10 He's .... **the shower**.
11 They're .... **the train**.
12 She's .... **town**.

3 Write the words / phrases in **bold** in **2** in the table.

at	*a party*	....
	....	....
in	....	....
	....	....
	....	....
on	....	....

4 Complete these sentences about you. Use phrases from **1**.

1 I'm .... now.
2 I was .... an hour ago.
3 I was .... three hours ago.
4 I was .... at seven this morning.
5 I was .... yesterday afternoon.
6 I was .... last Saturday evening.

VOCABULARY PLUS: PHOTOCOPIABLE

9 Irregular verbs

1 Match these verbs to pictures 1–10.

drive [4]   think [ ]   sleep [ ]
wake up [ ]   see [ ]   break [ ]
lose [ ]   find [ ]   send [ ]   read [ ]

① ② ③ ④ ⑤ ⑥ ⑦ ⑧ ⑨ ⑩

2 Write the verbs in **1** in the table.

verb	Past Simple
1 *think*	thought /θɔːt/
2	sent
3	broke
4	saw /sɔː/
5	slept
6	woke up
7	read /red/
8	drove
9	lost
10	found

3 **a)** Read Vicky's email. Did she have a good weekend?

new   reply   reply all   forward   print

Hi Harriet

How are you? Jason and I ¹ *went* (go) away last weekend. We ² _____ (drive) to an old town called Seaford and ³ _____ (stay) in a hotel near the beach. We ⁴ _____ (think) it was a four-star hotel, but it wasn't! The room was very small and the bed was awful. Jason ⁵ _____ (sleep) all night, but I didn't. I ⁶ _____ (wake up) at 4 a.m., then I ⁷ _____ (read) a book and ⁸ _____ (watch) TV. On Sunday we ⁹ _____ (go) sightseeing. We ¹⁰ _____ (see) some beautiful old buildings, but then I ¹¹ _____ (break) my camera. And in the afternoon Jason ¹² _____ (lose) his mobile! Of course, he ¹³ _____ (find) it again when we ¹⁴ _____ (get) home – it ¹⁵ _____ (be) in his bag. Next weekend Jason and I don't want to go anywhere!

Love Vicky

PS Did you get the DVDs I ¹⁶ _____ (send) you last week?

b) Read the email again. Put the verbs in brackets in the Past Simple.

4 **a)** Fill in the gaps with the Past Simple forms in **2**.

1 I *lost* some money last week.

2 I _____ a good film on TV last night.

3 I _____ at 7 a.m. this morning.

4 I _____ an English magazine last month.

5 I _____ about 100 emails last week.

6 I _____ for about eight hours last night.

7 I _____ to school today.

8 I _____ my arm when I was a child.

9 I _____ my last English lesson was easy.

10 I _____ some old photos last month.

b) Tick (✓) the sentences in **4a)** that are true for you.

10 The weather

1 Look at the pictures. Match sentences 1–10 to the cities.

1 It's **warm**.   Sydney
2 It's **hot**.   ....
3 It's **cold**.   ....
4 It's **wet**.   ....
5 It's **dry**.   ....
6 It's **sunny**.   ....
7 It's **cloudy**.   ....
8 It's **windy**.   ....
9 It's **foggy**.   ....
10 It's **26°**.   ....

TIP! • We write 26°. We say *twenty-six degrees*.

2 Look at the weather around the world tomorrow. Make sentences for the places.

Tomorrow's weather

Bogotá	
Cape Town	
Dubai	35°
Dublin	
Istanbul	
Lima	24°
Lisbon	FOG
Milan	20°
Moscow	0°
Tokyo	

1 In Bogotá it's going to be __wet__ .
2 In Cape Town it's going to be ....
3 In Dubai it's going to ....
4 In Dublin it's going ....
5 In Istanbul it's ....
6 In Lima ....
7 In Lisbon ....
8 In Milan ....
9 In Moscow ....
10 In Tokyo ....

3 **a)** Look at these questions. Fill in the gaps with *yesterday*, *today* and *tomorrow*.

1 What's the weather like .... ?
2 What was the weather like .... ?
3 What's the weather going to be like .... ?

b) Answer the questions for the town or city you are in now.

1 It's ....
2 It was ....
3 It's going to be ....

---

9 In Moscow it's going to be cold.   10 In Tokyo it's going to be sunny.   **3 a)** 1 today   2 yesterday   3 tomorrow
6 In Lima it's going to be 24°/warm.   7 In Lisbon it's going to be foggy.   8 In Milan it's going to be warm/20°.
it's going to be dry.   3 In Dubai it's going to be hot.   4 In Dublin it's going to be windy.   5 In Istanbul it's going to be cloudy.
2 2 In Cape Town   3 São Paulo   4 Berlin   5 Manchester   6 Cairo   7 Barcelona   8 Beijing   9 Chicago   10 Mexico City   **2** 2 In Cape Town

Progress Tests

Instructions

The Progress Tests (p164–p175) are designed to be used after students have completed each unit of the Student's Book. Each Progress Test checks students' knowledge of the key language areas taught in the unit. Some exercises and questions in Progress Tests 5 and 10 also test students' knowledge of language taught in previous units.

It is helpful for students to have done the Review section at the end of each unit in the Student's Book before doing a Progress Test. You can also encourage students to revise for the test by doing exercises for that unit on the CD-ROM and in the Workbook, and by reviewing the relevant Language Summary in the back of the Student's Book. Note that Progress Tests 5 and 10 also contain a listening section.

- Allow students 25 minutes for Progress Tests 1–4 and 6–9, and 50 minutes for Progress Tests 5 and 10. You may wish to adjust the time depending on the level of your class.

- Photocopy one test for each student. Students should do the tests on their own. You can either check the answers with the whole class at the end of the test, or collect in the tests and correct them yourself. Keep a record of the test scores to help you monitor individual students' progress and for report writing at the end of the course.

- Progress Tests can also be given as homework.

Listening tests

There is a listening section in Progress Tests 5 and 10 only. The recording scripts (R5.17 and R10.11) for these tests are in the Answer Key.

Both R5.17 and R10.11 have two separate sections. Focus on one section of the recording at a time. Allow students time to read through the questions for that section in the Progress Test before you start. Play that section of the recording without stopping and allow students time to answer the questions. Then play that section of the recording again without stopping. Repeat this procedure for the other section.

Answer Key and Recording Scripts

Progress Test 1 p164

1	2 your 3 my 4 you 5 You 6 you 7 I 8 you 9 I
2	b) eleven c) three d) eight e) twelve f) four
3	2 See you soon 3 home number 4 this is 5 to meet you 6 first name 7 your surname
4	2 His 3 he 4 He 5 Her 6 she 7 She
5	2 Spain 3 Australia 4 China 5 Brazil 6 Russia
6	2 repeat 3 sorry 4 What's 5 spell 6 mean 7 know
7	2 umbrella 3 iPod / MP3 player 4 apple 5 pen 6 bag 7 pencil 8 mobile (phone)
8	2 watches 3 people 4 babies 5 men 6 women 7 tables 8 countries

Progress Test 2 p165

1	2 Spanish 3 American 4 Chinese 5 Turkish 6 Brazilian 7 British 8 Russian
2	2 'm not, 'm 3 isn't, 's 4 aren't / 're not, 're 5 isn't / 's not, 's
3	2 a musician 3 a police officer 4 a doctor 5 a shop assistant 6 an actor 7 a waitress 8 a taxi driver
4	2 'm 3 Is 4 isn't / 's not 5 's 6 's 7 Is 8 is 9 Are 10 am 11 Am 12 aren't / 're not
5	(2 marks each) 2 What's your surname? 3 Are you married? 4 What's your nationality? 5 What's your address? 6 What's your mobile number? 7 What's your email address?
6	b) forty-six c) thirty-three d) fifteen e) fifty-eight f) a / one hundred

Progress Test 3 p166

1	2 small 3 unfriendly 4 expensive 5 cold 6 old
2	2 are 3 aren't / 're not 4 're (are) 5 aren't / 're not 6 're (are) 7 isn't / 's not 8 's (is) 9 'm not 10 'm (am) 11 's (is) 12 isn't
3	2 daughter 3 son 4 Pam's 5 sister 6 Steve's 7 father 8 Jane 9 grandfather 10 children 11 grandparents
4	2 your 3 she 4 Our 5 He 6 their
5	2 please 3 else 4 sandwich 5 away 6 in 7 that's 8 much 9 welcome
6	2 cheese 3 milk 4 chocolate 5 fruit 6 bread 7 eggs 8 vegetables 9 tea 10 meat 11 fish 12 water

Progress Test 4 p167

1	2 live 3 work 4 study 5 work 6 have 7 don't have 8 like 9 don't like
2	2 play 3 go 4 go to 5 go to 6 eat 7 watch 8 play
3	2 What music do you like? 3 Do you like Chinese food? 4 Where do their parents live? 5 What do you do in your free time? 6 Do your children study languages? 7 What food do they like?
4	2 chewing gum 3 batteries 4 tissues 5 a map 6 a newspaper 7 a magazine 8 a birthday card
5	2 over there 3 How much 4 each 5 These 6 can I have that 7 Anything else 8 that's all 9 Here you are
6a)	2 Wednesday 3 Thursday 4 Saturday
b)	a) week b) months c) hours d) seconds
7	b) **ten past** five c) (a) **quarter past** eight d) (a) **quarter to** eleven e) **ten to** nine f) **half past** four g) **twenty to** three h) **seven o'clock**

Progress Test 5 p168–p169

R5.17 See p161 for Listening Test instructions.

1

CUSTOMER Excuse me. Do you have any postcards?
ASSISTANT Yes, they're over there.
C Oh, OK. How much are they?
A They're 60p each.
C Thanks. And how much is this map?
A It's £5.95.
C OK. Can I have this map and eight postcards, please?
A Sure, anything else?
C Er … yes. Can I have that box of chocolates, please?
A The big box or the small box?
C The small box, please.
A OK, that's, um, £15.74, please.
C Here you are.
A Thanks very much. Bye.
C Goodbye.

2

TOBY Hi, Eric. How are you?
ERIC I'm fine, thanks, Toby. And you?
T I'm OK, thanks. Eric, this is my sister Vicky.
E Hi, Vicky. Nice to meet you.
VICKY You too. Do you work with Toby?
E No, I don't. We're old friends from school. I work for a computer company. I'm a manager.
V Oh, OK. Do you like your job?
E Yes, I do. But I'm always very busy. I start work at half past eight and I get home at half past seven in the evening.
V Do you work at the weekend?
E I sometimes work on Saturday, but never on Sunday.
V So what do you do on Sunday?
E Well, I always get up late and I usually go to the cinema in the evening. And what about you? Where do you work?

1 (2 marks each) 2 60p 3 £5.95 4 eight 5 small 6 £15.74

2 (2 marks each) 2T 3T 4F 5F 6T

3 2 has 3 works 4 leave 5 starts 6 has 7 doesn't have 8 finishes 9 gets 10 have 11 watch 12 go 13 work 14 don't work 15 watches 16 doesn't like 17 goes

4 2 do 3 have 4 does 5 work 6 does 7 start 8 Does 9 doesn't 10 do 11 have 12 Do 13 do 14 Do 15 don't 16 Does 17 doesn't

5 2 in 3 on 4 at 5 in 6 at 7 in 8 at 9 on 10 at

6 2 Can I have 3 mushroom pizza 4 would you like 5 for me 6 a bottle of 7 sparkling 8 a dessert 9 Not for me 10 for me 11 have the bill 12 Of course

7 2 burger 3 chips 4 salad 5 chicken 6 strawberry 7 ice cream 8 apple pie

8 2 We play tennis every week. 3 I'm sometimes late for class. 4 We never go to concerts. 5 He's usually tired on Mondays. 6 They eat out every week. 7 We don't usually get up early.

9 2 Spain 3 Where 4 this 5 for 6 their 7 with 8 past

10 2 I'm sorry, I **don't** understand. 3 My brother's **a** doctor. 4 **What's** your mobile number? 5 This is my **new car**. 6 I go to **the** cinema a lot. 7 She **studies** English at school. 8 What music **do** you like? 9 My **father's** name is Bill.

Progress Test 6 p170

1 2 there's 3 There isn't 4 there's 5 There's 6 there isn't 7 There aren't 8 there's 9 there aren't 10 there are

2 2 there is 3 Is there 4 there isn't 5 Are there 6 there aren't 7 Are there 8 there are

3 2 a supermarket 3 a market 4 a bank 5 a chemist's 6 a square

4 2 some 3 any 4 a 5 a lot of 6 three

5 2 a wallet 3 money 4 a camera 5 a credit card 6 keys 7 a passport 8 an ID card

6 2 Do you have 3 is it 4 When 5 from 6 to 7 on 8 day 9 where's 10 show 11 Here

7 2 a jacket 3 a skirt 4 shoes 5 a jumper 6 a dress 7 a coat 8 a shirt

Progress Test 7 p171

1 2 operas 3 watching 4 don't 5 visiting 6 likes, clothes 7 films 8 classical, doesn't 9 love

2 2 them 3 him 4 her 5 they, us

3 (2 marks each) 2 She can't cook. 3 She can ride a bike. 4 She can't play the guitar. 5 Brian can swim. 6 He can't sing. 7 He can't ski. 8 He can play basketball.

4 2 A Can your daughter speak Spanish? B Yes, she can. 3 A Can Tina's brother play the piano? B No, he can't. 4 A Can you speak English very well? B Yes, I can. (Yes, we can.)

5 2 Where's 3 right 4 on 5 opposite 6 Is 7 near 8 in 9 left 10 on 11 next to

6 2 send 3 chat to 4 buy 5 watch 6 book

Progress Test 8 p172

1 2 empty 3 right 4 short 5 terrible / awful 6 easy 7 unhappy 8 interesting

2 2 was 3 were 4 were 5 wasn't 6 was 7 weren't 8 were 9 wasn't 10 was 11 was 12 weren't

3 2 Were his brothers at the party? 3 they were 4 Was his sister there? 5 she wasn't 6 Where were Ewan's parents? 7 Was the food very good? 8 it was

4 2 ago 3 in 4 yesterday 5 ago 6 last

5 2 February 3 June 4 August 5 September 6 November

6 2 shall we 3 Let's 4 so 5 Why don't we 6 that's 7 Where 8 at 9 shall

7 d) 22nd e) 20,000,000 f) 1666 g) 31st h) 200,000
i) 2018 j) 950

Progress Test 9 p173

1 2 plane 3 boat 4 motorbike 5 bus 6 bike / bicycle

2 2 had 3 visited 4 met 5 bought 6 didn't stay 7 wanted
8 left 9 travelled 10 was 11 were 12 got 13 didn't sleep
14 stayed 15 went 16 wrote

3 2 go on 3 rent 4 go 5 stay with 6 go for 7 go 8 take
9 stay in 10 travel

4 3 Where **did you** go last weekend? 4 When did they
arrive at the party? 5 ✓ 6 **Did** Sue go out yesterday
evening? 7 ✓

5 2 returns 3 When 4 come 5 On 6 That's 7 your
8 next 9 does 10 in

6 2 How much 3 When 4 Why 5 How many 6 What
7 How old 8 Who

Progress Test 10 p174–p175

R10.11 See p161 for Listening Test instructions.

1

TOURIST Good morning.

ASSISTANT Hello, can I help you?

T Yes, please. Do you have a map of the city centre?

A Yes, of course. Here you are.

T Thank you. How much is it?

A It's £1.50.

T OK, thanks. Where's the theatre?

A It's in Market Street, opposite the cinema.

T Can you show me on this map?

A Yes, of course. Um, here it is. It's about 5 minutes away.

T Thanks. And where's the museum?

A It's in Park Road, near the station.

T Oh yes, I know. When is the museum open?

A It's open from nine thirty a.m. to six p.m.

T Is it closed on Mondays?

A No, it isn't. But it is closed on Sundays.

T OK, thank you very much.

A You're welcome. Goodbye.

T Bye.

2

BOB Hi, Louise. Did you have a good weekend?

LOUISE Yes, I did, thanks. It was my husband's birthday on Saturday.

B Oh, what did you do?

L We went to Paris for the weekend.

B Really? Did you fly?

L No, we went by train. It's only about two hours from London.

B Oh, right. And where did you stay?

L Oh, we stayed in a very nice old hotel in the city centre.

B Hmm. And what did you do in Paris?

L Well, on Saturday we went shopping and had dinner with friends. And on Sunday we went sightseeing. Paris is a very beautiful city.

B Yes, it is, isn't it? I went there two years ago with some friends. We had a great time.

L And guess what – it's my birthday next weekend!

B No! What are you going to do?

L We're going to visit my sister – and she lives in Berlin!

B Oh.

1 (2 marks each) 2b) 3a) 4b) 5b) 6b)

2 (2 marks each) 2 train 3 in a hotel 4 Sunday
5 two years ago 6 her sister

3 (2 marks each) 2 'm not going to look for
3 'm going to start 4 's (is) going to get 5 aren't/
're not going to have 6 are going to move
7 'm going to start 8 're going to look for
9 isn't/'s not going to look for 10 's going to do

4 2 go 3 go to 4 have 5 go to 6 have 7 go 8 watch

5 (2 marks each)
2 Are you going to do any exams next month?
3 Where are your parents going to go on holiday?
4 Is your sister going to get engaged next year?
5 When are you going to move to the UK?
6 Are you going to watch TV tonight?

6 2 bored 3 sad 4 excited 5 tired 6 angry 7 hungry
8 scared

7 2 with my brother 3 Have a good time 4 See you
next 5 Yes, see you 6 visit my parents 7 Have a
good weekend 8 good luck with 9 very much

8 2 I'm not from the USA. 3 I don't live in London.
4 They aren't / They're not from France. 5 I didn't
go out last night. 6 They weren't at work. 7 She
can't swim. 8 He doesn't like coffee. 9 There isn't
a market. 10 It wasn't expensive.

9 2 some 3 lives 4 their 5 watching 6 were 7 ago
8 opposite 9 Why 10 in 11 this 12 by

10 2 Let's go **to** the beach. 3 Where **were** you born?
4 I went **on** holiday last month. 5 Where did you
stay in London? 6 My birthday's **on** December
30th. 7 How **many** people were at the party?
8 His grandparents **weren't** at the wedding.
9 This is my **favourite jacket**. 10 I never listen **to**
the radio. 11 What **shall we** do this weekend?

Name _____ Score [50]

1 Fill in the gaps with I, my, you or your.

BOB Hello, ¹ _I_ 'm Bob. What's ² _____ name?

ANN Hello, ³ _____ name's Ann.

BOB Nice to meet ⁴ _____ .

ANN ⁵ _____ too.

KIM Hi, Liz.

LIZ Hi, Kim. How are ⁶ _____ ?

KIM ⁷ _____ 'm fine, thanks. And ⁸ _____ ?

LIZ ⁹ _____ 'm OK, thanks. [8]

2 Write the numbers.

a) 6 _six_   d) 8 _____

b) 11 _____   e) 12 _____

c) 3 _____   f) 4 _____ [5]

3 Fill in the gaps with these words and phrases.

~~Goodbye~~ home number this is first name
to meet you your surname See you soon

SALLY ¹ _Goodbye_ , Colin.

COLIN Bye, Sally. ² _____ .

SALLY Yes, see you.

PAUL What's your ³ _____ ?

DAVE It's 020 7845 5447.

ANDY Tom, ⁴ _____ Lily.

TOM Hello, Lily. Nice ⁵ _____ .

LILY You too.

KATE What's your ⁶ _____ , please?

MARIO It's Mario.

KATE What's ⁷ _____ ?

MARIO It's Maldini. [6]

4 Fill in the gaps with he, his, she or her.

A What's ¹ _his_ name?

B ² _____ name's Peter.

A Where's ³ _____ from?

B ⁴ _____ 's from the USA.

A What's her name?

B ⁵ _____ name's Lisa.

A Where's ⁶ _____ from?

B ⁷ _____ 's from the UK. [6]

5 Write the countries.

1 T_urkey_   2 S_____

3 A_____   4 C_____

5 B_____   6 R_____ [5]

6 Fill in the gaps with these words.

~~Excuse~~ spell mean know sorry repeat What's

1 _Excuse_ me.

2 Can you _____ that, please?

3 I'm _____ , I don't understand.

4 _____ 'merhaba' in English?

5 How do you _____ 'computer'?

6 What does 'diary' _____ ?

7 I'm sorry, I don't _____ . [6]

7 Write the words.

1 a _book_   5 a _____

2 an _____   6 a _____

3 an _____   7 a _____

4 an _____   8 a _____ [7]

8 Write the plurals.

1 chair _chairs_   5 man _____

2 watch _____   6 woman _____

3 person _____   7 table _____

4 baby _____   8 country _____ [7]

Name _____ Score ☐ 50

1 Write the nationalities.

1 Germany _German_   5 Turkey _____

2 Spain _____   6 Brazil _____

3 the USA _____   7 the UK _____

4 China _____   8 Russia _____

☐ 7

2 Fill in the gaps with the correct positive (+) or negative (–) form of *be*.

1 Serge _isn't_ (–) Italian. He _'s_ (+) from France.

2 I _____ (–) from the UK. I _____ (+) from the USA.

3 Marta _____ (–) from Brazil. She _____ (+) from Colombia.

4 You _____ (–) a teacher. You _____ (+) a student.

5 It _____ (–) a German car. It _____ (+) a Japanese car.

☐ 8

3 Write the jobs. Use *a* or *an*.

What's your job?

a teacher   _____

_____   _____

_____   _____

_____   _____

☐ 7

4 Fill in the gaps in these conversations. Use the correct form of *be*.

A Where ¹ _are_ you from?

B I ² _____ from Egypt.

A ³ _____ your teacher from the UK?

B No, she ⁴ _____ .

A What ⁵ _____ his name?

B His name ⁶ _____ Henry.

A ⁷ _____ Mrs Jones from London?

B Yes, she ⁸ _____ .

A ⁹ _____ you from Mexico?

B Yes, I ¹⁰ _____ .

A ¹¹ _____ I in this class?

B No, you ¹² _____ .

☐ 11

5 Karen is at the nine2five Employment Agency. Write the questions.

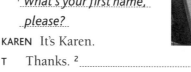

TONY Good morning. Welcome to the nine2five Employment Agency.
      ¹ _What's your first name, please?_

KAREN It's Karen.

T Thanks. ² _____ ?

K It's Brown.

T OK. ³ _____ ?

K No, I'm single.

T ⁴ _____ ?

K I'm Australian.

T ⁵ _____ ?

K It's 67 Park Road, Manchester, M17 3JT.

T OK, thanks. ⁶ _____ ?

K My mobile number? It's 07899 345768.

T ⁷ _____ ?

K It's karen.brown@webmail.net.

T Thank you.

☐ 12

6 Write the numbers.

a) 20 _twenty_   d) 15 _____

b) 46 _____   e) 58 _____

c) 33 _____   f) 100 _____

☐ 5

Name _____ Score ☐ 50

1 Write the opposites of these adjectives.

1 good _bad_   4 cheap _____
2 big _____   5 hot _____
3 friendly _____   6 new _____

☐ 5

2 Fill in the gaps with the correct positive (+) or negative (−) form of *be*.

☒

Hi Roberto

How ¹ _are_ (+) you? David and I ² _____ (+) in the UK! We ³ _____ (−) in London, we ⁴ _____ (+) in a big hotel in Brighton. The rooms ⁵ _____ (−) very big, but they ⁶ _____ (+) very nice. The hotel ⁷ _____ (−) very expensive and the manager ⁸ _____ (+) very friendly. I ⁹ _____ (−) in the hotel now, I ¹⁰ _____ (+) in an Internet café in Brighton. It ¹¹ _____ (+) a very beautiful city, but it ¹² _____ (−) very hot here! See you soon.

Love Julia

☐ 11

3 Look at Roy and Jane's family. Fill in the gaps in these sentences.

Roy ⊙⊙ Jane

Leo ⊙⊙ Pam   Nick

Steve   Jo

1 Jane is Roy's _wife_ .
2 Pam is Roy and Jane's _____ .
3 Nick is their _____ .
4 Leo is _____ husband.
5 Pam is Nick's _____ .
6 Jo is _____ sister.
7 Leo is Jo's _____ .
8 _____ is Pam's mother.
9 Roy is Steve's _____ .
10 Steve and Jo are Leo and Pam's _____ .
11 Roy and Jane are Steve and Jo's _____ .

☐ 10

4 Choose the correct words.

1 Where's *I* / *my* bag?
2 Where are *you* / *your* parents from?
3 Is *she* / *her* an actress?
4 *We* / *Our* teacher's name is Caroline.
5 *He* / *His* isn't from Mexico.
6 What's *they* / *their* dog's name?

☐ 5

5 Read this conversation in a café. Fill in the gaps with these words.

~~help~~ welcome that's else much
sandwich away please in

ASSISTANT Can I ¹ _help_ you?
CUSTOMER Yes, two coffees, ² _____ .
A Anything ³ _____ ?
C Yes, an egg ⁴ _____ , please.
A Eat in or take ⁵ _____ ?
C Eat ⁶ _____ , please.
A OK, ⁷ _____ £6.25, please.
C Thank you very ⁸ _____ .
A You're ⁹ _____ .

☐ 8

6 Write the words.

① ② ③
④ ⑤ ⑥
⑦ ⑧ ⑨
⑩ ⑪ ⑫

1 _sugar_   7 _____
2 _____   8 _____
3 _____   9 _____
4 _____   10 _____
5 _____   11 _____
6 _____   12 _____

☐ 11

© Cambridge University Press 2009   Answer Key p161

Name .... Score ☐ 50

1
Fill in the gaps with the correct positive (+) or negative (–) form of *like*, *have*, *live*, *work* or *study*.

My name's Brigitte and I ¹ *live* (+) in Paris with my husband, Bernard, and our two children. We ² .... (+) in a nice flat in the centre of the city. I ³ .... (+) for a French phone company and I ⁴ .... (+) English after work two days a week. I ⁵ .... (+) in an office near our flat. We ⁶ .... (+) two sons, but we ⁷ .... (–) a daughter. They ⁸ .... (+) rock music and tennis, but they ⁹ .... (–) football or homework!

☐ 8

2
Choose the correct verbs.

1 (go)/ watch out with friends
2 play / go computer games
3 go to / go shopping
4 go to / go the cinema
5 go to / go concerts
6 eat / play out
7 play / watch TV
8 go / play tennis

☐ 7

3
Make questions with these words.

1 do / Where / work / you ?
   Where do you work?

2 music / do / What / like / you ?
   ....

3 you / Chinese food / like / Do ?
   ....

4 live / do / Where / their parents ?
   ....

5 do / What / in your free time / you / do ?
   ....

6 your children / Do / languages / study ?
   ....

7 food / they / What / like / do ?
   ....

☐ 6

4
Write the words.

1 s *weets*
2 c ....
3 b ....
4 t ....
5 a m ....
6 a n ....
7 a m ....
8 a b ....

☐ 7

5
Read this conversation in a shop. Fill in the gaps with these words and phrases.

~~Excuse~~   over there   each   Here you are   How much
These   that's all   Anything else   can I have that

CUSTOMER ¹ *Excuse* me. Do you have any postcards?
SHOP ASSISTANT Yes, they're ² ....
C   Thanks. ³ .... are they?
SA   They're 40p ⁴ ....
C   OK. ⁵ .... four postcards, please. And ⁶ .... box of chocolates?
SA   Of course. ⁷ .... ?
C   No, ⁸ .... , thanks.
SA   OK, that's £8.59, please.
C   ⁹ ....
SA   Thanks a lot. Goodbye.

☐ 8

6
a) Write the days of the week.
¹ *Monday* , Tuesday, ² .... , ³ .... , Friday, ⁴ .... , Sunday

b) Write the time words.
a) 7 *days* = 1 ....   c) 1 day = 24 ....
b) 1 year = 12 ....   d) 1 minute = 60 ....

☐ 7

7
Complete the times.

a) ..... *five* ..... *to* ..... nine
b) .... five
c) .... eight
d) .... eleven
e) .... nine
f) .... four
g) .... three
h) ....

☐ 7

Answer Key p161

PROGRESS TESTS: PHOTOCOPIABLE

1 **R5.17** **Listen to a conversation in a shop. Choose the correct answers.**

1 The shop (has some / doesn't have any) postcards.
2 The postcards are *50p / 60p* each.
3 The map is *£5.95 / £5.99*.
4 The customer buys *six / eight* postcards.
5 The customer buys a *big / small* box of chocolates.
6 The customer spends *£15.24 / £15.74*. [10]

2 **Listen to Toby, Eric and Vicky. Are these sentences true or false?**

Vicky   Eric   Toby

1 Eric is Vicky's brother. *F*
2 Eric doesn't work with Toby. ____
3 Eric's a manager for a computer company. ____
4 He gets home at 8.30 in the week. ____
5 He sometimes works on Sunday. ____
6 He usually goes to the cinema on Sunday evening. ____ [10]

3 **Read about Andy's daily routine. Put the verbs in brackets in the correct form of the Present Simple.**

Andy

Andy is a taxi driver in London. He ¹ *gets up* (get up) at 6.00 and he ² _____ (have) breakfast at 6.30 with his wife, Kathy. She ³ _____ (work) in a café near their flat. Andy and Kathy ⁴ _____ (leave) home at about 7.00. Andy ⁵ _____ (start)

work at 7.30. He always ⁶ _____ (have) a coffee and a cheese sandwich at about 11.00, but he ⁷ _____ (not have) lunch. He ⁸ _____ (finish) work at 4.30 and usually ⁹ _____ (get) home at about 5.00 or 5.30. Andy and Kathy ¹⁰ _____ (have) dinner at about 6.30. Then they ¹¹ _____ (watch) TV and ¹² _____ (go) to bed at 10.00. Andy and Kathy ¹³ _____ (work) every Saturday, but they ¹⁴ _____ (not work) on Sundays. Andy usually ¹⁵ _____ (watch) football on Sunday afternoon, but Kathy ¹⁶ _____ (not like) football. She usually ¹⁷ _____ (go) out with friends. [16]

4 **Read about Andy and Kathy in 3 again. Then fill in the gaps in these questions and answers.**

A What time ¹ *does* Andy get up?
B At 6.00.
A When ² _____ Andy and Kathy ³ _____ breakfast?
B At 6.30.
A Where ⁴ _____ Kathy ⁵ _____ ?
B In a café near their flat.
A What time ⁶ _____ Andy ⁷ _____ work?
B At 7.30.
A ⁸ _____ he have lunch?
B No, he ⁹ _____ .
A When ¹⁰ _____ Andy and Kathy ¹¹ _____ dinner?
B At about 6.30.
A ¹² _____ they work on Saturdays?
B Yes, they ¹³ _____ .
A ¹⁴ _____ they work on Sundays?
B No, they ¹⁵ _____ .
A ¹⁶ _____ Kathy like football?
B No, she ¹⁷ _____ . [16]

5 **Fill in the gaps with *on*, *in* or *at*.**

1 *on* Sunday   6 ____ night
2 ____ the morning   7 ____ the afternoon
3 ____ Friday morning 8 ____ the weekend
4 ____ half past four 9 ____ Friday evening
5 ____ the week   10 ____ midday
[9]

6 Dan and Kerry are in a restaurant. Read the conversation. Then fill in the gaps with these words and phrases.

> order   for me (x 2)   have the bill   sparkling
> a dessert   a bottle of   mushroom pizza   Of course
> Not for me   Can I have   would you like

WAITER   Are you ready to ¹ _order_ ?

KERRY   Yes. ² _____ the lasagne, please?

DAN   And can I have the ³ _____ , please?

W   Certainly. What ⁴ _____ to drink?

K   An orange juice ⁵ _____ , please.

D   And can we have ⁶ _____ mineral water?

W   Still or ⁷ _____ ?

D   Still, please.

W   OK. Thanks very much.

W   Would you like ⁸ _____ ?

K   ⁹ _____ , thanks.

D   Fruit salad ¹⁰ _____ , please. And two coffees, please.

W   Certainly.

D   Excuse me. Can we ¹¹ _____ , please?

W   ¹² _____ .

D   Thanks a lot.

[11]

7 Write the words.

① a p_izza_

② a b_____

③ c_____

④ a s_____

⑤ c_____

⑥ a s_____

⑦ i_____ c_____

⑧ a_____ p_____

[7]

8 Make sentences with these words.

1 early / goes / She / to bed / always .
   She always goes to bed early.

2 week / play / We / every / tennis .
   _____

3 I'm / for class / sometimes / late .
   _____

4 to concerts / never / go / We .
   _____

5 usually / He's / on Mondays / tired .
   _____

6 eat out / They / week / every .
   _____

7 early / usually / We / get up / don't .
   _____

[6]

9 Choose the correct words.

1 What's *you* / *your* first name, please?
2 My wife is from *Spain* / *Spanish*.
3 *What* / *Where* do your brothers live?
4 How much is *this* / *these* watch?
5 I work *in* / *for* a British company.
6 This is a photo of *they* / *their* children.
7 I go out *with* / *for* friends a lot.
8 It's half *past* / *to* eleven.

[7]

10 Correct these sentences.

1 He ᐟs from the USA.

2 I'm sorry, I not understand.

3 My brother's doctor.

4 What your mobile number?

5 This is my car new.

6 I go to cinema a lot.

7 She studys English at school.

8 What music you like?

9 My father name is Bill.

[8]

Name .... Score ☐ 50

1 Fill in the gaps with *there's, there isn't, there are* or *there aren't*.

I live in Wolverhampton, a city in England.
¹ *There are* (+) a lot of nice buildings and
² .... (+) a beautiful old theatre called
The Grand. ³ .... (−) a river in the
centre, but ⁴ .... (+) a very nice park
called West Park. ⁵ .... (+) a station in
Wolverhampton, but ⁶ .... (−) an
airport. I live in Albert Road, near West Park.
⁷ .... (−) any shops in my road, but
⁸ .... (+) a small supermarket five
minutes away. And ⁹ .... (−) any
restaurants in my road, but ¹⁰ .... (+)
a lot of very good restaurants in the centre. ☐ 9

2 Fill in the gaps with the correct form of *there is / there are*.

A ¹ *Is there* a theatre in Wolverhampton?

B Yes, ² ....

A ³ .... an airport?

B No, ⁴ ....

A ⁵ .... any shops in Albert Road?

B No, ⁶ ....

A ⁷ .... any good restaurants in the centre?

B Yes, ⁸ .... ☐ 7

3 Write the words.

1 a b_us_ st_op_   4 a b........................
2 a s........................   5 a c........................
3 a m........................   6 a s........................ ☐ 5

4 Choose the correct words.

1 There's ⓐ/ *any* bus station.
2 There are *some / any* hotels.
3 There aren't *an / any* museums.
4 There isn't *a / some* cashpoint.
5 There are *any / a lot of* shops.
6 There are *a / three* cinemas. ☐ 5

5 Write the words.

1 a _purse_   5 a ....
2 a ....   6 ....
3 ....   7 a ....
4 a ....   8 an .... ☐ 7

6 Read the conversation. Choose the correct words or phrases.

ASSISTANT   Hello. Can I ¹(help)/ *helps* you?

TOURIST   Yes, please. ²*Do you have / You have* a map of the city centre?

A   Yes, of course. Here you are.

T   How much ³*is it / it is*?

A   It's free.

T   ⁴*When / Where* is the City Museum open?

A   It's open ⁵*from / to* 9.30 a.m. ⁶*from / to* 5.30 p.m.

T   Is it closed ⁷*in / on* Mondays?

A   No, it's open every ⁸*day / days*.

T   And ⁹*where's / there's* the Royal Theatre?

A   It's in Green Street.

T   Can you ¹⁰*help / show* me on this map?

A   Yes, of course. ¹¹*Here / Where* it is.

T   Thanks a lot. ☐ 10

7 Write the words.

1 ...._jeans_....   5 a ....
2 a ....   6 a ....
3 a ....   7 a ....
4 ....   8 a .... ☐ 7

face2face Starter Photocopiable   © Cambridge University Press 2009   Answer Key p162

Progress Test 7 25 minutes

1 Fill in the gaps with these words.

~~hates~~ love likes don't doesn't films
watching visiting classical clothes operas

1 My sister _hates_ flying.
2 My parents love soap ....
3 I like .... sport on TV.
4 My parents .... like dancing.
5 Mike and Julie like .... new places.
6 Gillie .... shopping for ....
7 My sons don't like horror ....
8 Zara likes .... music, but she .... like rock music.
9 We .... animals. We have five cats and three dogs! [10]

2 Choose the correct words.

1 (*I*) / *Me* love Italian food.
2 Do you know *they* / *them*?
3 I don't understand *he* / *him*.
4 Maria's nice. I like *she* / *her* a lot.
5 Do *they* / *them* live near *we* / *us*? [5]

3 Look at the things Yvonne and Brian can do (✓) and can't do (✗). Write sentences for pictures 1–8.

Yvonne		Brian	
1	✓	5	✓
2	✗	6	✗
3	✓	7	✗
4	✗	8	✓

1 Yvonne _can drive_ .
2 She ....
3 She ....
4 She ....
5 Brian ....
6 He ....
7 He ....
8 He .... [14]

4 Make questions with these words. Then complete the short answers.

1 A swim / you / Can ?
   Can you swim?
   B No, _I can't_ .
2 A Spanish / Can / daughter / your / speak ?
   ....
   B Yes, ...
3 A piano / play / brother / Tina's / the / Can ?
   ....
   B No, ...
4 A well / speak / you / Can / very / English ?
   ....
   B Yes, ... [6]

5 Tom is at ✳ on the map. Choose the correct words in these conversations.

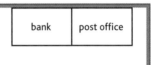

OLD STREET

museum

bank   post office   theatre

✳

TOM   Excuse ¹*you* / (*me*). ²*Where's* / *There's* the theatre?
MAN   Go along this road and turn ³*left* / *right*. The theatre is ⁴*in* / *on* the right, ⁵*next to* / *opposite* the museum.
TOM   Thanks very much.

TOM   Excuse me. ⁶*Is* / *Are* there a bank ⁷*next to* / *near* here?
MAN   Yes, there's a bank ⁸*at* / *in* Old Street. Go along this road and turn ⁹*left* / *right*. The bank is ¹⁰*on* / *in* the left, ¹¹*next to* / *opposite* the post office.
TOM   Thanks a lot. [10]

6 Choose the correct words.

1 (*download*) / *book* music
2 *send* / *buy* emails
3 *chat to* / *book* friends
4 *buy* / *watch* concert tickets
5 *listen* / *watch* videos
6 *book* / *send* flights [5]

PROGRESS TESTS: PHOTOCOPIABLE

Name .... Score [50]

1 Write the opposite of these adjectives.

1 young _old_
2 full ....
3 wrong ....
4 long ....
5 amazing ....
6 difficult ....
7 happy ....
8 boring .... [7]

2 Read about Ewan's birthday party. Fill in the gaps with *was, were, wasn't* or *weren't*.

[X]

Hi Stephanie

How are you? My weekend ¹ _was_ great! It
² .... (+) Ewan's 30th birthday party on
Saturday. There ³ .... (+) about 50
people at the party. Ewan's three brothers
⁴ .... (+) there, but his sister
⁵ .... (−) there. She ⁶ .... (+) in
the USA, I think. Also his parents ⁷ ....
(−) there, they ⁸ .... (+) in Spain. The
music ⁹ .... (−) very good, but the food
¹⁰ .... (+) fantastic! It ¹¹ .... (+) a
good party, sorry you ¹² .... (−) there!
Love Pia

[11]

3 Make questions with these words. Then fill in the gaps in the short answers.

A party / birthday / When / Ewan's / was ?
  ¹ _When was Ewan's birthday party?_
B On Saturday.
A his / at the party / Were / brothers ?
  ² ....
B Yes, ³ ....
A there / his / Was / sister ?
  ⁴ ....
B No, ⁵ ....
A were / Where / parents / Ewan's ?
  ⁶ ....
B In Spain.
A the food / good / very / Was ?
  ⁷ ....
B Yes, ⁸ .... [7]

4 Choose the correct words.

1 Peter was at a wedding (yesterday)/ ago.
2 I was in London two years *last / ago*.
3 Our son was born *last / in* 2007.
4 Where were you *yesterday / last* afternoon?
5 Kim was at home an hour *ago / yesterday*.
6 I wasn't at work *last / yesterday* week. [5]

5 Write the months.

¹ _January_ , ² .... , March, April, May,
³ .... , July, ⁴ .... , ⁵ .... ,
October, ⁶ .... , December [5]

6 Read this phone conversation. Choose the correct words or phrases.

IAN Hi, Eve. How ¹*is /* (are) *you*?
EVE I'm fine, thanks. And you?
IAN I'm OK, thanks. What ²*we shall / shall we* do this afternoon?
EVE ³*Why don't / Let's* go to the park.
IAN No, I don't think ⁴*that / so*. We always go to the park.
EVE OK. ⁵*Why don't we / Shall* go to that new shopping centre?
IAN Yes, ⁶*that's / that* a good idea. ⁷*Where / When* shall we meet?
EVE Let's meet ⁸*at / to* the bus station.
IAN What time ⁹*shall / do* we meet?
EVE About three o'clock.
IAN Great. See you there. Bye! [8]

7 Write the years, dates and big numbers.

a) nineteen seventy _1970_
b) seventh _7th_
c) three thousand _3,000_
d) twenty-second ....
e) twenty million ....
f) sixteen sixty-six ....
g) thirty-first ....
h) two hundred thousand ....
i) twenty eighteen ....
j) nine hundred and fifty .... [7]

Answer Key p162

1 Write the words.

1 a _car_

2 a ....

3 a ....

4 a ....

5 a ....

6 a ....   ☐5

2 Read about Paul and Sarah's holiday in India. Fill in the gaps with the Past Simple of the verbs in brackets.

> Hi Mum and Dad
> How are you? Sarah and I ¹ _arrived_ (arrive) in Goa last night. We ² .... (have) a fantastic time in Mumbai and Sarah and I ³ .... (visit) some amazing museums. We also ⁴ .... (meet) some nice people and Sarah ⁵ .... (buy) some clothes. We ⁶ .... (not stay) in Mumbai very long because we ⁷ .... (want) to go to Goa. We ⁸ .... (leave) Mumbai at 5 a.m. yesterday and we ⁹ .... (travel) to Goa by train. It ¹⁰ .... (be) a 12-hour journey and we ¹¹ .... (be) very tired when we ¹² .... (get) to our hotel. Sarah ¹³ .... (not sleep) very well, so this morning she ¹⁴ .... (stay) in bed and I ¹⁵ .... (go) to the beach.
> Love Paul
> PS I ¹⁶ .... (write) you an email from Mumbai. Did you get it?

☐15

3 Choose the correct words or phrases.

1 go / (go to) the beach
2 go on / go to holiday
3 travel / rent a car
4 go / go to sightseeing
5 stay with / stay in friends
6 go for / go to a walk
7 go on / go swimming
8 take / rent photos
9 stay with / stay in a hotel
10 rent / travel around

☐9

4 Look at these Past Simple questions. Tick (✓) the correct questions. Correct the wrong questions.

1 Did you ~~watched~~ TV last night?   _watch_
2 What did Dave do yesterday? ✓
3 Where you did go last weekend?
4 When did they arrived at the party?
5 Did your parents like the present?
6 Do Sue go out yesterday evening?
7 Where did you meet your wife?   ☐5

5 Read this conversation at a station. Choose the correct words.

TICKET SELLER   Hello. ¹(Can) / Do I help you?
CUSTOMER   Two ²singles / returns to London, please.
TS   ³When / Where do you want to ⁴come / go back?
C   ⁵On / In Sunday evening.
TS   OK. ⁶That / That's £54.60, please. Here are ⁷you / your tickets.
C   Thanks. What time's the ⁸next / near train?
TS   There's one at 10.23.
C   What time ⁹does / is it arrive ¹⁰to / in London?
TS   At 12.15.
C   Thanks a lot. Bye.   ☐9

6 Fill in the gaps with these question words.

> ~~Where~~   Who   What   Why   When
> How much   How many   How old

1 A _Where_ are you from?
  B I'm from Colombia.
2 A .... is that green bag?
  B It's £45.
3 A .... did you buy your phone?
  B Six months ago.
4 A .... were you late for class?
  B Because I got up late.
5 A .... people were at the party?
  B About a hundred.
6 A .... did you do last night?
  B I went to the cinema.
7 A .... is your daughter?
  B She's thirteen.
8 A .... 's your English teacher?
  B Kate Robertson.

☐7

1 [R10.11] Listen to a conversation in a tourist information centre. Tick (✓) the correct answers.

1 When is the conversation?
   a) In the morning. ✓   b) In the afternoon.
2 How much is a map of the city centre?
   a) £1.00.   b) £1.50.
3 Where's the theatre?
   a) It's opposite the cinema.   b) It's next to the cinema.
4 Where's the museum?
   a) It's in Station Road.   b) It's near the station.
5 What time does the museum open?
   a) Nine o'clock.   b) Half past nine.
6 When is the museum closed?
   a) On Mondays.   b) On Sundays.   [10]

2 Listen to Bob and Louise talk about last weekend. Choose the correct words.

1 It was *Louise's* / *Louise's husband's* birthday on Saturday.
2 Louise and her husband went to Paris by *train* / *plane*.
3 They stayed *in a hotel* / *with friends*.
4 They went sightseeing on *Saturday* / *Sunday*.
5 Bob went to Paris *last year* / *two years ago*.
6 Louise is going to visit *her sister* / *a friend* next weekend.   [10]

3 Fill in the gaps with the correct positive (+) or negative (–) form of *be going to* and these verbs.

| ~~leave~~ start |
| get   have |
| look for |

Carolina from Spain

I ¹ *'m going to leave* (+) school next month.
But I ² .... (–) a job
because I ³ .... (+)
university in September. And my brother
⁴ .... (+) married in
September. They ⁵ .... (–)
a big wedding, only about 25 people.

| look for (x 2) |
| move   do |
| start |

Brad and Amy from the USA

Amy and I ⁶ .... (+)
to San Francisco in August because I
⁷ .... (+) a new job
there. We ⁸ .... (+)
a flat in the centre of the city. But Amy
⁹ .... (–) a job because
she ¹⁰ .... (+) a computer
course.   [18]

4 Choose the correct verbs.
1 *watch* / *have* the news
2 *go* / *go to* shopping
3 *go* / *go to* a party
4 *have* / *go* dinner with friends
5 *go* / *go to* the gym
6 *have* / *watch* a party
7 *go* / *go to* running
8 *watch* / *go* sport on TV   [7]

5 Make questions with these words.

1 after class / you / are / What / do / going to ?
   What are you going to do after class?

2 any exams / next month / going to / you / Are / do ?
   ....

3 your parents / on holiday / Where / go / are / going to ?
   ....

4 get / next year / Is / engaged / going to / your sister ?
   ....

5 move / going to / you / to the UK / are / When ?
   ....

6 going to / you / Are / tonight / TV / watch ?
   ....

   [10]

6 Write the adjectives.

① h_appy_   ② b.................

③ s.................   ④ e.................

⑤ t.................   ⑥ a.................

⑦ h.................   ⑧ s.................

   [7]

7 Fill in the gaps with these phrases.

> ~~after class~~   Yes, see you   with my brother   very much
> Have a good weekend   Have a good time   See you next
> visit my parents   good luck with

ULI   What are you going to do ¹ _after class_ ?
JIN   I'm going to have coffee ² ....
ULI   ³ .... !
JIN   Thanks a lot. ⁴ .... class.
ULI   ⁵ ....

MEG   Are you going to go away at the weekend?
PHIL Yes, I'm going to ⁶ ....
MEG   ⁷ .... !
PHIL Thanks a lot. Oh, and ⁸ ....
      your new job.
MEG   Thanks ⁹ ....

   [8]

8 Make these sentences negative (−).

1 She's a doctor.   _She isn't a doctor._
2 I'm from the USA.   ....
3 I live in London.   ....
4 They're from France.   ....
5 I went out last night.   ....
6 They were at work.   ....
7 She can swim.   ....
8 He likes coffee.   ....
9 There's a market.   ....
10 It was expensive.   ....

   [9]

9 Choose the correct words.

1 I don't know they / (them).
2 There are some / any people in the park.
3 My brother live / lives in New York.
4 This isn't they're / their bag.
5 I like watch / watching TV.
6 Where was / were you last night?
7 I was in Peru two years last / ago.
8 The café is next / opposite the bank.
9 What / Why are you always late?
10 I play tennis in / on the evening.
11 Is this / these your camera?
12 He goes to work by / in car.

   [11]

10 Correct these sentences.

          don't
1 I ~~not~~ have a car.

2 Let's go at the beach.

3 Where did you born?

4 I went to holiday last month.

5 Where did you stayed in London?

6 My birthday's in December 30th.

7 How much people were at the party?

8 His grandparents wasn't at the wedding.

9 This is my jacket favourite.

10 I never listen the radio.

11 What we shall do this weekend?

   [10]

Acknowledgements

Chris Redston would like to thank everyone at Cambridge University Press for their continuing dedication and commitment to the *face2face* project. In particular he owes a huge debt of gratitude to Sue Ullstein and Ruth Atkinson, the other two members of the 'Starter Team'. Sue and Ruth both worked so tirelessly and with such enthusiasm on every component that their names deserve to be on the cover of every Starter book. He would also like to thank Dilys Silva and Karen Momber for their in-house project management; Gillie Cunningham for all her help and support since we started writing *face2face* together six years ago, and everyone at pentacor**big** for artwork and book design. He would also like to thank the following people for their help and support during the writing of the Starter level: Mark Skipper, Will Ord, Katy Jarrett, Dylan Evans, David Earle, Nick Tims, Jean Barmer, Mary Breen, Margie Fisher, Joss Whedon, SMG, JJ Abrams, Tom Rowlands, Ed Simons, Matt Stone, Trey Parker, Sarah Connor, his two sisters, Anne and Carol, and of course his ever-supportive father, Bill Redston. Finally, he would like to thank Adela Pickles for making him extraordinarily happy (and for all the big cups of coffee!).

The author and publishers are grateful to the following contributors:

pentacor**big**: cover and text design and page layout
Hilary Luckcock: picture research

The author and publishers acknowledge the following sources of copyright material and are grateful for the permissions granted. While every effort has been made, it has not always been possible to identify the sources of all the material used, or to trace all copyright holders. If any omissions are brought to our notice, we will be happy to include the appropriate acknowledgements on reprinting.

The Council of Europe for the table on p13 from the *Common European Framework of Reference for Languages: Learning, teaching, assessment* p26 (2001) Council of Europe Modern Languages Division, Strasbourg, Cambridge University Press. Copyright of the text is held by the Council of Europe exclusively © Council of Europe. Reprinted with permission. *English Pronunciation in Use* Elementary by Jonathan Marks, Cambridge University Press, 2007 and *English Pronunciation in Use* by Mark Hancock, Cambridge University Press, 2003 for the diagrams on p28, p37, p45, p53, p61, p69, p77, p84, p92. Reprinted with permission.

The publishers are grateful to the following for permission to reproduce copyright photographs and material:

Key: l = left, c = centre, r = right, t = top, b = bottom

Alamy Images/©Blend Images for p118(Paco & Ana), /©Redchopsticks.com LLC for p118(Kang & Li), /©BlueMoon Stock for p152(1), /©SundayPhoto Europe a.s. for p152(2), /©Itani for p152(3), /©Tetra Images for p152(4), /©Dennie Cody for p152(6), /©Radius Images for p152(8), /©UpperCut Images for pp152(9), /©SundayPhoto Europe a.s. for p152(10), /©Justin Kase Zsixz for p168(b), /©UpperCut Images for p172(r), /©Joseph Lawrence Name for p174(t), /©OJO Images Ltd for p174(b); Corbis/©Corbis RF for p171(r); Getty Images for p113(Fatboy Slim); Photolibrary/©Digital Vision for p118(Ian & Sonia), /©PhotoDisc for p118(Tom & Alice), /©Thinkstock for p126, /©Thinkstock for p127, /©Blend Images for p152(5), /©Ken Weingart for p156, /©Age fotostock for p168(t), /©Pierre Bourrier for p171(l), /©Age fotostock for p172(l); Punchstock/©Stockbyte for p152(7), /©moodboard for p167; Rex Features/©Matt Baron/BEI for p113(Bono), /©Sipa Press for p113(Elle Macpherson), /©Charles Sykes for p113(Nicolas Cage), /©Matt Baron/BEI for p113(Winona Ryder), /©David Fisher for p113(Stevie Wonder), /©Greg Allen for p113(Elton John), /©Alex Berliner/BEI for p113(Demi Moore); Trevor Clifford for p165.

The publishers would like to thank the following illustrators:

Dirty Vectors, Mark Duffin, F&L Productions, Andy Hammond (Illustration), Graham Kennedy, Joanne Kerr (New Division)